The Mosque
in Early Ottoman
Architecture

Ulucami of Bursa

The Mosque
in Early Ottoman
Architecture

Aptullah Kuran

The University of Chicago Press, Chicago and London

University of Chicago
Publications of the Center for Middle Eastern Studies, Number 2
William R. Polk, General Editor

Publications of the Center for Middle Eastern Studies

Library of Congress Catalog Card Number 68-16701

THE UNIVERSITY OF CHICAGO PRESS *60637*
THE UNIVERSITY OF CHICAGO PRESS, LTD., LONDON W.C.1

General Editor's Preface

The Center for Middle Eastern Studies at The University of Chicago was founded in October 1965. The more than two dozen members of its faculty offer courses on subjects ranging from the geography of Morocco to the literature of Iran, and from the beginnings of the Muslim state in the time of Muhammad to contemporary political problems. The Center and the Oriental Institute, which deals with the more ancient periods of the Near East, enable the University to offer perhaps the most complete program on the Middle East available anywhere in the world.

It is the purpose of the Center to encourage and disseminate scholarly work on the Middle East. To this end, the Center provides fellowships and research funds and brings to the University visiting scholars.

Professor Aptullah Kuran, Dean of the School of Architecture of the Middle East Technical University of Ankara, was a guest of the University during the fall of 1966. At that time he gave a series of lectures on Ottoman architecture in Turkey. These lectures will be published by the University of Chicago Press. *The Mosque in Early Ottoman Architecture,* the first of three volumes on the history of architecture of the Ottoman Empire, is a continuation of Professor Kuran's scholarly research.

This and other forthcoming volumes in the series will illustrate the extent and diversity of the interests of the Center for Middle Eastern Studies at The University of Chicago.

WILLIAM R. POLK
Director of the Center for Middle Eastern Studies

Author's Preface

This book is the first part of a proposed trilogy on Ottoman mosque architecture. It deals with what I consider to be the most significant Ottoman mosques of the fourteenth and the fifteenth centuries. The second and third books will take up the Golden Age (sixteenth and seventeenth centuries) and the Decline (from the early eighteenth century to the end of the World War I), respectively.

I began studying Ottoman mosques in 1961. Three years later my first book on early Ottoman mosque architecture was published in Turkish. The present book, however, is not a translation of the earlier work; it includes a great deal of new material—some of it heretofore neither published nor widely known—as well as a number of alterations and corrections.

At the start of this undertaking I decided to see, measure, and photograph as many mosques as possible and not to include in my book any that I had not actually seen and studied on location. I have not been to the Balkan countries and am familiar with Ottoman architecture in these countries only through scholarly works. For this reason, with the exception of one mosque in Dimetoka, Greece, which had to be included because of its unique place in the evolution of Ottoman mosque architecture, all examples in this book have been taken from within the boundaries of modern Turkey. Whenever possible they have all been especially photographed for it and, even when measured drawings existed, were remeasured for accuracy and newly drawn.

The plans and sections in this book were prepared from my measured sketches by Miss İnci Aslanoğlu. The photographs are the works of Mustafa Niksarlı. Both have accompanied me on numerous trips in Anatolia and eastern Thrace and I am indebted to them not only for their invaluable contribution but also for their unfailing interest and enthusiasm. I am equally indebted to Miss Suna Gebizli for her secretarial assistance.

My former Robert College teacher and friend Professor Hilary Sumner-Boyd, my colleague Mrs. Jeanne D. Tifft and my wife, Sylvia Kuran, have at various times read the manuscript and made many constructive suggestions. To all three my deepest gratitude and heartfelt thanks.

Contents

Illustrations

Introduction

Complex of Bayezid II, Edirne

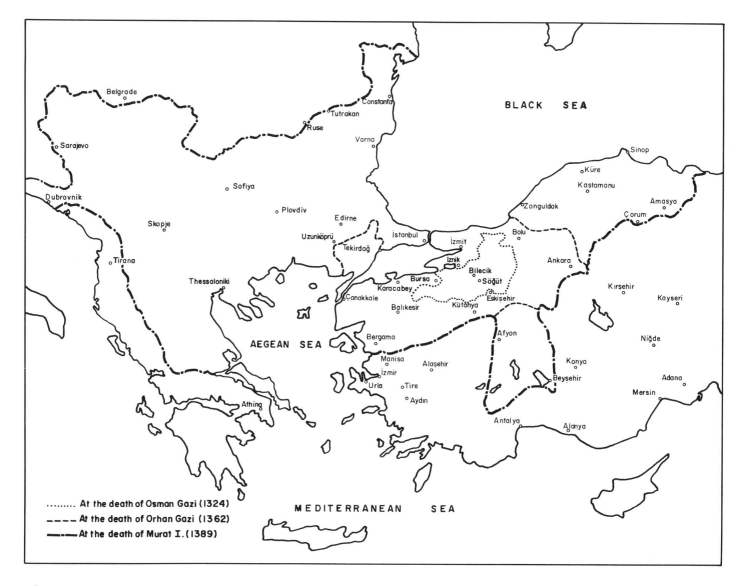

BLACK SEA

Belgrade

Constanta

Tutrakan

Ruse

Sarajevo

Varna

Sinop

Küre

Kastamonu

Sofiya

Dubrovnik

Zonguldak

Amasya

Skopje

Plovdiv

Çorum

Edirne

İstanbul

Bolu

Tirana

Uzunköprü

İzmit

Ankara

Tekirdağ

İznik

Bilecik

Thessaloniki

Bursa

Söğüt

Kırşehir

Karacabey

Eskişehir

Kayseri

Çanakkale

Kütahya

Balıkesir

AEGEAN SEA

Afyon

Niğde

Bergama

Manisa

Konya

Adana

İzmir

Alaşehir

Beyşehir

Urla

Mersin

Tire

Athina

Aydın

Antalya

Alanya

MEDITERRANEAN   SEA

.... At the death of Osman Gazi (1324)
‒ ‒ ‒ ‒ At the death of Orhan Gazi (1362)
‒·‒·‒·‒ At the death of Murat I. (1389)

The Ottoman State

2

Comparatively little attention has been given to date to the architecture of the Ottoman Turks despite the fact that, as they evolved from a small community to one of the biggest and longest-lasting empires the world has ever known, they left behind them a rich architecture. The Ottoman Turks were great builders, engaging in extensive building activity as early as the first half of the fourteenth century. Initially in their first capital city of Bursa, then in Edirne and Istanbul, the principles of Ottoman Turkish state architecture were developed, formulated, and disseminated. Monumental or modest examples of their architecture remain today wherever Ottoman Turks have been.

No civilization that comes in contact with other civilizations can claim immunity from outside influences. The Ottoman Turks were no exception. It would be unrealistic to assume that a tribe of Turkish people who migrated from central Asia to western Anatolia, building an empire that stretched from Istanbul to Iran, Yemen, Egypt, Algiers, Hungary, and the Crimea were not interested in, or influenced by, historic or contemporary works of art and architecture which they encountered and that these influences did not play a part in the formulation of Ottoman Turkish state architecture. It would be equally unrealistic to suppose, however, that superior building techniques, limitless financial means, and the desire for grandeur could in themselves be sufficient to attain architectural excellence and that significant works of art could be produced outside a cultural ambient that kindles the imagination of the artist and the architect.

It would be too easy to draw quick parallels between the monumental mosques of Istanbul and the Hagia Sophia, or to dismiss Ottoman Turkish works as the anticlimax of Byzantine architecture. The influences of Byzantine or Seljuk works on Ottoman Turkish architecture can easily be detected. This is only natural because architecture is a continuum. One cannot think of Gothic architecture without the preceding Romanesque, or the Renaissance without the Roman. The question is not so much what each era took from an earlier period but what it has been able to do with what it found and whether what it left behind is significant. Ottoman Turkish architecture of the sixteenth century can stand comparison with any great style of architecture of its day and Süleyman the Magnificent's chief architect Sinan (1490–1588), can easily compete with any Renaissance architect of the fifteenth or sixteenth centuries.

The purpose of this book, however, is not to discuss the golden age of Ottoman architecture, or the architect Sinan, but to study the nature and the evolution of only one type of Ottoman Turkish building—that of the mosque—during the first two centuries of the Ottoman Empire. The book covers the period from the early thirteenth century to 1506, when the Mosque of Bayezid II in Istanbul, generally considered to be the first of the monumental Ottoman mosques, was inaugurated. In other words, it will not primarily be concerned with the masterpieces of Ottoman Turkish architecture, but with those modest and experimental buildings which must precede the peak and prepare the groundwork for it.

The Ottoman Empire at the end of the
fifteenth century

The year 1506 may seem an arbitrary date for the termination of the initial period of Ottoman architectural development, since the Turkish conquest of Constantinople in 1453 marks the beginning of the new era in Ottoman history. It is true that with the conquest of Constantinople the Ottomans entered a more sophisticated phase. The struggling, modest sultanate gave way to a more secure and mature empire. Mehmed II not only conquered a city of strategic and psychological importance but critically changed the social and administrative structure of his state. Architectural advances, however, do not necessarily coincide with political development. The conquest of Constantinople had its influences on the Ottoman architect who gained the opportunity to study significant Byzantine buildings in the city, especially Hagia Sophia. It would be unrealistic not to accept, for instance, that the halfdome and the conch were not Byzantine contributions to Ottoman architecture. But the influences of Constantinople or, to put it differently, the architectural vocabulary of the new era, were not immediately evident. It took at least another fifty years for the experimental, or the medieval, Ottoman architecture to transform itself into the rational "classical" style. Although the elements of the classical Ottoman style are to be found in the mosques built during the reign of Bayezid II (1481–1512), there are also those of the early period. They have not been totally freed from the Anatolian Seljuk vocabulary. The ornate, decorative minarets of the Mosque of Bayezid II in Amasya (Fig. 194) or the side wings of the same sultan's mosques in Edirne (Fig. 46) and Istanbul (Fig. 218) clearly indicate early Ottoman influences.

The Mosque of Bayezid II in Istanbul (1501–6) has always been accepted as the first of the imperial mosques. This mosque, as well as the now nonexistent Mosque of Fâtih (the Conqueror), differ from the earlier sultans' mosques because of the use of halfdomes in their upper structures. For this reason, they are generally considered to be different from the monumental mosques built before 1453. I take exception to this argument, since the adoption of the halfdome is not all that significant. Byzantine elements and construction techniques as well as others have always been used in Ottoman architecture. The important thing, it seems to me, is not the incorporation of new elements but the creation of a clearly defined Ottoman style devoid of traditional Anatolian and Seljuk forms and medieval spirit. I do not believe that this transformation took place during the reigns of Mehmed the Conqueror or of his son Bayezid II, but at a later time, during the reign of Süleyman the Magnificent.

A second factor which necessitated the prolongation of this work beyond 1453 was the eyvan mosque, an early Ottoman mosque type not found in the classical era. It continued to be built throughout the fifteenth century and ceased to exist after that. The eyvan mosque, I must admit, lost some of its initial characteristics during the second half of the fifteenth century; but despite that, it retained its identity for another fifty years after the conquest.

For the reasons stated above, I do not end this study on early Ottoman mosques with the conquest of Constantinople—although the introductory notes of exposition do not go beyond 1453—but stretch its scope to include the significant mosques dating from the second half of the fifteenth century. In this way, I have tried to show the development patterns in early Ottoman mosques up to the threshold of the emergence of the mature, rational "classical" style.

THE ORIGIN AND THE RISE OF THE OTTOMANS

The Osmanlıs—or Ottomans, as they came to be known—descended from a small tribe called Kayı of the Oğuz family of Turks. The Kayı tribe migrated westward from central Asia in the early years of the thirteenth century to avoid the onslaught of Genghis Khan's armies, crossed Iran in a relatively short time, and settled for a while near Ahlat, to the northwest of Lake Van. It is strongly suspected that in the Battle of Yassıçemen (1230) the Kayı Turks fought in the ranks of the Anatolian Seljuks against the Khwarizm shahs. About this time their leader, Gündüz-Alp, died and his place was taken by Ertuğrul Bey (d. 1281). Soon the Kayı Turks were in the vicinity of Ankara, and around 1235 they were settled by the Seljuk sultan Alâeddin Key-Kubâd I in the Söğüt-Bilecik sector in western Anatolia.

The Anatolian Seljuk empire was composed of a number of principalities which paid tribute to the Seljuk sultan in Konya. In the mid-thirteenth century the strongest principality in northwestern Anatolia was that of Çobanoğulları, whose capital city was Kastamonu. One strongly suspects that the small Kayı tribe was subject to the principality of Çobanoğulları during its first fifty years in Anatolia, and after the decline of this dynasty, the Kayı Turks paid tribute to the House of Germiyan in western Anatolia. It was not until halfway through the reign of Ertuğrul Bey's son Osman (Othman) Bey (1281–1324[?]) that the principality of Osman acquired sufficient strength and stature to be subject directly to the Anatolian Seljuk court in Konya.

When the Anatolian Seljuk empire was finally dissolved in 1308, the principality of Osman started paying a token tribute to the Ilhanids in Tebriz. With the Anatolian Seljuks no longer in power, Osman Bey started pushing the frontiers of his territory toward the Black Sea and the Sea of Marmara. By the end of the first decade of the fourteenth century the Ottomans had captured the town of Hendek, 20 kilometers from the Black Sea, and, by taking Mudanya in 1321, had reached the shores of the Sea of Marmara.

The siege of Bursa (Brussa), one of the Byzantine strongholds in Anatolia had been undertaken about 1315. The fortified city resisted Ottoman attempts for ten years, however, and was not captured until April 6, 1326. Nephritis inactivated Osman Gazi after 1320; the administration of the state was left to his son, Orhan Bey. It is not definitely known how long Osman Gazi lived after that date or whether or not he had abdicated in favor of Orhan Bey. A document dated 1324 mentions Orhan Bey as the ruler and a coin minted the same year bearing his name attests to the fact that by 1324 Orhan Bey had ascended the Ottoman throne.[1] Osman Gazi is buried in Bursa. It may be that he died in 1324, was buried in Söğüt in his father's mausoleum, and his remains were later brought to Bursa in accordance with his will to be buried in the Silver Mausoleum on the citadel. It is also possible that he lived to see Bursa captured by his son and was directly entombed in the Silver Mausoleum.

Like that of his father, the reign of Orhan Gazi, who first used the title of sultan, was also long (1324?–62) and equally full of military campaigns. After the capture of Bursa, which was made the capital city, the next Ottoman objective was İznik (Nicaea), the capital city of the Byzantine Empire from 1204 to 1261. It fell during the month of May in 1329. The Byzantine emperor Andronicus Paleologos III made an effort to force the Ottomans back but was defeated by Orhan Gazi in the Battle of Pelekanon, which took place near Gebze on the Bay of İzmit (Nicomedia), 40 kilometers from the Bosporus. The Ottoman victory eased the Ottoman conquest of Byzantine territory in Anatolia. Gemlik was taken in 1334 and three years later İzmit fell.

Between the principality of Karasi in Balıkesir and the Ottoman state, there remained uncaptured the fortresses of Ulubad, Mihaliç, and Kirmastı. Orhan Bey took them in 1342, and soon afterwards led a campaign against the neighboring principality to the west, seizing most of its territory. Some of the Karasi forces retreated westward and held a strip of land from the Bay of Edremit to Troy; but this land, too, was annexed during the reign of Murad I.

The capture of the southern shores of the Sea of Marmara constituted the initial step of Ottoman conquest in Thrace and a struggle for power in Constantinople gave them the opportunity to land and to establish a stronghold on European soil. When Emperor Andronikos died in 1341, his son Ioannis was too young to ascend the throne; and Kantakuzinos was made regent. His regency, however, was not accepted in Constantinople and Adrianople; therefore, he moved to Dimetoka and proclaimed himself emperor. This action was contested by Adrianople and resulted in internal wars, during which Kantakuzinos requested assistance from Orhan Bey. With the help of six thousand Ottoman troops, he seized most of the Byzantine provinces on the Black Sea as well as Adrianople. He then moved on to Constantinople in 1347 and took it. Along with the rest of Kantakuzinos' forces Orhan Bey's six thousand men entered the city. In the meantime, Kantakuzinos had betrothed his daughter Theodora to Orhan Gazi.

Two years later the Ottomans came to the aid of the Byzantines once again. Orhan Bey's able son and crown prince, Süleyman Paşa, crossed the Dardanelles with twenty thousand men to keep Saloniki from falling into the hands of the Serbs and, in 1352, dealt a severe blow to the Serbian-Bulgarian armies in the Battle of Dimetoka. For this campaign, Orhan Bey had requested from Kantakuzinos a fortified position to secure his rear in case Ottoman units were forced to retreat and was given the Castle of Tsimpe on the Gallipoli Peninsula. After the Slavic danger had been eliminated, the Ottomans settled in the Castle of Tsimpe and began using it as a base to expand northward. By 1365 the whole peninsula was in the hands of the Turks. Ottoman expansion in Rumelia had begun. Toward the end of Orhan Bey's reign the Ottoman territory had increased to 95,000 square kilometers, which was 10,000 square kilometers larger than the territory held by the Byzantines at the time.

Süleyman Paşa was killed in 1359 by falling off his horse. His younger brother, Murad Bey, took over as commander of Ottoman forces in Rumelia. Murad Bey (the Hüdavendigâr), who was to ascend the Ottoman throne upon the death of his father in 1362, extended the boundaries of the Ottoman state both in Rumelia and Anatolia. He captured Adrianople in 1361 and the environs of Ankara in 1362.

The rapid Ottoman expansion on European soil forced the Balkan States to unite. Hungary, Serbia, Bosnia, and Wallachia joined hands in a new crusade under the leadership of the Hungarian king Layosh. The crusaders moved toward the River Maritza in 1364. Sultan Murad I (1362–89) was in Bursa at the time, and the main bulk of the Ottoman forces were with him. But the Ottoman commander in Gallipoli had a force of 10,000 colonizer-dervishes at his command. He took the initiative and conducted a surprise attack on Layosh's armies, crippling them to inactivity. This Ottoman victory paved the way for further westward expansion. By 1371 the Ottomans reached the border of Serbia and the Adriatic Sea. A second crusade against the Ottomans also failed. In 1374 Serbia agreed to pay tribute to the Ottomans, as the Bulgarians and Byzantines had agreed to do earlier. The most important city in southern Serbia, Niş, fell in 1375; Monastir, the key to northern Macedonia was taken in 1382. By 1383 the Ottomans were pushing forward in eastern Albania and southern Montenegro.

In the meantime, the Ottomans had been extending their borders in Anatolia. The city of Kütahya fell in 1378. The principality of Hamidoğulları, located to the south of Eskişehir and the principality of Candaroğulları, to the east of Bolu and stretching along the Black Sea all the way to Amasya, were annexed between 1382 and 1385.

The first confrontation between the principality of Karaman, which considered itself the natural heir of the Anatolian Seljuks, and the Ottomans occurred in 1386. The Karamans challenged the Ottoman ascendancy to power by capturing Beyşehir, which the Ottomans had bought from the Hamids. Murad I could not let this onslaught go unchallenged. He met the Karaman forces near Konya and easily defeated them. Beyşehir was retaken and Sultan

Murad returned to Bursa. While the Ottomans were occupied in Anatolia, a third crusade was being prepared in Europe. The allied forces were composed of contingencies from all Balkan principalities and kingdoms and their commander-in-chief was Lazar, the king of Serbia. They met the Ottoman army in Kosova on June 20, 1389. The battle lasted eight hours and ended in another Ottoman victory but also in the death of Murad I, who was fatally wounded by a Serbian nobleman toward the end of the battle. Murad's place was immediately taken by his son, Bayezid, whose epithet Yıldırım (Thunderbolt) was given to him because of his quick and decisive actions in battle.

It is estimated that at the death of Ertuğrul Bey in 1281, the Ottomans possessed 4,800 square kilometers of territory. During Osman Bey's reign this was enlarged to 16,000 square kilometers. When Murad I ascended the throne the Ottoman state had reached 95,000 square kilometers, and at his death it had increased to approximately 500,000 square kilometers, 291,000 of which were on European soil.

Despite the Ottoman victory in the Battle of Kosova, the death of Sultan Murad I gave new hope to the beys of Anatolia, who felt that they could weaken the influence of the Ottomans in Anatolia and possibly overthrow them. They had underestimated Yıldırım Bayezid's power and ability. He may have been young, but he was as capable a military commander and administrator as his father. He quickly organized his forces, which included Serbian and Byzantine troops, marched on Kütahya and annexed the principality of Germiyan; he then moved further south to dissolve the principalities of Saruhan, Aydınoğulları, and Menteşeoğulları in Manisa, Aydın, and Muğla, respectively. Thus the Ottomans reached the shores of the Aegean Sea in 1390. The harbors, shipyards, and vessels of the seaside principalities were turned over to Yıldırım Bayezid. For the first time in their history, the Ottomans now possessed a naval force. After seizing Antalya, the sultan crossed the borders of the principality of Karaman in early 1391. The bey of Karaman had already realized that he had misjudged the Ottoman strength. He retreated without giving battle and Yıldırım Bayezid entered Konya unchallenged and accepted the peace offer of Alâeddin Ali Bey, who happened to be his son-in-law.

Yıldırım Bayezid decided that the time to conquer Constantinople had come. He now had a sixty-piece navy which could check Venetian and Genoese assistance to the city by way of the sea. The first Ottoman siege of Constantinople lasted seven months during which time six thousand men were stationed outside the walls. At the same time Yıldırım Bayezid crossed the Danube to annex Wallachia. In 1393, he was back again in Anatolia to deal with Kadı Burhaneddin, a central Anatolian feudal lord who had sided with the Karamans. During this campaign he recaptured some of the northern provinces which had changed hands. The second siege of Constantinople took place during the summer months of 1395. This alarmed the European countries, which by 1396 were once again united against the Ottomans. A large Christian army was organized whose objective it was to defeat the Ottomans and conquer all Turkey. Yıldırım Bayezid lifted the siege of Constantinople and marched to Adrianople. On September 25, the European alliance comprising 130,000 troops met the Ottoman army of 70,000 men in Nikopolis and in the ensuing battle the Ottomans overpowered their opponents.

After the Battle of Nikopolis, Yıldırım Bayezid turned his attention to the Greek peninsula. In 1397 he crossed Thermopylae and entered Athens. Later that year the conquest of the entire Morean peninsula was completed. Soon afterwards the principality of Karaman and the provinces under Kadı Burhaneddin were annexed and the third siege of Constantinople was undertaken. This siege, as well as the fourth one which began in the spring of 1400, was not successful. Yet what with the Ottomans in complete control in Anatolia and eastern Europe it seemed only a matter of a few years before Constantinople would fall to the Ottomans. A new threat, however, this time from the east, was to upset the balance of power in Anatolia and eastern Europe, to throw the Ottomans into a period of confusion and internal struggles, and to postpone the fall of Constantinople for another half a century. This was the onslaught of Tamerlane (Timur Leng).

The rivalry between the Ottomans and the Ak Koyunlu dynasty in eastern Anatolia had reached a new stage after the elimination of Kadı Burhaneddin. The Ak Koyunlu paid tribute to Tamerlane, and with their encouragement Tamerlane marched on Sivas, whose population at the time was 120,000, captured the city in 1400, and destroyed it. He then took the city of Malatya. Yıldırım Bayezid immediately moved his forces to Anatolia and reached Kayseri; Tamerlane, not wishing a confrontation with the Ottomans, retreated. He wanted to fight at a time and in a place of his own choosing, which were to be July 28, 1402, and Ankara. Despite heavy losses, which are estimated to have been 40,000 men, Tamerlane defeated the Ottomans in the Battle of Ankara. Yıldırım Bayezid was captured and died in captivity on March 3, 1403, in Akşehir. Principalities subdued earlier by the Ottomans, re-established themselves. Some of the Rumelian provinces declared their independence. The Ottoman throng faced the danger of partition. Yıldırım Bayezid's sons Süleyman, İsa, and Mehmed each proclaimed himself ruler in Edirne, Bursa, and Amasya, respectively. Mehmed strengthened his position first and marched on Bursa to take it away from his brother. İsa lost the Battle of Ulubad and took refuge with Süleyman in Edirne, although he made a number of attempts to restore his position. He was finally captured and put to death in 1410. İsa Çelebi's elimination forced Süleyman to take a stand against Mehmed. He moved his forces into Anatolia and for a while it looked as if he were the sole Ottoman ruler. It proved not to be so. For Mehmed had convinced his younger brother Musa to march against their elder brother and while Musa and Süleyman fought in Thrace, he himself extended his domination over Anatolian provinces. Although Süleyman initially defeated Musa in battle, he was weakened by the latter's persistent attacks, and his forces were finally dispersed in a confrontation near Sophia. He escaped but was captured and slain. Musa, victorious, entered Edirne in 1411. Although a good military commander, Musa lacked the political ability and insight of his brother Mehmed. He ruled for two years but was finally defeated and eliminated by his brother. The death of Musa left Mehmed the only heir to the Ottoman throne, which he ascended on July 5, 1413.

At this time the boundaries of the Ottoman territory had shrunk considerably as compared with the size of the state during the reign of Yıldırım Bayezid. But Ottoman prestige in Anatolia was still strong. In his eight years as sultan, Mehmed I (1413–21) managed to extend Ottoman territory to 870,000 square kilometers, only 70,000 short of what it had been before the Battle of Ankara. More important than this, he re-established the supremacy of the Ottomans.

When Mehmed's son Murad II arrived in Bursa to assume the sultanate he was seventeen years old. During the reign of Mehmed I, the Byzantine emperor had given asylum to Mustafa Çelebi, the fifth son of Yıldırım Bayezid, who now claimed Ottoman provinces in Rumelia. Assisted by the Byzantines, Mustafa soon acquired the allegiance of the Ottoman commanders in Europe and crossed the Dardanelles in 1422. The forces of the uncle and nephew met near Bursa and in the ensuing battle the young sultan overpowered Mustafa, who was caught and hanged. A direct outcome of this development was a new siege of Constantinople, which lasted sixty-four days and was lifted only when Murad's younger brother, also named Mustafa, revolted against the sultan, a matter that was quickly settled. During the next twenty years, Murad II continued to struggle in Anatolia and Rumelia to retain the status quo. Anatolian principalities often changed sides or turned rebellious. The Karamans especially, who had never really accepted Ottoman supremacy, challenged it frequently. In Europe, the Turco-Venetian wars (1425–30) and the war with Hungary (1427–30) required constant attention.

The Hungarians, who often pressured Ottoman borders, were finally defeated and pushed back in 1438. This campaign led to the siege of Belgrade in 1439 but the Ottomans failed to capture the city at this time. The Turks had once again begun to threaten Europe, and Europe once again united against the Ottomans when Murad II abdicated in 1444 in favor of his son Mehmed II, who was then twelve years old. The ascension to the throne of a very young sultan encouraged European powers. Their united army of 100,000 men reached Vidin by September of that year and marched on to the Black Sea. The Ottoman Council of State held in Edirne decided that Murad should come back to lead the Ottoman army, which met the allies at Varna and defeated them. After the battle, the army made it known that they did not want to see the young Mehmed as sultan while Murad was alive. So Mehmed was sent to Manisa, and in 1445 Murad ascended the throne for the second time. A new European alliance did not take long in organizing. With Hungary as the leader, Poland, Bohemia,

Wallachia, Moldavia, and Sicily united and confronted the Turks in Kosova on October 17, 1448. The battle lasted for three days and three nights. After the second day, the allied units began to retreat. Those that resisted were encircled and taken prisoner. The second Battle of Kosova marks the end of European attempts to push back the Turks from the Balkans. From 1448 on, for two and a half centuries, European rulers were to fight to defend their countries but ceased to challenge the Ottoman supremacy over the lands south of the Danube.

Murad II died in 1451. At twenty-one Mehmed II became sultan for the second time. Mehmed's big ambition was to capture Constantinople, which had withstood countless sieges and attempts. He had a Rumelian fortress built on the Bosporus across from the Anatolian fortress erected by Yıldırım Bayezid. He thus gained full control of the straits. Having spent the winter of 1453 in Edirne preparing for the siege, Mehmed ordered his army to march on the city in the spring. The land and sea siege began on the sixth day of April. The Byzantines had secured the mouth of the Golden Horn by a chain. During the night of April 22, the 67-vessel Ottoman fleet was drawn by oxen over the hills to sail in the Golden Horn. This feat and the pontoon bridge which the Ottomans erected on the Golden Horn demoralized the Byzantines. What worried Mehmed II was the destruction of Constantinople's walls under the fire of his large cannons. He wanted to take the city intact. On May 23 when the fall of Constantinople became a certainty he sent an emissary to the emperor to surrender the city. According to Turkish law, fortresses, towns, or cities that were not taken by force could not be pillaged or their inhabitants taken prisoners. The proud emperor Constantine XI Palaeologus Dragases refused the offer and died fighting on the ramparts on May 29, 1453, when Constantinople finally fell.

With the conquest of Constantinople, the wounds of the Battle of Ankara were healed and the Ottomans, after having put an end to the Seljuk empire, now inherited the rule of a second one. The Ottomans had not yet reached the Taurus Mountains or the River Euphrates in Anatolia. But there was hardly a state in the east to counter an Ottoman thrust. The Timurids were no longer strong. The Kara Koyunlu state was engaged by its enemy, the Ak Koyunlu state. The Mamluks were too far away and could hardly be expected to threaten Anatolia. In western Anatolia, no principality remained and the central Anatolian principalities of Candar, Karaman, and Dulkadir continued to exist under Ottoman suzerainty. On the European continent the political scene was the same. There was not a single country that alone could withstand an Ottoman offensive. In the mid-fifteenth century the Ottoman state had a young, able, and ambitious sultan as her ruler and would continue to expand for more than a century. Mehmed the Conquerer's grandson, Yavuz Selim I, "the Grim" (1512–20), would conquer Syria and Egypt, put an end to the Mamluk dynasty and assume the title of halife (caliph) in 1517 adding new luster to the House of Osman. Selim's son, Süleyman the Magnificent (1520–66), reached the walls of Vienna. The Ottoman state was destined to become a world empire.

EARLY SULTANS OF THE HOUSE OF OSMAN

According to Turkish law and tradition, a state was owned by a ruling family, and a member of that family was elected *ulu bey* (great leader) to head the family and state. This tradition was respected through the reign of Murad I. Afterwards, the election of the new ruler was restricted to the immediate family, or the sons, of the late sultan. Ottoman sultans, as sole owners and absolute rulers of the state, enjoyed unlimited authority over the lives and possessions of their subjects; but they did not exercise their power unduly or arbitrarily. All matters of state were deliberated in the divan (Council of State) and the sultan often consulted with his viziers (ministers) before issuing decrees, since an imperial edict automatically became law. Even at the peak of their power, Ottoman sultans were most careful to abide by the decisions of the divan, and hardly ever overruled them. As a matter of fact, until Mehmed the Conquerer, Ottoman sultans always participated in and acted as the chairman of the divan and only in their absence did the prime minister assume the role of head of government. The sultan was also the commander-in-chief of the Ottoman army. In large campaigns he led his troops in person; in smaller campaigns a deputy of his own choosing was given the command.

Through the reign of Murad II, Ottoman sultans kept in contact with the people, mixed with them, often heard and judged court cases, and treated their comrades in arms as friends. Mehmed the Conquerer put an end to this. The relationship between the sultan and his subjects became formal. During the reigns of his successors, the separation of the court and the people was further widened so that in time the ruler and the ruled neither saw nor knew one another.

Although Osman Bey was the founder of the Ottoman dynasty, he was not a sultan; neither coins nor inscriptions minted or written in his name have ever been discovered. During his reign (1281–1324[?]) Osman Bey expanded his territory but paid tribute to, and remained semidependent on, the Anatolian Seljuks and the Ilhanids.

The first Ottoman ruler to assume the title of sultan was Orhan Bey (1324[?]–1362), who was an organizer endowed with clear thinking and perseverance. Not only did he plan and execute the Ottoman crossing to Europe, but the civil and military institutions of the new state were first established during his reign. In Orhan Bey's military campaigns the contributions of his two sons, Süleyman Paşa (1316–59) and Murad, who later succeeded him, and of his brother Alâeddin Bey (d. 1331) were of importance. In administrative and organizational matters Orhan Bey's vizier, Alâeddin Paşa and his *kadı* (judge), Cendereli Kara Halil, played significant roles.

Murad I (1362–89) was an equally capable military commander and administrator. He had strong will power and mental flexibility and was quick in action. He was also known for his just and impartial attitude toward his subjects. All of Murad I's military campaigns were painstakingly planned and cleverly executed. He strengthened his administration by new laws, and his farsighted policy in settling large numbers of Turkish families in the newly conquered territory in Rumelia proved an asset in later decades. The most important viziers and commanders during the reign of Murad I were Çandarlı Kara Halil Paşa and his son Ali, Lala Şahin Paşa, Timurtaş Paşa, Hacı Il Beyi, and Evrenuz Bey.

Although Murad I had repose and restraint, his son Yıldırım Bayezid I (1389–1402) was nervous, cruel, and inflexible. Bayezid I was quick and decisive in action. He removed from the map a number of Anatolian principalities in one swift move, capturing Amasya, Samsun, Sivas, and Malatya. His victory at Nikopolis was another example attesting to his agility. Bayezid I's defeat by Tamerlane, however, may also have been due to the impulsive action of his head-on offensive against a superior military commander and master tactician. The Battle of Ankara threw Ottoman conquests back by fifty years.

Following the era of the War of the Princes after Bayezid's death, Mehmed I (1413–21) reorganized and revitalized the disaster-stricken country. For this, Mehmed I may be considered the second founder of the Ottoman state. In his eight-year rule he recaptured the territory returned to the Byzantines by his brother Süleyman, and the cities of Manisa, Aydın, and Samsun and annexed the principality of Menteşe. It has been estimated that Mehmed I took part in twenty battles and skirmishes and had on his body not less than forty wounds.

Mehmed's son Murad II (1421–44 and 1445–51) was seventeen when his father died. It was with the assistance of his able ministers that he ascended the throne and could withstand the serious threat from his uncle. He was a brave, good-hearted man with a wild but artistic disposition. But he did not possess the will power or the resolution of either his father or his son. The affairs of state were administered throughout his reign by his vizier, Çandarlı İbrahim Paşa, and his son Halil Paşa.

Ottoman royal princes were called *şehzade*, or *şahzade* (son of the shah). During the early period they were given the title Çelebi (Gentleman) and were assigned to important provincial governorships between the ages of ten and fifteen to be trained in military and administrative matters in the field by an experienced tutor (*lala*) who accompanied his charge to the *sancak* (province) and remained there with him.

If his age and prior training permitted it, the Çelebi Sultan (the prince who governed a *sancak*) established his own divan and, with the assistance of his *lala*, ruled semi-independently from his father. In royal edicts he fixed his own seal but had to inform the central administration of his appointments and acquire the sultan's approval.

Until the mid-fifteenth century the cities that the princes were appointed to govern as *sancak beyi* (provincial governor) were Balıkesir, Isparta, Antalya, Amasya, Manisa, and Sivas, all in Anatolia. It was against the law to appoint them governor of a *sancak* in Rumelia.

EARLY OTTOMAN ADMINISTRATIVE ORGANIZATION

The highest administrative body in the early Ottoman state was the divan, or the Council of State, which met at the capital city, or where the sultan happened to be, under the chairmanship of the sultan himself. In his absence, his vizier presided over the meeting. Up to the reign of Mehmed the Conquerer the authority was in the hands of viziers and commanders of Turkish origin. With Mehmed it passed to those who had either converted to Islam in adulthood or had risen from the ranks in the janissary organization, who were, again, not Turkish in origin.

During the reign of Orhan Gazi, the viziers were civilian scholars and not military commanders. When Candarlı Kara Halil assumed the offices of both vizier and army commander, the trend changed, and afterwards the authority of the grand viziers was extended to include military as well as civilian affairs. Until the end of the fifteenth century the number of the viziers never exceeded three. Their symbol of office was three *tuğs* (crest of horsehair painted red) given them by the sultan.

The second important position was that of *beylerbeyi* (governor general), and he was given two *tuğs*. Orhan Gazi's son Süleyman Paşa was a *beylerbeyi*. At his death the title passed on to Lala Şahin Paşa. During the early part of the fourteenth century, there was only one *beylerbeyi*. But as the Ottoman state grew in territory, a second governor generalship was created, one for Rumeli (Rumelia) and the other for Anadolu (Anatolia). Later on, their numbers were further increased. The seat of the *beylerbeyi* of Rumelia was the city of Monastir, that of Anatolia was Kütahya, except for a short period when it was moved to Ankara.

The third post in the hierarchy of Ottoman administration, whose symbol of office was one *tuğ*, was that of *sancak beyi* (governor). A *sancak beyi* had under his jurisdiction a number of *kazas* (towns) and villages. He was not only the military commander of the *sancak*, but was responsible for its civil administration and security.

BUILDING COMPLEXES

The rapid growth of the Ottoman state, from a tiny principality possessing approximately 4,800 square kilometers of territory to the southeast of the Sea of Marmara at the death of Ertuğrul Bey in 1281 to a world empire covering an area 20,000 times larger and spreading over three continents by the mid-sixteenth century, cannot simply be attributed to military strength and strategy. It is true that for two and a half centuries the Ottoman state was endowed with ten successive strong sultans, from Osman Gazi to Selim II. All ten were either gifted commanders or able administrators—in most cases both. Furthermore, most of them had the good fortune to have long reigns. Although the first ten capable sultans must be accepted as an important factor in the development of the Ottoman state, the role of other elements, such as the administrative and military organization, social and judicial institutions, or settlement policies, must also be given due credit.

I have already commented on the administrative organization of the Ottomans. I would now like to say a few words about the colonizer-dervishes (*gazi-dervişler*), who played an important part in the foundation of the Ottoman social structure. These dervishes served as the organizers of the migrating Turkish families from Khurasan to Anatolia. They took command of the incoming Turkish people, first training and educating them, and later leading them in battle. When a town was seized, some of the colonizer-dervishes settled in it with their units while the others pushed on to the next objective.

Since Turkish families from central Asia continued to arrive in Anatolia, both the vanguard forces and the newly settled towns were periodically replenished. When the Ottomans captured a Byzantine town, the largest church was immediately converted into a mosque but the second largest church was left to the Christian population for their services. If the town had only one church, the Christians were given permission to erect a new church for themselves. The mission of the Turkish colony which remained in the town began at once. First the *hamam* (bath), then the *zâviye* (convent) for the colonizer-dervishes, the *medrese* (school), public kitchens, fountains, roads, bridges, and caravanseries were built, and the process of colonization and urbanization was launched. The colonization process was especially swift in Rumelia.

The Ottomans did not favor religious intolerance. Indeed, mass conversion to Islam was against their policy. Apart from religious freedom, the Ottoman Christians enjoyed judicial, educational, and cultural non-interference. They had their own schools, social institutions, and law courts. This policy of extreme tolerance and non-involvement in the affairs of non-Muslim subjects affected the development pattern of Ottoman towns. Since the integrity of the non-Muslim communities was retained, the urbanization of the Turkish families migrating from central Asia demanded the creation of new neighborhoods. These were established outside the boundaries of the existing towns. Thus the Ottomans did not leave the foundation and the growth of new neighborhoods to chance but developed a pattern of settlement that would promote community spirit. They also adopted the already developed system of commerce of the Anatolian Seljuks and applied it widely to encourage trade.

During the fourteenth and fifteenth centuries, new neighborhoods were founded by the erection of a *külliye*, or a complex of buildings, generally located outside the city walls. Starting with Orhan Bey, all Ottoman rulers erected at least one building complex during their reign. Until the conquest of

Constantinople royal building complexes were modest in size. After the conquest they became monumental, comprising a great number of structures and, more often than not, constituting the nuclei of fairly large urban redevelopment schemes.

The first Ottoman building complex was founded in İznik by Orhan Gazi. It is located outside the city walls approximately 400 meters to the south of the Yenişehir Gate, and consists of a mosque, a bath, and an *imâret* (public kitchen). Not much remains of the three buildings. Recent excavations unearthed the lower part of the mosque's walls as well as a portion of the marble inscription slab which gives the date of completion as A.H. 735, or A.D. 1334.

A second, and bigger, complex built by the same sultan is found in Bursa. These buildings date from the fourth decade of the fourteenth century and again are located approximately 400 meters to the east of the citadel. Although they are now situated right at the center of the city of Bursa, historians note that at the time they were built the area was a lonely one and that it required courage to go out after dark.

The complex of Orhan Gazi in Bursa was composed of a mosque, a bath called Bey Hamamı (Prince's Bath), an *imâret*, a *medrese*, and a *han*, known as Bey Hanı or Emir Hanı (Prince's Inn). The mosque and the bath exist today in more or less their original form. Bey Hanı was burned down in the fire of 1955, which destroyed most of the historical commercial center of Bursa, but has since been reconstructed in its original form and style. It is known that the *imâret* was located to the east of the mosque. Unfortunately, it no longer exists. As for the *medrese*, there is no indication where it was situated.

Ottoman building complexes were not only erected but were also maintained by their founders by means of a *vakfiye*, or a foundation charter. The founder of a complex prepared a foundation charter in which he specified the salaries of the clergy and the teaching staff of the *medrese* and the primary school, the stipends of the students, and even the number of meals and the amount of food to be served daily to the above as well as to the poor of the neighborhood. These varied from charter to charter depending on the stature of the means of the founder, but there was generally an accepted minimum level which no foundation charter could fall below. Even the most modest foundation charters specified one *fodla* (flat bread), soup, and meat once a day, and *pilav* (rice) and *zerde* (sweetened rice colored with saffron) twice a week. To meet the expenses of the mosque, the *medrese*, and the *imâret*, the founder generally erected a commercial building, the management of which, along with the responsibility for the maintenance of the complex, was given to the trustees of the foundation. In the case of Orhan Gazi's building complex in Bursa, the sultan built a *han*, a combination office building and hostel, and the accrued income of this commercial enterprise supported the various religious, educational, and public welfare activities of his complex.

A fairly large complex in Bursa is that of Yıldırım Bayezid located to the northeast of the city. Only the mosque, the *medrese*, and the *türbe* (mausoleum) remain intact. According to the *vakfiye* dated A.H. 802 (1399), which is in the archives of Bursa but not yet published, the buildings erected by Bayezid I were numerous and, in addition to the above, included an *imâret*, a *hamam*, a second *medrese*, a *han*, and a *saray* (palace). Based on this information Professor Gabriel proposed a site plan which shows the existing buildings and the probable location of the others.[2] The complex of Yıldırım sits on the crest of a hill. Remains of a wall suggest that it was fortified and was accessible through two gates, one situated on the north leading from the Plain of Bursa, the other on the east connecting the complex to the neighborhood. The mosque is placed on a plateau occupying the highest ground. Farther to the north, the *medrese*, which today houses a medical clinic, occupies a second plateau. It is a rectangular structure built around an arcaded fountain court. The cells (small rooms for students and scholars), each with a fireplace, are placed on three sides, the fourth side being taken up by the classroom built in the form of a domed eyvan and, like the prayer eyvan of the mosque, protrudes from the main rectangular mass of the structure. The *türbe* is in front of the *medrese*. It is a simple domed-square structure with a three-bay porch. The *hamam* is located to the southeast and the *saray* to the northwest of the mosque. J. Dallaway remarks that on his way to İznik he saw the *saray* and that it was in ruins.[3] All that remains of it today are some foundations and low walls. The second *medrese* mentioned in the *vakfiye* must be the *darüşşifa* (hospital) located outside the walls some 250 meters to the southeast of the mosque. In plan it is very similar to the *medrese* with the exception that the main hall across from the entrance, which, in all probability, was the operating theater, is enclosed and does not project from the rectangular mass. The hospital collapsed in the earthquake of 1855 and, like the *saray*, is in ruins today.

In the complex of Bayezid I the eyvan mosque occupies the dominant position. In the complex of Mehmed I, known as the Green Complex, the crowning element is the *türbe*, a tall octagonal structure surmounted by a dome, 15 m. in diameter, and faced with turquoise ceramic tiles within and without. Along with the mosque, it represents the peak of craftsmanship in early Ottoman architecture. Part of the *imâret* of the Green Complex still exists, providing us with an early model. It comprises a rectangular hall, or refectory, with a two-unit kitchen and two baker's ovens on one wall, and a storeroom. The *medrese* is not unlike that of the Bayezid complex, except that it is square in form and has two additional eyvans on the sides. The *hamam*, comprising a domed-square hall, a domed tepidarium, and a two-unit caldarium, is also similar to the *hamam* of the Bayezid complex.

As one can readily observe, although the individual buildings of early Ottoman complexes may be symmetrical and orderly in their design, the general composition is not. The buildings are placed following the contours of the terrain, but there is no geometric relationship between them. Instead one finds the medieval approach of arbitrary grouping. But rational and geometric site planning was not far away. Some forty years after the Green Complex was erected, Mehmed the Conquerer built the complex in Istanbul in which we see not only a grand concept but also an articulated balance, symmetry, and harmonious order.

The complex of Fâtih (the Conquerer) was designed by the architect Atik Sinan and was built between 1463 and 1471. It is located on top of one of Istanbul's seven hills. At the center is a huge square plaza measuring 270 m. per side, defined by four *medreses* each on the east and west and by walls on the south and north. The mosque that stands today in the middle of the plaza is not the original Mosque of Fâtih, which collapsed in the earthquake of 1766 and was rebuilt in 1771 on a larger plan. The old mosque had one full and one halfdome; the new one supports one full and four halfdomes. Because of this expansion, which occurred toward the south, the *türbe* of the Conquerer, located near the south wall behind the mosque, was also rebuilt farther to the south in the eighteenth century. A second and smaller *türbe*, that of the Conqueror's wife, Gülbahar Hatun, stands at right angles to the first.

Although the mosque and the *türbe* do not date from the mid-fifteenth century, the *medreses* do. The four in the east overlooking the Golden Horn are called Karadeniz (Black Sea) *medreses;* those on the west overlooking the Sea of Marmara, the Akdeniz (Mediterranean) *medreses.* All eight are constructed of alternating stone and brick courses in the style of the day and are similar in plan: a rectangular, arcaded court at their center, cells on three sides, the closed classroom at one end with the toilets placed next to it, and the portal on the side to make it accessible from the plaza. The *medreses* are arranged in a line with two ramped passages between them on each side. Thus the end ones are independent but the two in the middle are built back to back. Historical records mention eight more *medreses*—one below each of the existing ones. Unfortunately, we do not know what these looked like for they have disappeared. It is assumed that they were linear in plan—that is to say, the cells overlooked a long terrace and not a court—and that they were either attached to the exterior walls of the court *medreses* at a lower level down the slope or arranged independently below them with an alley in between. I find both these hypotheses unacceptable; it is difficult to imagine that while all the existing *medreses* —despite their introverted plans—exhibit the additional security measure of having their doors opening on the walled plaza, the other eight were not only arranged outside the framework of the central plaza but were also totally unprotected, having no courts upon which the cells opened. I am of the opinion that the cells of the lower *medreses* opened to narrow courts of their own and that these lower courts were connected to the upper courts by staircases placed across the entrance portals.

In addition to the two gates mentioned above, on the east and west between the *medreses*, there are two more gates each on the north and south. On the inner sides of the northern gates two small, elevated, domed-square buildings perched on walls. The western one was the library and still exists; the other, a primary school, has disappeared. On the other side of the plaza, outside the walls, there also were two buildings, both built inside protective walls of their own. The one on the east was the hospital and no longer exists. The other, the *tabhane*, or hospice, is in fairly good condition. Its plan resembles those of the *medreses*. Around the arcaded court there is a domed eyvan for recreation. Two more eyvans are placed on the sides, each composed of two adjacent domed units. The rest of the building comprises halls, guest rooms, and a kitchen wing at the southwest corner. A small two-room structure located to the west of the *tabhane* is believed to be a part of the *imâret*. Evliya Çelebi remarks that it had seventy domes.[4] This, perhaps, is a slight exaggeration. But it obviously was a fairly large building with adequate facilities to serve food to hundreds of students as well as to the poor of the neighborhood.

Another monumental complex worthy of note is the complex of Bayezid II located next to the River Tunca in Edirne. Designed by the architect Hayreddin, it was built between 1484 and 1488. Although less symmetrical than the complex of Fâtih, it is nonetheless as orderly and geometric in its general composition.

At the center is the mosque, comprising a large, single-unit sanctuary flanked by twin convents, all three giving on to a spacious fountain court. Two tall minarets rise at the northern corners of the convents. To the east of the mosque, there stand two buildings of equal width separated by a yard. The longer is the *imâret*, composed of a good-sized kitchen with two huge fireplaces in it, a long dining room, and three dormitories for the staff, arranged around a court. The other building, north of the *imâret*, consists of a large storeroom and a bakery whose ovens were so located and designed that they could be stoked from the service yard where the wood was kept. The yard also served as a passage to the back door of the storeroom through which food staples in quantity were brought in.

Undoubtedly, the most original and well-thought-out section of the complex is the hospital and medical college wing on the west. Placed at right angles to each other, the two buildings are linked by a narrow structure containing the toilets which served both. The medical *medrese* is a square structure planned around an arcaded fountain court. Each student cell is provided with a fireplace and storage niches. The classroom is high and, like operating theaters until recent years, has a gallery at the back from which the students watched surgical operations.

The hospital is divided into two sections: the out-patient and the in-patient departments. Six examination rooms and a passageway leading to the toilets take up one side of the out-patient court. Across from these there are four rooms serving as the laundry, storeroom, kitchen, and cook's room. This shows that dietary cooking and laundry of the in-patients were not handled in the *imâret* but inside the hospital itself. It is hard to determine the function of the two big halls on the south. Both have two domes and two fireplaces. I am of the opinion that one was the pharmacy and the other was for surgery. Or, alternatively, one could have been a combination pharmacy and surgery and the other the patients' dining room.

Through a second portal one passes into the smaller in-patient court on either side of which there is an eyvan flanked by two rooms for patients. A third door leads to a domed, hexagonal central hall. Here again, patients' quarters are arranged in an alternating pattern of rooms and eyvans. Four eyvans on the sides served as sitting areas. The fifth, across from the entrance, is deeper than the others because of its polygonal projection at the back. It is supposed to have served as a dais for musicians who played for the patients. This eyvan is oriented toward the *kıble* (the direction of Mecca) and, it seems to me, was probably designed as a prayer eyvan.

The combination hospital and medical college of the complex of Bayezid II in Edirne marks the first occurrence of such an institution in Ottoman architecture. It is, however, by no means the first of its kind founded by the Turks in Anatolia. The Seljuks built one, called the Çifte Medrese (Double Medrese) in Kayseri as early as 1205. They even established and strictly enforced a licensing system for physicians and surgeons to keep quacks out of the medical profession. During the Ottoman era, a medical student submitted a "thesis" and received his diploma not from his teacher but from the head physician of the province. In the palace school of Mehmed the Conquerer diplomas bore the *tuğra* (the monogram) of the sultan.

The first Ottoman *medrese* was founded in İznik in 1331, and a leading scholar of the day, Davud-i Kayseri, was appointed *müderris* (professor) with a high salary of thirty akçe (asper) a day (one akçe is today equivalent to $2.00). After İznik, the center of Ottoman education shifted to Bursa, where not only the sultans but their viziers as well competed with one another to establish new schools. By the end of the fourteenth century the *medrese* of İznik had lost its importance. And when Edirne became the capital city, and Murad II built his *medrese* there (Peykler Medresesi) the center of learning again shifted. The *müderris* of the Green Medrese in Bursa received fifty akçe a day, whereas the *müderris* of the Peykler Medresesi in Edirne was paid twice that amount. The supremacy of Edirne as a center of learning did not last long. When Mehmed the Conquerer erected his *külliye* in Istanbul which included sixteen *medreses* offering courses in a variety of theological and scientific subjects, the first Ottoman university was founded. Others would follow and Istanbul would remain the cultural and educational center as well as the seat of government of the government of the Ottoman Empire until its dissolution.

The schools erected and maintained by the sultans and others who could afford to found them were instrumental in the dissemination of Turkish culture, especially in Rumelia. New *medreses* were built in the territory conquered from the Christians. In Anatolia, the Seljuks and the principalities had their schools. As the Ottomans annexed their territory, the schools, as well as other public buildings, were repaired and restored and their *vakfiyes* were recognized and honored. In this manner, the Ottomans preserved the old institutions and reinstated some that had been discontinued.

I have already mentioned that a *külliye*, or a complex of public buildings, was maintained by its founder through a foundation charter (*vakfiye*) administered by a board of trustees which took care of the salaries and wages of personnel as well as their meals. The food of a *külliye* was cooked in the building called the *imâret* (also *aşhane* or *dar-ül ziyafe*) which served not only the officials and the students but also the poor of the neighborhood.

The first Ottoman *imâret* was built along with the *medrese* in İznik, and, following tradition, Orhan Bey in person distributed soup to the needy. During the fourteenth century there were seven *imârets* in the city of İznik. In Bursa, apart from those of the royal *külliyes*, there existed in the early fifteenth century, twenty-four *imârets* erected and founded by viziers or philanthropists.

To finance the activities and to meet the expenditure of the *külliye*, its founder specified in the *vakfiye* a continuous source of revenue. This could be a village, the taxes from which were turned over to the trustees, or it could be a commercial enterprise such as a row of shops or a *han*. A *han* is a two-story structure consisting of rooms arranged around a courtyard behind open arcaded galleries. The rooms on the ground floor were used as offices and storerooms. Those on the upper floor were rooms for bachelors or out-of-town visitors.

The Ottoman *han* has its origins in the Anatolian Seljuk *han* or caravanseries which were built approximately fifteen miles apart, or at intervals of a day's journey, on the main trade routes to offer travelers and merchants comfort, recreation, and protection. They were sturdily constructed like fortresses, their massive outer walls strengthened by turrets. Anatolian Seljuk caravanseries are separated into three groups: the summer type with an open central court; the winter type which is totally enclosed; and the combined summer and winter type. Evdir Han (1210–19) on the Antalya-Korkuteli road and Şerefza Han (1243) near Alanya represent the first and second types, respectively. The third group is exemplified by the Sultan Han (1230) on the Kayseri-Sivas road. The latter is a monumental stone building with a magnificent portal which leads to a large court. The rooms on either side of the entrance eyvan are the innkeeper's quarters and the long hall on the right is the storeroom where the goods of the caravans were kept under lock overnight. To the left of the court are the stables; to the right, the guest rooms and a bath. At the center of the court stands a mosque elevated on four piers and accessible by an external staircase. The space below houses the sheltered ablution fountain. The enclosed wing behind the courtyard is a large pillared hall covered by a flat roof on either side and a barrel vault over the center aisle. Light and air were provided through the perforations in the mammoth domed lantern.

Seljuk *hans* and caravanseries were not generally built in towns. The Ottomans brought them into their towns and organized the big ones as wholesale centers for specific goods for efficient distribution and trade. The İpek Hanı (silk market) built by Mehmed I to finance the Green Complex was the center for merchants and businessmen dealing in silk. The Pirinç Hanı (1507), the Fidan Hanı, and the Koza Hanı (1489) were the markets for rice, seedlings, and cocoons. All the *hans* mentioned above are in Bursa and all of them are similar to the Bey Hanı in plan and architectural character, except that the Koza Hanı has a small, elevated, octagonal mosque at the center of its courtyard in the manner of the Sultan Han.

A second type of Ottoman building for commerce is the *arasta*, which simply means "market" in Turkish. The *arasta* consists of a row of one-story shops arranged on either side of a street which may be open to the sky or vaulted. Similar to the early *hans*, *arastas* were generally erected, separately or as part of a building complex, to provide a permanent source of revenue for a building complex. Unlike the *hans*, the *arasta* was not inspired by a Seljuk model, since the Anatolian Seljuks did not have them. Nor is the *arasta* found in Ottoman architecture before the sixteenth century.

A third type of commercial building is the *bedesten*. The word is a corruption of *bezistan* or *bezzazistan*, cloth market or market for cloth dealers. Architecturally, it is a pillared hall surmounted by domes. Like the covered *arasta*, it offered shopkeepers protection because it was enclosed. *Bedestens* were built at the heart of towns, usually in the neighborhood of the great mosque, and served for the sale of silk or other precious fabrics as well as jewelry, spices, and other valuable goods. They also served as a primitive kind of bank, since shopkeepers and businessmen left their money for safekeeping with watchmen of the *bedesten*, who were locked in at night. Some *bedestens* have exterior shops and big ones have small storage cells built along their walls on the inside. But the hall itself is not divided into compartments. Salesmen put their goods inside large wooden crates whose lids were opened during the business hours to display their contents but were otherwise kept locked.

All major Ottoman towns had a *bedesten* which generally was two bays wide and anywhere from two to seven bays deep. The Bedesten of Tire (late fourteenth century) has an eight-bay interior. That of Bursa has fourteen domes and four doors, one at the center of each wall, and probably dates from the reign of Yıldırım Bayezid. Its twin is to be seen in Edirne. The two *bedestens* constituting the focal points of the Covered Bazaar in Istanbul follow the pattern set by earlier *bedestens* of Bursa and Edirne, but they break tradition in one respect. The Old Bedesten, or Suk al-Bezzaziye as it was originally called, has an odd number of bays in three rows. It was built by Mehmed the Conquerer and is surmounted by fifteen domes. The second, called Sandal Bedesteni —sandal is a cloth woven of silk and cotton—is a sixteenth-century structure and has twenty domes in four rows of five domes each.

AN OUTLINE OF MOSQUE ARCHITECTURE

In Islam, buildings for prayer are called mosques. The English word "mosque" (or the French *mosquée* and the German *Moschee*) derived from the Arabic word *masgid* (spelled *mescid* in Turkish), which means a "place for prostrating oneself in worship." A second word used for a religious meeting place of the Muslims is *jami* (*cami* in Turkish), meaning a place of assembly for the congregation. In Turkish usage the *mescid* refers to a small, and *cami* to a large, place of worship. Those built by royalty, which generally have two or more minarets—the erection of more than one minaret being a royal prerogative—are known as the *selâtin cami* (sultans' mosques).

It is a known fact that the very first mosque was built by the Prophet himself in Kuba near Medina; but we know nothing about its architecture. On the other hand, judging from some of the earliest mosques, one may deduce that it comprised a rectangular courtyard enclosed by walls with a flat-roofed sanctuary (*harem*) on one side. It is possible that the Prophet's mosque was modestly constructed of mud brick walls and that its roof was made of mud-plastered palm leaves supported by rows of palm trunks, much like the Arab dwelling houses of the period. Another mosque of the Prophet was in Medina. This mosque was later (in 712) rebuilt on a monumental scale by the caliph al-Walid and became the prototype of the pillared mosque with courtyard.

During the first half of the seventh century the fighters for the faith erected mosques in conquered lands. The Mosque of Amr was built at Fustat in 641–642. It was pulled down and rebuilt on a larger plan in 673, at which time the first known minarets in Islam were constructed on each of its four corners. Two other mosques dating from this period are those built in the new towns of Basra and Kufa. Like the Mosque of Amr, however, both were rebuilt in 665 and 670, respectively. The architecture of these three mosques must have closely followed the prototype set by the mosque at Medina. In Syria, on the other hand, mosque architecture followed a totally different pattern. There, instead of building new mosques, the conquerers converted existing basilicas into mosques. This was executed by the simple process of reorienting the basilica to face south (*kıble*) instead of east. The western door or doors were either closed or converted into windows, new entrances were opened in the north wall, and the axis of the building was thus altered from length to width. The Church of St. John at Damascus grew into the Umayyad Mosque, and parts of the Basilica of Constantine in Jerusalem were used for the Aksa Mosque.

The Syrian model of an oblong pillared hall with aisles defined by rows of arches was transplanted in Maghreb, as can be seen in the Zituna Mosque in Tunis (732) or in the Great Mosques of Kairawan (begun in 670) and Cordova (begun in 786).

In Iraq, on the other hand, the Abbasids continued to build mosques patterned after the early models of Basra and Kufa. The Great Mosque at Samarra, built by the caliph al-Mutawakkil (848–852), measures approximately 245 m. by 158 m. externally. Thick walls (2.65 m.) of brick strengthened by semicircular bastions and by square corner towers enclose an interior developed around a courtyard. To the south is the main prayer hall, where originally there were twenty-four rows of nine piers. On the two sides and at the rear, the courtyard was surrounded by *revaks* (arcades) four and three bays deep, respectively. A free-standing minaret known as the *malwiya* (spiral) rises to the north of the main structure.

A second Abbasid mosque of the same type is the Mosque of Abu Dulaf (861–862) located to the north of Samarra, and a third is the Mosque of Ibn Tulun in Cairo built in 877–879. Ibn Tulun was obviously influenced by the Samarra mosque and, in turn, influenced the Fatimid mosques in Egypt. Another source of influence for the Fatimid mosques of al-Azhar (970–972) or al-Hakem (990–1003) seems to have been the Maghreb, from which the use of small domes in front of the *mihrab* and at the corners of the prayer hall must have come.

In Iran the earliest mosques were flat-roofed pillared structures much like the hypostyle halls of Persian kings. The Friday Mosque at Kazvin (early eighth century) was known as the "Bull Mosque," which suggests that the columns of the prayer hall had Persian double-headed capitals, or even an actual conversion into a mosque of an apadana. Later mosques in Iran dating from the era of the Great Seljuks add a new spatial quality to mosque architecture. This is the four-eyvaned court. The eyvans were placed at the centers of the four sides of a rectangular courtyard in a cross-axial pattern and behind the main eyvan on the *kıble* side was a domed hall in which the *mihrab* was located. A typical example of the Seljuk mosque is the Masgid-i Jum'a of Isfahan, which was built by Nizam al-Mulk for the sultan Malik Shah (1072–92). It was burned down by the Batinis in 1121, but the main section to the southwest was saved and forms a part of the larger mosque as it exists today.

Although the eyvaned Seljuk mosque greatly influenced the mosque architecture of the Ilhanids, the Timurids, the Safavids, and the Indian Mughals, it curiously had little effect on Anatolian Seljuk mosques. I say curiously because eyvaned buildings are not alien to Anatolia—Anatolian Seljuks erected a large number of them—but with the sole exception of the Ulucami (Great Mosque) of Malatya (1247) the eyvaned mosque is virtually unknown in Anatolia. One possible reason for this may be that the Syrian type was already established in southeastern Anatolia when the Seljuks began penetrating Asia Minor. A second factor may have been that Asia Minor had a tradition of its own and that the elements of Anatolian architecture which evolved from local conditions, materials, and climate could easily be adapted to new requirements.

The Ulucami of Diyarıbakır, which looks very similar to the Umayyad Mosque of Damascus with its clearly defined high central aisle and low side wings, probably dates from the first half of the eleventh century. Another important early mosque in the area is the Ulucami of Silvan (Mayyafarikin). According to some sources it was built in 1031. This date, however, has been questioned by many scholars because it seems to be too early for the large dome in front of the *mihrab*, which suggests that either the mosque was rebuilt in the late twelfth century or that the dome was added to it at this time. A similar mosque, the Ulucami of Kızıltepe (Dunaysır) dating from 1200 provides us with an acceptable point of reference.

Ortokid great mosques of southeastern Anatolia have, as a rule, prayer halls which are wider than they are deep, with walled courtyards in front of them. The same is not necessarily true for early mosques built in central Anatolia. The Ulucami of Sivas built by the Danishmends during the twelfth century has an oblong interior and a simple courtyard in front of this. So does the Seljuk Mosque of Alâeddin in Konya (begun in the mid-twelfth century). On the other hand, the Ulucamis of Niksar (1145) and of Kayseri (mid-twelfth century) are both basilical structures whose interiors are longer than they are wide, and neither of them has a courtyard. The latter, however, had one central, uncovered bay serving as a small interior court to provide light and air for the large pillared hall.

The Ulucamis of both Niksar and Kayseri, as well as the Alâeddin Mosque in Konya have domes in front of their *mihrabs*. This practice of covering a section of the roof with a dome was further accentuated during the thirteenth century, when in some mosques not one but three of the bays were covered by domes. The Mosque of Alâeddin in Niğde (1223) is three bays wide and five bays deep, with its three bays adjacent to the *kible* wall surmounted by three domes. A slightly different scheme is seen in the Burmalı (twisted) Mosque (so called because of the fluted spirals on its minaret's shaft) in Amasya (1242), in which the three domes are placed perpendicularly to the *mihrab* over the central aisle. A further example of the three-domed upper structure is the Gök (sky) Medrese Mosque in the same city (second half of the thirteenth century), the interior of which is covered by a series of three-domed units arranged longitudinally and transversally in an alternating pattern.

Anatolian Seljuk mosques despite certain common features such as portals, pillared interiors, or domes in front of their *mihrabs*, nonetheless vary a good deal. They are generally classified in two major groups according to the orientation of their rectangular masses. A few mosques whose roof structures are supported on wooden posts instead of the usual stone piers may be considered to form a subgroup, although timber-posted mosques are represented in both the basilical and the transept types. The Ottoman mosques, on the other hand, are more standardized and definable in their basic forms. Judging them to be so, I shall attempt a typological study. I am fully aware, of course, that any generalization has its exceptions and that there will also be the odd example which will not fit a type perfectly.

In terms of exterior form and organization of inner space, the Ottoman Turkish mosques built during the fourteenth and fifteenth centuries can be classified into three major groups, which I shall call (1) the "single-unit" mosque, (2) the "eyvan" mosque, and (3) the "multi-unit" mosque.

The typical single-unit mosque consists of a square, or near square, prayer room, a two- or three-bay porch (*son cemaat yeri*), and a minaret. The prayer room is generally surmounted by a dome; the porch by vaults, domes, or a combination of the two.

The multi-unit mosque has a large interior space which is divided into compartments by means of columns or piers in order to provide shorter spans. Seljuk mosques of this type usually have flat roofs; but for reasons of emphasis, one or more of the compartments may be covered by domes. The Ottoman multi-unit mosques, on the other hand, are more standardized, for in them all the compartments are domed-square units.

Undoubtedly the most interesting type of early Ottoman mosque is the eyvan mosque. There is a kinship between the eyvan mosque and the Seljuk *medrese* with its central dome. Both types of buildings have two or four focal points that occur at the ends of only the longitudinal axis or both the longitudinal and transverse axes around a domed interior court. The number or the arrangement of the rooms other than those which constitute the focal elements vary but never interfere with the basic axial system. The porch of the eyvan mosque has five bays and there may be one or two minarets.

The two groups which I referred to as the single-unit and the multi-unit mosques have been called to date the "one-domed" and the "many-domed" mosques. In this work, I have preferred the term "unit" to "domed" because, although the hemispherical dome is the main feature of the Ottoman mosque, and indeed of all types of Ottoman buildings, it merely refers to the upper structure. The term "unit," however, describes the basic structural and spatial system of architecture, which in this case is a square space defined by walls or by four piers at the corners and covered by a dome.

Obviously, it cannot be said that the "domed-square unit" is an architectural feature peculiar to Ottoman Turkish architecture. It probably originated in Mesopotamia and played an important role in the architecture of the Sassanians, the Armenians, and the Byzantines. It constituted the focal point of the centrally planned Greek-cross church and the domed basilica. It was also used by other peoples of Islamic faith though not as the basic unit of their architecture. But in no era of architecture—pagan, Christian, or Islamic—were the architectonic and spatial potentialities of the domed-square unit so persistently explored or its inner logic so well understood as they were in the Ottoman Turkish period. For this reason, one of the main objectives of this work will be to place particular emphasis on this domed-square unit, which, in my opinion, is the common denominator in early Ottoman Turkish buildings and forms the backbone of this architecture.

1 The Single-Unit Mosque

Altıparmak Mosque, Bursa

The main architectural theme during the early years of the Ottoman state is the domed-square structure, the walls of which are generally of roughly cut stone placed between courses of brick. The solidity of the masonry surface is broken only by small window or door openings which are not of a shape or size to weaken the sturdiness of the walls or to soften their massive quality.

The exterior form of the single-unit structure has a simple expression devoid of surface plasticity. The rectangular windows with pointed-arch heads are cut into the walls with precision. At times there is a decorative pattern of bricks inside the window arch. The saw-toothed—or porcupine—cornice which is built of courses of flat, square bricks placed diagonally into the wall in staggered rows is usually the only plastic feature of the wall surface, providing the mass of the wall with a rhythmic termination. The restrained and geometric air of the exterior form is reflected in the interior, where the space, defined by the basic geometric shapes of the square, the circle, and the triangle, has a static quality. It exhibits no tendency to expand. The dome completely dominates the interior and draws the space toward the center.

The domed-square structure, with the addition of a porch and a minaret, establishes the basic mass of the typical single-unit mosque. This type of simple mosque is characteristic not only of early Ottoman Turkish architecture but was favored throughout the six centuries of Ottoman rule and is widely used in Turkey even today. After the sixteenth century single-unit mosques became rather sophisticated in decoration. But the early ones are uncomplicated and plain. One senses the conscious effort of their founders and architects to avoid unnecessary or superfluous ornamentation. Carved marble antique or contemporary column capitals in the porch, or decorative corbeling under the balcony of the minaret, or a sculptured *mihrab* and an ornamental *minber*, or an interesting transitionary system to transmit the load of the dome onto the walls and frequently serving to infuse an element of plasticity into the otherwise austere interior are often all there is in the way of ornamentation.

In early single-unit mosques the transition from the hemispherical brick dome to the square base is carried out in three ways: the dome rests either on an octagonal base produced by squinches, or pendentives, or on a polygonal structural belt composed of broken triangular surfaces. During the fourteenth century the last of these systems was often preferred. Squinches were also used, but pendentives only rarely. Systematic incorporation of the pendentive into Ottoman building did not begin until the second quarter of the fifteenth century.

Squinches and pendentives are old systems. Examples of the squinch can be seen in the earliest works of Islamic architecture, such as the Great Mosques in Kairawan and in Cordova, or the Masgid-i Juma of Isfahan (eleventh century), to name a few. The use of pendentives goes even further back, as magnificent examples are found in the Basilicas of St. Irene (fifth century) and of Hagia Sophia (532–537) in Istanbul. But the belt of triangles, commonly called Turkish triangles, is an innovation that is basically Anatolian Turkish.

For the earliest single-unit Ottoman mosques, we must go back to the period of Orhan Gazi because the very first examples that are still in existence date from his reign. Unfortunately, no mosque, or for that matter any other type of building, remains from the earlier period of Osman Gazi the founder of the Ottoman state.[1]

The most important examples of typical single-unit mosques built during the first part of the fourteenth century are those of Alâeddin Bey in Bursa, Hacı Özbek in İznik, and Orhan Gazi in Gebze. I shall now consider these three mosques, as well as several others regarded to be significant, in order to show the development of the typical single-unit mosque in early Ottoman Turkish architecture from the reign of Orhan Gazi through that of Bayezid II.

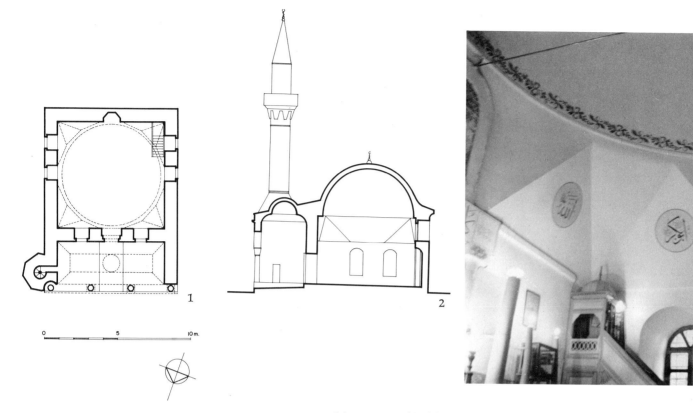

1

2

3

Mosque of Alâeddin Bey in Bursa

This small mosque was built by, or for, Alâeddin Bey (d. 1331), the younger brother of Orhan Gazi. It bears no inscription, but a plate above the entrance door, installed in 1890 (A.H. 1306), supplies the following information: *"736 bina-i evvel, 1278 bina-i sâni."* Thus we learn that the mosque was erected in 1335 (A.H. 736) and underwent a major restoration in 1862 (A.H. 1278).[2]

The interior of the Mosque of Alâeddin Bey comprises a square room measuring 8.20 m. by 8.20 m. (Fig. 1) surmounted by a hemispherical dome that rests on a sixteen-sided belt of large triangular planes. The dome, the transitional belt, and the walls are clearly differentiated, and despite a smooth visual flow from the walls to the dome the integrity of each geometric shape has been preserved (Figs. 2, 3). The walls are 1.05 m. thick and are constructed of rubble stone masonry with bricks placed horizontally and vertically between each stone. At eye level there are six windows: two on either side of the door and two on each side wall. A seventh window is located above the *mihrab*. Although the windows opposite the *mihrab* are symmetrically placed, those on the side walls are not (Fig. 1). Of the two windows on the west, one is located on the transverse axis passing through the center of the dome and the other at the mid-point between the central window and the southwest corner. Such order cannot be found on the east wall. Since the building is essentially symmetrical, this incongruity leads one to suspect that the window openings on the east may have been shifted during the restoration work in 1862.

4

5

Mosque of Alâeddin Bey, Bursa
1 *Plan*
2 *Section*
3 *Interior*
4 *Exterior*
5 *Minaret*

The porch has partially lost its authenticity. In earlier monographs the Mosque of Alâeddin Bey is shown with a pedimented façade.[3] This pediment, built in 1862, has in recent years been torn down and replaced by a roof structure bearing a saw-toothed cornice (Fig. 4). This is more in keeping with early Ottoman Turkish architecture. It would not be unrealistic to suggest that the mosque, in its present form, may be quite close to the original. The porch has four columns, all bearing Byzantine capitals, two of which are located in front of the side walls. As seen from the exterior, the three bays are defined by pointed arches; but the ceiling of the porch is a long, flat-topped barrel vault running from one wall to the other. At the center, over the door, it builds up to a small dome which rises above the roof and can be seen from the outside.

The minaret clutches the east end of the porch. Its base is constructed of mixed stone and brick masonry, but the rest of the structure is of brick. The upper section is new. The shaft, including the supports of the balcony (*şerefe*), however, may be original, in which case the minaret of the Mosque of Alâeddin Bey in Bursa would be the first known Ottoman minaret in existence (Fig. 5).[4]

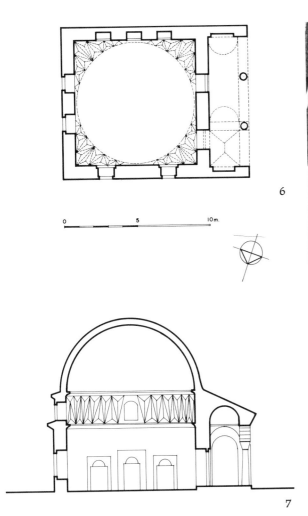

6

8

Mosque of Hacı Özbek in İznik

Mosque of Hacı Özbek, İznik
6 *Plan*
7 *Section*
8 *Exterior*

The mosque of Hacı Özbek in İznik—also known as Çarşı Mescidi (Market Mosque)—dates from the first half of the fourteenth century. It is the oldest Ottoman building whose original inscription plate has survived. Therefore, it is known with certainty that the Mosque of Hacı Özbek was erected in 1333 (A.H. 734).[5] The original building was composed of a domed-square prayer room and a three-bay porch on the west. A minaret was never built.[6]

The interior is a square measuring 7.92 m. per side (Fig. 6). The hemispheric dome, which is slightly elongated at the base, rests on a belt of triangular planes (Fig. 7). This belt is accentuated by two tiers of molding below and above it. Thus on the vertical plane the interior is divided into three sections that are of different geometric shapes. The same characteristic may be observed on the exterior: the dome, the dodecagonal drum, and the base walls are clearly expressed and are separated from one another by means of saw-toothed cornices. The lower structure and the drum are constructed of rubble stone leveled by

34

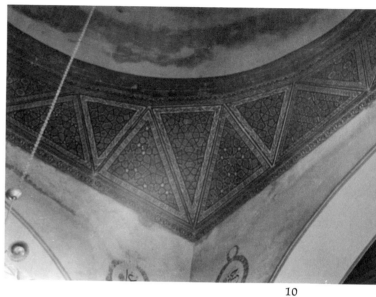

9

10

Medrese of Karatay, Konya
9 Interior. Turkish triangles

Mosque of Alâeddin, Konya
10 Maksure dome. Turkish triangles

courses of brick. The brick dome is covered with a curved terra-cotta tile designed to face spherical surfaces—a typical early Ottoman construction feature (Fig. 8).

The original porch was a three-bay structure whose arch openings on the façade were supported by two marble columns with Byzantine capitals. A barrel vault ran the length of two bays, and the third bay was surmounted by a cross-vault. Unfortunately, the original porch no longer exists. It was torn down in 1959 when the street it faced was widened. It is replaced by a vestibule whose sole merit may be its location opposite the *mihrab*. The new street elevation has four windows, the southernmost of which is the original window that looked onto the porch. Next to it is the original door opening which has now been converted into a window. The other two date from the recent alteration.

Unlike the porch which no longer exists and the exterior, which has been changed and partially rebuilt, the interior retains most of its original character. There are three simple niches cut into the south wall, the central niche being the *mihrab*, and eight windows, five at eye level and three on the transitional belt. The latter are placed at mid-points of the belt above the *mihrab*, on the north and the east. On the west, where the original porch stood, the belt is unperforated.

As one can readily see, the Turkish triangles of the Mosque of Alâeddin Bey look somewhat different from those of Hacı Özbek. Despite a visual dissimilarity, however, there is a structural affinity between the triangular corner panels of the first mosque and the triangular faceted belts of the second, because

35

Taş Medrese, Akşehir
11 *Interior of the mescid. Turkish triangles*

both systems have the function of distributing the load of the dome along the mass of the walls. I do not agree with Gabriel, who finds a kinship between the triangular corner panels of the Mosque of Alâeddin Bey in Bursa and the Medrese of Karatay in Konya.[7] In the Karatay the fan-shaped structure (Fig. 9) composed of long triangular panels whose sharp points meet at one spot collects the load at the corner, and, as such, acts much like a pendentive. In the Alâeddin Bey, the triangular panels are arranged with their apexes alternatively placed upward and downward. In this manner the load is distributed along the length of the wall instead of being focused at the corners.

If we must look for earlier examples of the structural belt of the Ottoman mosque, the transitional systems of the dome in front of the *mihrab* in the Mosque of Alâeddin in Konya (twelfth century), or the *mescid* of the Taş (stone) Medrese in Akşehir (1250) come to mind as more pertinent examples.

The dome in front of the *mihrab* in the Mosque of Alâeddin in Konya does not define a square space but merely covers one compartment of a large interior. It rests on an icosagonal base provided by a transitional belt (Fig. 10) composed of thirty-six triangular panels arranged in an alternating manner with the exception of the four mid-points of the square where adjacent triangles are placed with apexes in the same direction.

One finds the same alternating arrangement in the transitional belt of the Hacı Özbek, with this difference: the triangular panels are many more in number and are doubled—or each panel is broken into two—resulting in a system where coupled triangles alternate. The *mescid* of the Taş Medrese in Akşehir is not an independent structure but it closely resembles fourteenth-century single-unit mosques in terms of form and interior space. For in this *mescid* not only the interior but also the general massing, complete with porch and minaret, follow the basic program of the typical early Ottoman single-unit mosque. The brick minaret is tall and out of proportion with the small (6.30 m.^{2}) prayer room. There is, however, nothing unusual in this, since Seljuk minarets as a rule are tall, thick structures that are often not even integrated with the main body of the mosque.

The transition to the dome in the *mescid* of the Taş Medrese is effected by a belt of sixteen large triangular panels (Fig. 11)—an arrangement that is in no way different from that of the Mosque of Alâeddin Bey.

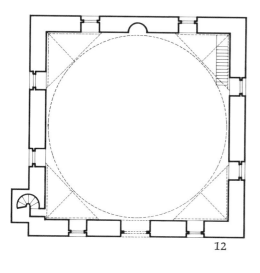

12

14

Mosque of Orhan Gazi in Gebze

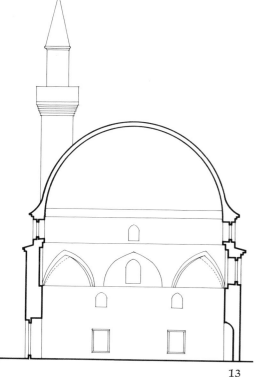

13

Mosque of Orhan Gazi, Gebze
12 *Plan*
13 *Section*
14 *Exterior*

Another mosque erected during the reign of Orhan Gazi is located in the town of Gebze near Istanbul. Although the building has no inscription plate and was repaired in 1775 (A.H. 1189),[8] a few features typical of early fourteenth-century Ottoman Turkish works, such as the use of coarse rubble masonry, rather squat lower structure, presence of Byzantine building elements, and the poor, unrefined workmanship enable us to attribute this structure to the period of Orhan Gazi.

The square prayer room is covered by a dome that measures 12.30 m. in diameter and 15.70 m. in height at the center (Figs. 12, 13). It sits on squinches whose arches are tied by iron bars. The stone walls are 1.15 m. thick and are constructed of horizontal layers of rubble stone without any brick courses in between. Despite twenty-three windows, arranged in four tiers, the interior is not light, for the windows are all small. The *mihrab* is a simple niche with a pointed arch.

The iron hooks above the entrance door and the presence of Byzantine column capitals, which were used as bases for posts, indicate that at an earlier time a timber porch stood in front of the north wall of the mosque. Since there are no traces of a masonry porch, it may be suggested that the timber porch was not a later addition built to replace a collapsed masonry porch but was built simultaneously with the mosque in the fourteenth century (Fig. 14).

The minaret is to the east of the entrance. Its base belongs to the original building; the shaft is of a later date, probably no older than three hundred years.[9]

37

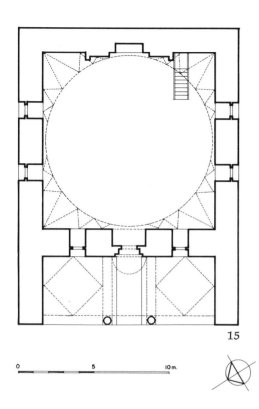

15

0 .... 5 .... 10 m.

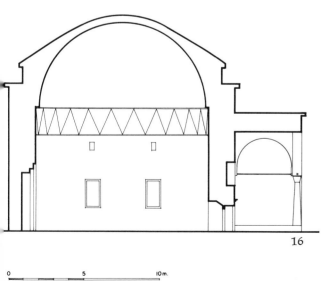

16

0 .... 5 .... 10 m.

Mosque of Hüdavendigâr in Behramkale

The small mosque that perches over the village of Behramkale on the northern slope of the acropolis of the ancient Greek city of Assos is another typical example of the single-unit mosque. This building, too, does not have an inscription plate, but its founder is known to be Murad I (the Hüdavendigâr) and it has all the characteristic features of early Ottoman Turkish architecture. The city of Assos was taken by the Ottomans during the reign of Orhan Gazi. It is, therefore, possible that the mosque dates from the period of Murad I, or even as early as the mid-fourteenth century.

The Mosque of Hüdavendigâr is composed of a domed-square prayer room and a three-bay porch (Fig. 15). It has no minaret, probably because of the high, wind-blown location of the building. The prayer room measures 11.00 m. per side and the dome is fitted onto the square lower structure by means of a belt of triangles (Fig. 16). There are a total of six windows: two flanking the door and two on each side wall. No windows have been opened on the south wall. The interior, as it exists today, is devoid of any plastic element or color save for the plaster of Paris *mihrab*, which is decorated with geometric patterns. On the exterior, the corners of the walls on which the low, octagonal drum was placed, are shaved off (Fig. 19) thus softening the severity of the bulky lower structure. In this way a crude but architectonic expression of transition from the walls to the dome was achieved.

The two side compartments of the three-bay porch are square in shape and covered by vaults. Four pendentives build up to the apexes of the arches to form a flat ceiling of brick constructed in a pattern of rotating, diminishing squares. The central bay is narrower but higher than the two side bays and is surmounted by a barrel vault (Fig. 17). Today the porch is in ruins (Fig. 18), the two columns and the central section of the roof having collapsed. According to the inhabitants of the village, the eastern column was intact until 1961; it now lies on the ground in front of the porch. The shaft and the capital are of Byzantine origin. Similarly, the window lintels with carved acanthus leaves, the door lintel with an inscription in Greek, and the semicircular window arches on the side walls are all indicative of a strong relationship to Byzantine architecture. As a matter of fact, in all probability, the lower structure of the mosque belongs to a Byzantine church. Two different masonry techniques that are observed on the walls (Fig. 19) show that when the Ottomans took the city, the church must have been dilapidated. It is difficult to know without an excavation what the interior of the church was like. But it probably was not covered by a single dome. Considering that the interior is square, it is possible that the church had a Greek-cross plan supporting a small central dome at the crossing that sat on four columns. This upper structure, however, must have been nonexistent in the fourteenth century; otherwise the Ottoman Turks would not have felt the need to build a dome which was fairly large for its time. They would merely have converted the church into a mosque as they did in other places.[10]

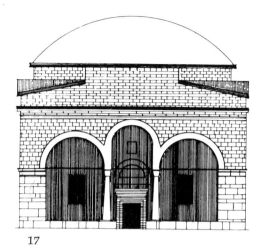

17

18

19

Mosque of Hüdavendigâr, Behramkale
15 Plan
16 Section
17 Restored front elevation
18 Exterior. Front view
19 Exterior. Side view

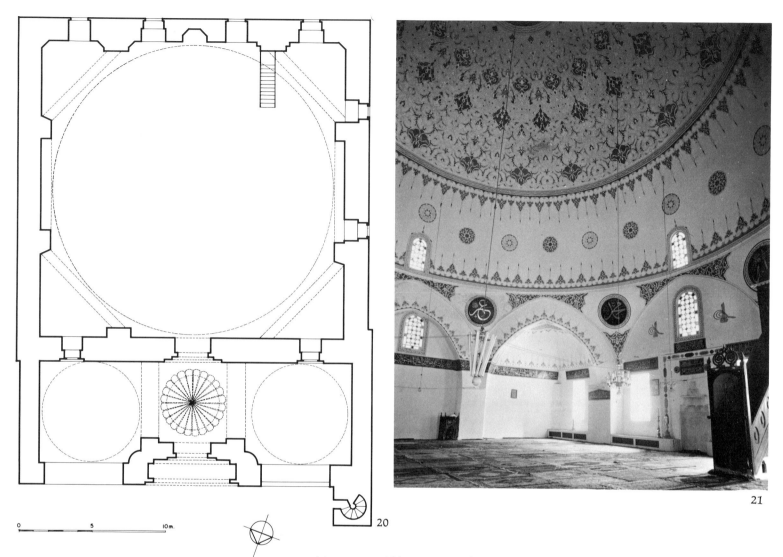

20

21

Mosque of Yıldırım Bayezid in Mudurnu

The Mosque of Yıldırım Bayezid in Mudurnu, because of its huge dome (19.65 m. in diameter), is perhaps the most important single-unit mosque of the fourteenth century. This building, too, has no inscription plate, but that of the *hamam*, which formed a part of the complex along with the now nonexistent *medrese*, indicates that this building complex was built in 1382 (A.H. 784).[11] There are four dates written at the base of the mosque's dome: A.H. 1190 (1776), A.H. 1225 (1839), A.H. 1318 (1900), and 1960. These represent the dates of major restoration the mosque has undergone.

The Mosque of Yıldırım Bayezid in Mudurnu is a building that measures 31.27 m. by 24.13 m. including the porch. The prayer room is slightly wider than it is deep, or 20.70 m. by 19.65 m. (Fig. 20). Thus the 19.65 m. dome sits on two narrow arches on the sides, and the transition from the hemispherical dome to the

Mosque of Yıldırım Bayezid, Mudurnu
20 *Plan*
21 *Interior*
22 *Exterior*

rectangular base is effected by four large squinches (Fig. 21). The walls are massive—1.60–1.70 m. wide—and are further thickened where the squinches press down to safeguard against the heavy load of the dome, which was unusually big for its time (Fig. 22).[12]

Similarly, the walls were kept low—8.80 m. at the arch springs—to secure the building further against the lateral thrust of the dome. There are ten windows at the lower level (of which two have been sealed), three windows at the upper level of the walls, and three more in the drum.

The three-bay porch is closed on the sides. The center bay is narrower and lower than the side bays and is covered by a small, fluted dome. The two side compartments are also domed, but these are fairly large, measuring over 5.00 m. in diameter.

The minaret rises on the northwest corner of the porch. This, however, is not the original minaret, which, according to local belief, was an independent structure at some distance from the porch.[13] The new minaret dates from 1744 (A.H. 1157).[14] It was partially destroyed in the earthquake of 1957 and has since been rebuilt, but the inscription plate bearing the date 1744 is still in place above the minaret's door.

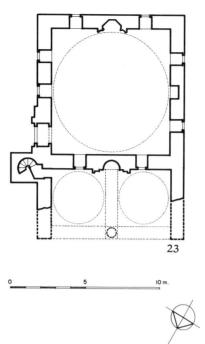

Mosque of Hacı Şahabeddin Paşa, Edirne
23 Plan
24 Exterior
25 Porch. Outer mihrab

24

25

Mosque of Hacı Şahabeddin Paşa in Edirne

This building in Edirne, commonly known as Kirazlı Cami (Cherry Mosque), was built, according to its inscription, in 1436 (A.H. 840) by Hacı Şahabeddin Paşa. Except for the tiny (dome diameter: 6.30 m.) but charming Mosque of Sarıca Paşa (1435), it is the oldest single-unit mosque in that city. Although in poor repair and not in use, it is also an important example of this type of mosque.

The composition follows the general outlines of the fourteenth-century pattern: a square prayer room covered by an 8.00 m. hemispherical dome, a minaret and a now nonexistent porch (Fig. 23). In certain features, however, one observes deviations from the prototype. Instead of a belt of triangles or squinches, the dome is supported by pendentives. Also, three of the outer walls are externally faced with cut stone (Fig. 24). The fourth, or the northwestern wall, as well as the octagonal drum, are less carefully constructed. These were not exposed, as is evident by the bits of plaster that can still be seen on the northern wall. Although it is now unprotected, this wall, of course, was covered by the porch, before the latter collapsed. Another feature worthy of mention is the double *mihrab*, one in the interior, the other on the porch placed at the center of the wall. The outer *mihrab* is a fine specimen of stone cutting, complete with moldings and a stalactite niche (Fig. 25). Above it one can see traces of an arch, which, together with the remains of walls that project from the corners on either side of the porch, clearly indicate that the porch was a two-bay structure, probably covered by two small domes.

42

26   27

Taş Medrese, Akşehir
26 *Porch (after Sarre)*

Mosque of Yavuz Ersinan, Istanbul
27 *Porch*

Early single-unit Ottoman mosques generally have three-bay porches. But two-bay porches were also occasionally built. So far as I know, the two-bay porch of Kirazlı Cami is the oldest one built by the Ottomans. However, it is by no means the very first occurrence of this element in Muslim Anatolia. The *mescid* of the İnce Minareli Medrese in Konya (1258) had a two-bay porch. Unfortunately, except for the lower portion of its minaret nothing remains of this *mescid* today. Another example is again the *mescid* of the Taş Medrese. Despite its utmost importance this very last two-bay Anatolian Seljuk porch lost much of its character during a recent restoration. But photographs taken before the crude restoration work give a good idea of what the original porch looked like (Fig. 26).

As for later examples of the single-unit Ottoman mosques with two-bay porches, one can name the Mosques of Selçuk Hatun in Edirne (1455, or A.H. 860), Yavuz Ersinan (*ca.* 1455) (Fig. 27), Yarhisar (1461, or A.H. 866), İshak Paşa and Yavaşca Şahin (both second half of the fifteenth century) in Istanbul, or Kilerî Süleyman Ağa in Amasya (1486, or A.H. 891).

The interesting thing about the two-bay porch of Kirazlı Cami, however, is that it functioned as a semi-independent, open prayer area and not as a pre-entrance element to the mosque, because the door does not open onto the porch but is located next to the minaret on the east. The base of the minaret is original. The shaft, the balcony, and the cap are definitely of a later date. Judging from the stone cap, the upper section of the minaret was probably built in the eighteenth century after the earthquake of 1751 in Edirne, which may also have destroyed the porch.

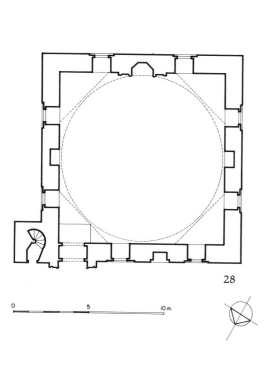

28

0   5   10 m.

29

Mosque of Kasım Paşa, Edirne
28 *Plan*
29 *Exterior. Side view*
30 *Exterior. Front view*
31 *Interior*

Mosque of Kasım Paşa in Edirne

A more developed example of the same type of single-unit mosque is to be found on the eastern shore of the River Tunca in Edirne. It was built in 1478 (A.H. 883) by Evliya Kasım Paşa, a minister of Sultans Murad II and his son Mehmed II. The building, in poor condition until recently, was partially restored in 1964.

The exterior of this mosque is completely finished in dressed stone. The window arrangement has a definite order—at least on three of the elevations: two rectangular windows, placed in a slightly recessed frame, at the lower level; two others directly above these; and the fifth, at dead center on the drum (Fig. 29). The entrance (northwest) elevation, however, is not symmetrical, owing to the location of the door which is to the side. Nor is the outer *mihrab* centrally located. It stands flanked by two windows about 1.00 m. off-center toward the west (Fig. 30).

30   31

The 11.00 m. dome sits on squinches that are placed fairly high on the walls (Fig. 31). They are expressed on the exterior by the pitched-roofed triangular projections which fill the space between the corners of the building and the drum. The tops of the walls are marked by a profile cornice. Below the drum there is a string of tiny arches. A similar band of arches can also be seen below the shaft of the minaret, which stands on the northeast corner of the mosque. The transition from the square lower portion of the minaret to the base of the circular shaft is effected by broken triangular planes, similar to those found under the domes of the fourteenth-century mosques.

The Mosque of Kasım Paşa does not have a porch. Earlier there existed a timber structure in front of the building. But this was definitely a later addition. The character and the fine workmanship of the mosque clearly suggest that if a porch had ever been considered for the original building, it would have been of masonry, in keeping with the rest of the structure.

32

Mosque of Firuz Ağa, Istanbul
32 *Exterior. Side view*
33 *Plan*
34 *Exterior. Front view*

Mosque of Firuz Ağa in Istanbul

The Mosque of Firuz Ağa was founded in 1490 (A.H. 896) by the head of the treasury of Sultan Bayezid II (1481–1512).[15] It is located near the Hippodrome in Istanbul. In this building one finds the most mature single-unit mosque at the threshold of the classical Ottoman Turkish architecture of the sixteenth century (Fig. 32).

The interior is a perfect square, surmounted by a 10.50 m. dome that sits on pendentives (Fig. 33). There are four windows on each wall, two below and two above the lower ones. The former are rectangular. The latter have arch heads and are fitted on the exterior with gypsum screens. The portal is placed on the longitudinal axis of the mosque, so that one enters the building directly across from the *mihrab*.

The three-bay porch is open at the ends (Fig. 34). On the façade it is supported by four columns which were produced specifically for this mosque. They have small octagonal bases, simple shafts of marble, and typical Ottoman Turkish stalactite capitals. Three small domes of equal size cover the bays of the porch. Each dome rests on pendentives and rises on an octagonal drum above the cornice of the porch.

The minaret is located on the northeast corner of the prayer room slightly behind the inner line of the porch. It, too, sits on an octagonal base. Its balcony is supported by stalactite corbels and is terminated by a pencil point cap sheathed with sheet lead.

The whole structure is faced with the hard, white *küfeki* stone of which most of Istanbul's Ottoman buildings are constructed. The arches are pointed and, in the porch, secured in both directions by light iron tie bars.

Single-unit mosques built by the Ottoman Turks during the fourteenth and fifteenth centuries are plentiful, and a large number of them are still in existence. Except for minor constructional or decorative differences and particulars they all conform to the prototype. Therefore, I shall not discuss the typical single-unit mosque any further but will proceed to study the major examples of single-unit mosques either in terms of interior space or exterior form to show deviations from the prototype. I shall consider these in two groups: "The Single-Unit Mosque with Complex Massing" and "The Single-Unit Mosque with Articulated Interior."

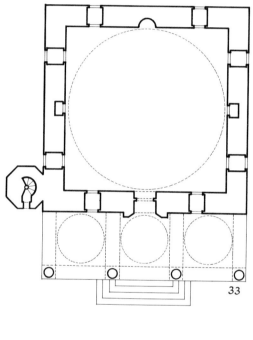

0   5   10 m.

33

34

SINGLE-UNIT MOSQUE WITH COMPLEX MASSING

In terms of space and form, the main difference between the single-unit mosque with complex massing and the simple single-unit mosque does not lie in the design of the domed-square prayer room but in the general composition which includes architectural elements other than the three-bay porch and the minaret. The additional element may be convent rooms (*zâviye*) or hospices attached to one or both sides of the prayer hall, an entire front section, or a monumental fountain court. But in this type of early Ottoman mosque, regardless of how complex the massing may be, and how large the prayer room may get, the integrity of the latter as a domed-square architectural unit is completely retained.

Mosque of Umur Bey in Bursa

Part of a group of buildings including a *hamam*, a *türbe*, and an independent ablution fountain, this mosque in Bursa bears the name of its founder, Umur Bey (d. 1461), son of Timurtaş Paşa. A foundation charter of great historic value written in Turkish on two separate plates placed to the right and to the left of the door provides much information about Umur Bey and the numerous other buildings he founded in Bursa and elsewhere. The inscription is dated A.H. 859 (1454).[16]

The mosque comprises two adjacent square rooms, one slightly smaller than the other, a five-bay porch, and a minaret (Fig. 35). The larger of the square rooms is 8.25 m. across. The small room measures approximately 6.50 m. on each side and is spatially connected to the other by an arched opening. I cannot say what function the smaller room in the Mosque of Umur Bey served. It is difficult to be definite, since it is a unique example; there is no other Ottoman mosque like it. I can only say that the smaller room was probably not a part of the prayer area because there is no *mihrab* in it.

An octagonal structure decorated with blind arches on each face serves as the base to the brick minaret, which is located at the junction of the large square room and the porch. The circular shaft rests on a sixteen-faceted belt of alternating triangles of stone and brick. Six rows of saw-toothed corbels project out to provide a platform for the balcony. The cap is in the form of a small onion dome.

The ends of the five-bay porch are closed. Four columns of Byzantine origin bearing stylized acanthus leaf capitals divide the façade into one narrow and four approximately equal bays. The former occurs in front of the entrance to the larger room which holds the *mihrab*. A second *mihrab* niche is cut into the inner wall of the porch on the north end of the wall in between the two rooms.

The entire structure of the Mosque of Umur Bey is covered by a pitched timber roof. Consequently, both rooms, as well as the porch, have flat ceilings. This upper structure, however, is not original. It was built in 1858 after the earthquake of 1855.[17] One can safely suppose that originally both square rooms were surmounted by domes and the porch by vaults. Likewise, the upper part

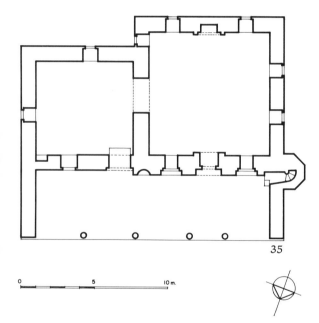

35

48

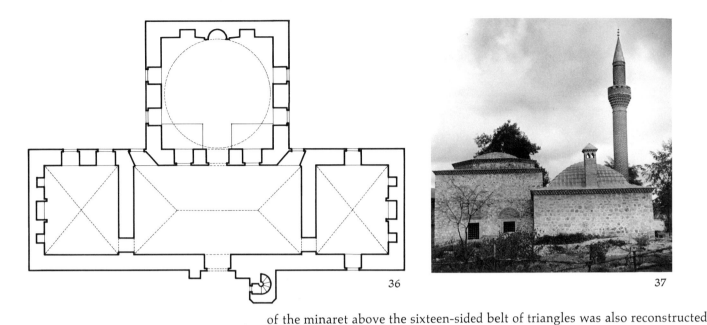

36

37

of the minaret above the sixteen-sided belt of triangles was also reconstructed in the nineteenth century.[18]

Yukarı Cami in Kurşunlu

Mosque of Umur Bey, Bursa
35 *Plan*

Yukarı Cami, Kurşunlu
36 *Plan*
37 *Exterior*

Yukarı Cami (Upper Mosque) in the town of Kurşunlu near İnegöl does not have an inscription plate and unfortunately no archive records are available to determine its date of construction. The construction techniques and certain architectural features, however, suggest that it was probably erected toward the end of the fourteenth century during the reign of Murad I or Bayezid I, more likely the latter.[19]

Yukarı Cami does not have a porch and its minaret, located to the right of the entrance, is decidedly of a later date. The main building comprises four well-defined spaces—three in a row and the fourth, behind the central space on the longitudinal axis—in a simple T formation (Fig. 36). The central hall is a rectangular area, its longer side at right angles to the entrance. The two side rooms on either side of the central hall, as well as the prayer room, are square in plan. The central hall and the side rooms are cross-vaulted but the prayer room is surmounted by a dome which rests on pendentives.

The significant aspect of the Kurşunlu mosque is its prayer room, which is an independent unit, clearly separated from the central hall by a wall. The duality of form, space, and function between the prayer room and the rest of the building is also indicated by the massing. The depth and the height of the central hall and the convent rooms (*zâviye*) are similar and the three spaces are united in one long, rectangular form. The domed-square prayer room is attached to this rectangular mass but without compromising the integrity of its form (Fig. 37). In short, the single-unit character of the domed square is clearly retained visually, spatially, and structurally.

38

Hatuniye Mosque, Tokat
38 *Exterior. Top view*
39 *Plan*
40 *Portal*

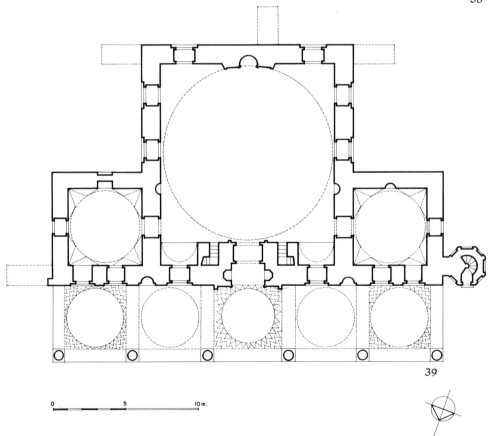

39

0   5   10 m.

Hatuniye Mosque in Tokat

40

A more developed example of the single-unit mosque combined with a *zâviye* (convent)[20] is the Hatuniye Mosque in Tokat, which, according to its three-line inscription, was built in 1485 (A.H. 890) by Bayezid II in honor of his mother, Gülbahar Hatun.[21]

The square prayer hall is flanked by two symmetrical and smaller convent rooms to the east and the west. A five-bay porch crosses the width of the building (Fig. 38). The minaret is located near the northwest corner of the western convent room. It is a semi-independent structure joined to the main building only on one side of its octagonal base (Fig. 39).

The prayer hall is 11.80 m. across and covered by a dome on pendentives finished with honeycomb decorations. It is illuminated by two rows of superposed windows. On the north wall, there are two low rectangular niches. The balcony above these is reached by two staircases on either side of the entrance.

The two convent rooms have domes which rest on belts of Turkish triangles. They are not accessible from the prayer room, though each has a window looking into it, but from the porch.

The porch is composed of five square bays of equal dimensions, all domed. The domes of the center and outer bays sit on stalactite corbels. The other two are on pendentives. The six marble columns of the porch are typical Ottoman columns. Their capitals are decorated with alternating stalactites and lozenges, and their bases are circumscribed by bronze circlets. The highly decorative portal is decidedly one of the best produced during the fifteenth century (Fig. 40). Unlike the Yukarı Cami, the Hatuniye is not a single occurrence. The İmâret Camii in İnecik, Tekirdağ (1498)[22] and even an earlier example, the Mosque of Uzun Hasan—of the White Sheep dynasty (1453–78)—in Fethiye, Malatya[23] are both almost exact replicas of the Hatuniye Mosque. The Mosques of Davud Paşa and Mehmed Paşa must also be considered within the same group. They are more developed versions of the same type.

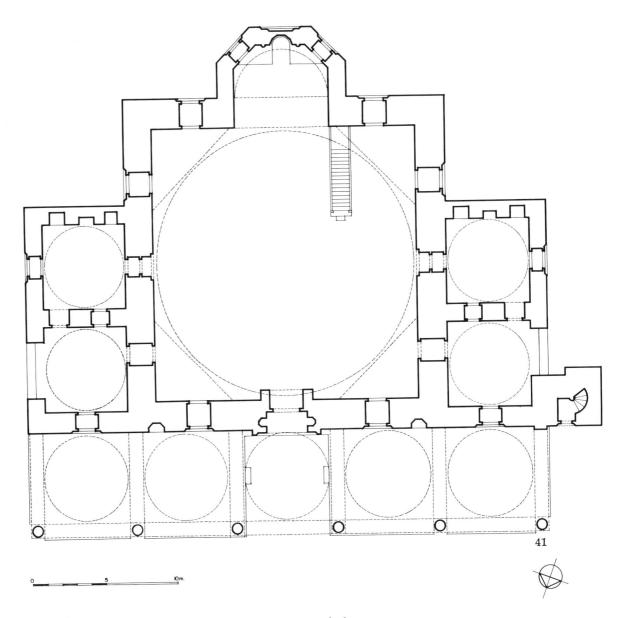

41

Mosque of Davud Paşa in Istanbul

Another mosque of the same type is the Mosque of Davud Paşa in Istanbul.
It was erected by Davud Paşa (d. 1498), the grand vizier (1482–97) of Bayezid II,
in 1485 (A.H. 890),[24] the same year the Hatuniye Mosque in Tokat was built.
The two mosques show a great many similarities.

    Like the Hatuniye in Tokat, the Mosque of Davud Paşa has a large, domed-
square prayer hall, two convent rooms, a five-bay porch and a semi-independent
minaret on the west (Fig. 41). But unlike the Tokat mosque, here the *mihrab*
is placed in a polygonal apse like a niche which protrudes from the south wall,
and there are two additional domed-square units flanking the prayer hall in front

52

42

Mosque of Davud Paşa, Istanbul
41 *Plan*
42 *Exterior*

of the convent rooms (Fig. 42). These units function as vestibules to the convent rooms and they, in turn, have large arch openings not to the porch but to the east and west. The domed-square vestibules with their arch-openings on one side bring to mind the domed eyvans that were developed earlier in Bursa, about which I shall have more to say when I discuss the eyvan mosque in chapter 2.

The interior of the Mosque of Davud Paşa measures 18.20 m. by 18.00 m. The walls are heavy and thick—1.90 m.—to resist the load and the lateral thrusts of the huge dome, which sits on corbeled spherical squinches with stalactites. The minaret is original up to the top of its base. Of the porch, unfortunately, only the six columns remain, its upper structure having collapsed in an earthquake.

In the introductory paragraph to this section I stated that the integrity of the domed-square prayer room is completely retained in the single-unit mosque with complex massing. One may take slight exception to this statement in the case of the Mosque of Davud Paşa, because of its apsidal protrusion—an affectation seen in a great number of Istanbul mosques of the fifteenth and later centuries. In my opinion, the apsidal protrusion cannot be considered a spatial extension of the domed-square interior. It is relatively too small and structurally insignificant to constitute a second unit. Beylerbeyi Mosque in Edirne, which will be discussed in chapter 2, also has a polygonal protrusion. But there it is as wide and as deep as the domed-square unit to which it is attached and does form a second unit. Since the same distinction cannot be made for the apse-like projection of Davud Paşa, we must accept it as a variation on the single-unit theme.

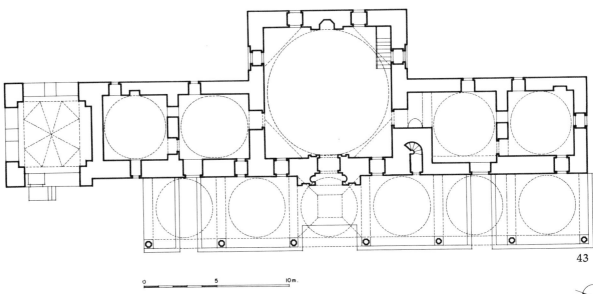

43

Mosque of Mehmed Paşa in Amasya

44

Mosque of Mehmed Paşa, Amasya
43 *Plan*
44 *Exterior. Front view*

A more complex variation on the theme defined by the Hatuniye and the Davud Paşa is found in the Mosque of Mehmed Paşa in Amasya located on the west bank of Yeşil Irmak. The two-line inscription above the door give the date of construction as 1486 (A.H. 891) and the name of Mehmed Paşa as the founder. This Mehmed Paşa was the regent of Şehzade Ahmed, son of Bayezid II, who was appointed governor of Amasya by his father.

The structure is composed of a prayer hall, four small convent rooms, a six-bay porch, the minaret, and a *türbe* (Fig. 43). The prayer hall is a square 8.70 m. across, surmounted by a dome on squinches. On the northwest of the prayer hall rises the minaret. Behind it there is a tiny, barrel-vaulted passage that connects the prayer hall with a square room. This room, in turn, leads to another square room located farther west. Both rooms measure approximately 4.50 m. across and are covered by domes on pendentives. The outer room has a fireplace indicating domestic use. The inner one has a door opening onto the porch which suggests that it was an antechamber. A similar two-room arrangement, minus the passage, is on the opposite side. This unique transversal composition is further stretched by the *türbe* of Mehmed Paşa's father[25] on the eastern tip of the building. Although now enclosed, the *türbe* gives one the impression that it was originally open on three sides and that its eight-sided domical vault sat not on walls but piers on the east.

A second unique feature of the Mosque of Mehmed Paşa is its porch of six bays (Fig. 44) instead of the usual three or five. Because of the even number of bays it is placed asymmetrically with respect to the portal. Probably a seven-bay porch extending the width of the façade was designed, but for some reason the seventh bay was either never built or later destroyed.

54

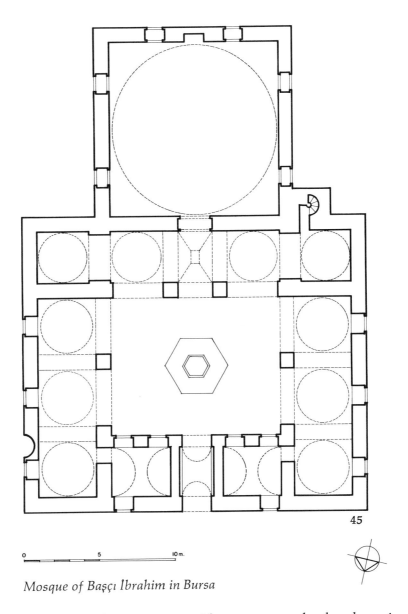

45

0   5   10 m.

Mosque of Başçı İbrahim in Bursa

Mosque of Başçı İbrahim, Bursa
45 Plan

A typical single-unit mosque with an even more developed massing than
the Mosque of Davud Paşa was built by a merchant of sheeps' heads, Başçı
İbrahim, in Bursa. The mosque has no inscription plate and the exact date of its
construction is not known. But it can be attributed to the second half of the
fifteenth century, since its founder, who lies buried behind the *mihrab* of the
mosque, died in A.H. 896 (1490).

In the Mosques of Umur Bey, Hatuniye, and Davud Paşa, the domed-square
prayer room is flanked by smaller domed-square units, and the whole complex
is tied together by a porch running the width of the building. In the Mosque of
Başçı İbrahim, the domed-square prayer hall does not have rooms on the sides
but is enhanced by a courtyard placed in front of it (Fig. 45).

The entrance to the rectangular court is on the north. The barrel-vaulted vestibule is located directly across from the door of the prayer hall. On either side of the vestibule, there are two barrel-vaulted rooms. The other relevant units that form an arcade around the court are open on one or two sides and, except for the narrow unit in front of the door of the prayer hall which is covered by a flat-topped cross-vault, are all domed. Like the other mosques whose side units were convent rooms, the units around the court here also belonged to a *zâviye*.[26]

There are signs to indicate that the three sides—east, west, and north—of the arcade were not included in the original design but were added to the mosque later, probably soon after it was completed.[27] In any case, the high shield wall on top of the three units in front of the prayer hall segregates these units from the others. If one is to visualize the mosque without a court, what remains is a typical single-unit mosque with a large prayer hall (11.00 m. across), a minaret, and a three-bay porch similar to those of other single-unit mosques in Bursa, such as the Mosque of Kamberler (Sitti Hatun, 1459), the Mosque of Ahmed Daî (1471), or Tuzpazarı Camii (second half of the fifteenth century).

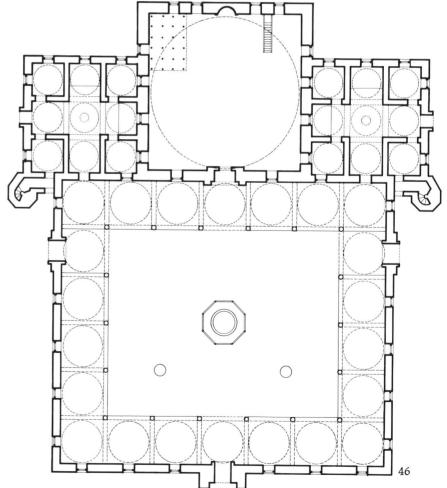

46

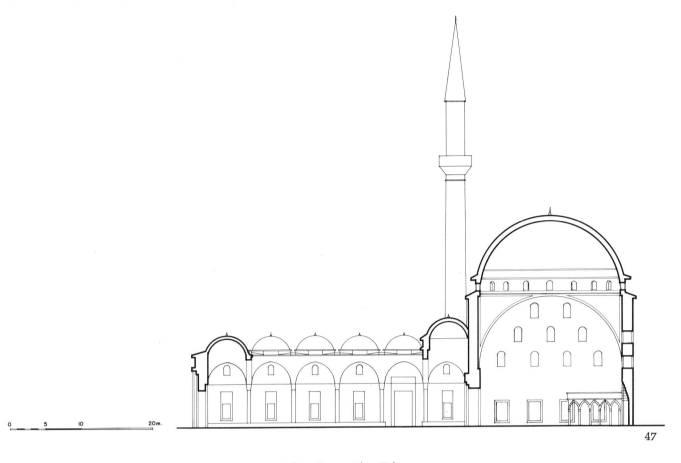

47

Mosque of Sultan Bayezid in Edirne

The highlight of the single-unit mosque with complex massing in early Ottoman architecture is the Mosque of Sultan Bayezid II,[28] which occupies the focal point of a large complex of buildings on the River Tunca in Edirne. Designed and built for Bayezid II by the architect Hayreddin between the years 1484 and 1488 (A.H. 889–893), the mosque comprises a fountain court, a domed-square prayer hall with two hospices (*tabhane*) attached to it on either side, and two minarets (Fig. 46).

The domed arcade (*revak*) around the rectangular court is seven bays wide and six bays deep. There are three exterior doors; one center front and the other two on the sides. The twin hospices fill in the southern corners of the court. Their interiors are divided into nine equal domed-square compartments. Four corner units are individual rooms. The other four serve as eyvans between the corner units, and the ninth unit, which supports a lantern above its dome, is the central hall. Thus the eyvans and the central unit form a quadrifoil interior space. The minarets are located at the outer north corners of the hospices. They are accessible directly from the outside as well as from inside the hospices.

The prayer hall is a typical domed-square structure with very high exterior walls. There are eight windows overlooking the fountain court, fourteen in the opposite wall, and eleven each on either of the side walls, arranged in four tiers. Another twenty are to be found in the drum. Aside from these, at the lowest level, three window openings on the east and the west look into the hospices.

48

The simplicity of expression observed on the exterior continues inside the prayer hall, which is a simple square room 20.25 m. per side. The huge dome rests on four pendentives and completely envelops the interior space (Fig. 48).

In terms of organization of space, the domed prayer hall does not have any relationship with the hospices. Not even a direct access exists between the prayer hall and two hospices, whose doors open to the fountain court or to the outside on the east and the west. Nor are the hospices tall buildings; they stand about a third as high as the prayer hall, allowing the latter to dominate the scene and to retain its identity as a single-unit structure (Fig. 49).

The evolution of the courtyard in Ottoman Turkish architecture will be discussed in chapter 3. I shall, therefore, refrain at this time from commenting about the courtyards of the Mosques of Başçı İbrahim and Sultan Bayezid. But I would like to comment on what I consider to be an important point regarding the organization of interior space and its outward expression in the typical domed-square structure. I have already discussed the types of transition from the dome to the walls in early Ottoman mosque architecture and pointed to the two systems of transition: one type distributing the load onto the length of the walls and the other type collecting it at the corners. I shall now go a step further and analyze how the two systems effect the expression of form and space in architecture. The former system, or the belt of triangular planes, is fitted on top of the walls at a predetermined level. The building, which is square on the lower horizontal plane, retains the same rectangular character on the vertical plane up to the level of the Turkish triangles. In other words, the lower structure is in the form of a cube. The same cubic form can be found on the exterior form and interior space. In short, this system brings out the true geometric and rational expression of the wall as a load-bearing structural element.

In the Mosques of Orhan Gazi in Gebze or Yıldırım Bayezid in Mudurnu, the transition is effected by squinches. The arches of the squinches placed at 45° angles in the corners occur at a level high up on the walls. The lower structure retains its cubic form up to the line of the transition and the spherical surfaces of squinches fill the corners above it. But where pendentives are used, such as in the Mosques of Firuz Ağa or Sultan Bayezid, the lower structure with a cubic exterior hides behind it an interior space whose upper corners curve inward. The only feature on the outside to suggest the presence of the pendentives may be the window arrangement. In the Mosque of Sultan Bayezid, there are five windows in the second, three in the third, and two in the fourth row, thus forming a pyramid (Fig. 50). The pendentive is a structural means of transmitting the load of the dome to the corners. When the load is transmitted to the corners, the wall surfaces lose their architectonic quality, as they have in the

49

50

Mosque of Mihrimah, Istanbul
51 *Exterior*

Mosques of Firuz Ağa and Sultan Bayezid. It was to take another sixty years before the pendentive would be sensitively employed under similar conditions. The architect Sinan, in his Mosque of Mihrimah in Edirnekapı, Istanbul (1555), achieved a strong and singularly effective architectonic expression by indicating the curved form of the pendentive on the exterior. Furthermore, he pushed in the walls and opened a great many large windows in them to obtain a screen-like quality in order to emphasize the essential structural nature of the big arches where pendentives are used (Fig. 51). The pendentive is meaningful when the dome sits on four arches and not on walls. In a single-unit building which has a strict cubic form the use of pendentives results in a misleading geometry. Turkish triangles or squinches are more appropriate transition systems, since they define the relationship between the walls and the dome in a straightforward manner. The Ottoman Turkish architect seems to have sensed this aesthetic subtlety. The early architects did not use pendentives in their solidly built square structures. When they did adopt the pendentive, they did not consider it simply another structural system but developed it into an element of visual appeal both within and without.

SINGLE-UNIT MOSQUE WITH ARTICULATED INTERIOR

In single-unit mosques with complex massing, regardless of how involved the over-all composition may get, the basic unit, or the prayer room, retained its simple character. The interior space is defined by four walls under a dome. In single-unit mosques with articulated interiors the development takes an opposite path. The external form remains more or less the same; but the interior of the basic domed-square unit is enriched by auxiliary spaces.

The expansion of the interior space occurs on one side or more, the mosques in this group showing a variety of form. But there is one thing common to all. The single central dome above the prayer room does not totally cover it. In other words, in this group of single-unit mosques, the interior area contained by the walls is larger than that defined by the dome, the additional areas being covered by vaults, halfdomes, smaller domes, or a combination of these.

52

Yeşil Cami in İznik

Yeşil Cami, İznik
52 Fluted dome of the porch

The Yeşil Cami (Green Mosque) of İznik was constructed by the architect Hacı bin Musa between the years 1378 and 1392 (A.H. 780–794). Its founder was Hayreddin Paşa of Candar.

The porch of the mosque has the usual three-bay arrangement with bipartite open ends. All three bays are surmounted by flat-topped cross-vaults. The center bay supports an additional fluted dome on a belt of Turkish triangles (Fig. 52) that rests on a high octagonal drum. This dome rises above the roof and is easily seen from the outside.

53

55

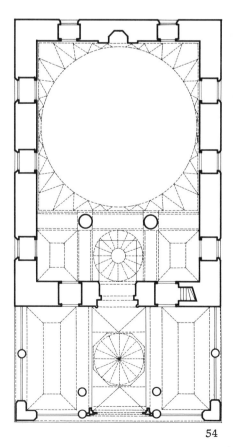

54

0   5   10 m.

0   5   10 m

The prayer hall is basically a typical domed-square space. In this mosque, however, one finds a second three-bay space located between the prayer hall and the porch (Figs. 54–56). Like the porch, the side bays of the vestibule are covered by flat-topped cross-vaults and the center bay supports a dome which is much lower than that of the porch but has an unperforated lantern on top.

The main dome measures 11.00 m. in diameter and unlike the two smaller domes, which are pointed, is hemispherical. It sits on a wide belt of Turkish triangles (Fig. 55) very similar to that of the Mosque of Hacı Özbek. There are three window openings in the dodecagonal drum. Below it, there are a total of twelve windows, eight on the two side walls and two each flanking the door and the *mihrab*.

The exterior walls of Yeşil Cami are faced with finely cut stone (Fig. 57). The interior is finished, up to the height of 3.30 m., with large plates of richly textured marble. The brick minaret is in the best Seljuk tradition, decorated with yellow, green, turquoise, and dark purple colored glazed terra-cotta.

56

Yeşil Cami, İznik
53 Portal
54 Plan
55 Section
56 Interior
57 Exterior

57

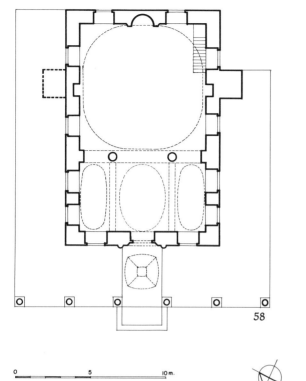

58

59

Dar-ül Hadis in Edirne

Another structure of the same type is located in Edirne. This building was not designed as an independent mosque but, as its name suggests, as part of a *dar-ül hadis* which no longer exists. It was built in 1434 (A.H. 838) by Murad II.

Dar-ül Hadis is a rectangular building of cut stone whose exterior dimensions are 15.40 m. by 9.85 m. Like the Yeşil Cami in İznik, the interior is divided into two, comprising a square section that measures 8.00 m. across in front of the *mihrab*, and a deep three-bay vestibule behind that (Fig. 58). Unlike the Yeşil Cami, however, the main dome on pendentives is not a hemisphere but a domical vault with rounded corners like a hassock in plan. The three bays of the vestibule are also covered by similar spherical vaults but, owing to the excessive depth of the vestibule, these are basically elliptical in shape.

On the exterior, attached to the west wall on the center line of the main dome, there is a buttress-like stone tower. Since it is obviously a nonstructural element one is puzzled by it at first glance. But originally the base of the minaret, which was of equal dimensions, occupied a similar position in front of the east wall (Fig. 59). The minaret was destroyed by bombs during the Balkan War (1912) and its remains were later completely removed, so that today the only trace of it is the patchwork on the masonry wall against which the minaret once stood (Fig. 60).

64

60

61

Dar-ül Hadis, Edirne
58 *Plan*
59 *Exterior (after Gurlitt)*
60 *Exterior. Side-view*
61 *Exterior. Front view*

Nor is there much left of the original porch. What remains is a cross-vaulted canopy on four antique columns in front of the door and four more free-standing columns suggesting a five-bay porch (Fig. 61). Actually, the earlier porch was an eleven-bay structure surrounding three sides of the mosque. Whether the eleven-bay porch that was still intact in 1911 when Gurlitt photographed the building (Fig. 60) dates from the fifteenth century, however, is questionable. The soft, curved movement of the cornices, false weight towers around the main dome, and the over-all character of the canopy with its undulating roof lines are in the style of early nineteenth-century Ottoman baroque architecture. As a matter of fact, the name, Mimar Koç Ahmet (Koç Ahmet the Architect), and the date, A.H. 1224 (1809), carved on a stone near the now nonexistent minaret show that the building was restored in the nineteenth century. The present character of Dar-ül Hadis undoubtedly dates from this period. I strongly suspect that the eleven-bay porch was also an Ottoman baroque innovation. In all probability, the fifteenth-century porch was a three-bay structure and the four free-standing columns originally served as the supports of the two side bays.

62

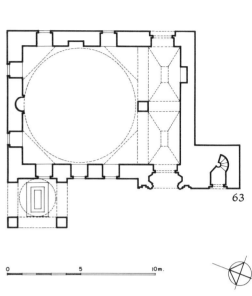

63

Mosque of Şahmelek Paşa in Edirne

This little mosque was built in 1428 (A.H. 832) by Şahmelek Paşa, an important personage during the reigns of Mehmed I and Murad II; he lies buried in a modest, open mausoleum adjoining the mosque on the east (Fig. 62).

The outer dimensions of the building are 12.80 m. by 9.90 m. (Fig. 63) and, like the last two mosques described above, its interior is split into two sections. The prayer room is surmounted by a dome on squinches, and lit by five windows—two rows of two superposed openings in the walls, the fifth in the drum—on the south and the west (Fig. 64). The east wall has an additional sixth window between the two lower ones. The basic elements of the domed-square prayer room follow the general outline of the other two mosques. But the vestibule does not. For, here, not only is the vestibule a two-bay structure covered by flat-topped cross-vaults but, in the absence of a porch, it also serves as one. There are two doors placed across from each other. The entrance on the west is simple and undecorated (Fig. 64). The east entrance, on the other hand, is richly ornamented with a carved arch opening, side niches, and small engaged columns (Fig. 62).

The minaret located on the south of the portal is attached to the building in a most awkward manner, leading one to suspect that it might be a later addition. If not, the base, the shaft, and the balcony (the cap does not exist) are definitely not original but were built in the nineteenth century.

In analyzing these three mosques I find that the most significant development is the vestibule added between the domed prayer hall and the porch. In the Yeşil Cami, the vestibule, in terms of proportion and general character, is not unlike

64

Mosque of Şahmelek Paşa, Edirne
62 *Exterior. Side view*
63 *Plan*
64 *Exterior. Rear view*

the porches of the Alâeddin Bey or the Hacı Özbek, except that here the front columns and the east wall have changed places. Moreover, the porch was made deeper than was customary, resulting in an elongation of the mosque on the *kible* axis. The small dome at the mid-points of the porch and the vestibule accentuate this longitudinal expansion. I feel that the depth of the porch probably was not an arbitrary decision but the outcome of a conscious desire to achieve a balanced building,[29] since measurements of the mosque indicate that the combined depth of the porch and the vestibule is equal to the depth of the prayer room, with the bisecting line passing through the centers of the internal columns (see Fig. 55). An even more significant innovation is the appearance of columns in the interior. So far as I know, the Yeşil Cami in İznik and the Dar-ül Hadis in Edirne are the only edifices among early Ottoman mosques which have internal columns—not piers—and in which the load of the main dome is partially transmitted to columns. The direct structural relationship between the dome and the wall, a major feature of architecture in the typical single-unit mosque, begins to give way to more articulate solutions starting with the Yeşil Cami in the second half of the fourteenth century.

Actually the direct relationship between the dome and the walls is broken in the Mosques of Orhan Gazi and Hoca Yadigâr even before the Yeşil Cami. In the Yeşil Cami, the main dome sits on three walls and only on the fourth side does it rest on columns. In the Orhan Gazi and the Hoca Yadigâr, the walls are totally detached by the concentration of the load at the corners. This system encourages the expansion of space under the arches and permits the walls to be pushed out. The exterior walls do not appear to have a direct structural affinity to the main dome but serve merely as containers of space.

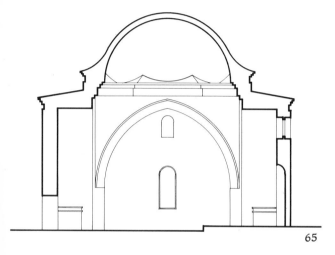

65

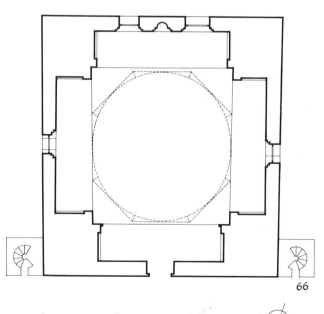

66

Mosque of Orhan Gazi in Bilecik

The construction date of the building in Bilecik referred to as the Mosque of Orhan Gazi is not definitely known but the construction technique and the use of materials lead one to believe that it dates from the first half of the fourteenth century.[30] So far as its exterior massing is concerned, the mosque is in the form of a typical single-unit structure. The almost square lower structure—approximately 16.50 m. by 17.50 m.—rises to a height of 9.50 m. and is surmounted by an egg-shaped dome circumscribed by a low, octagonal drum. But, in terms of interior space, the Mosque of Orhan Gazi does not conform to the prototype; for here the load of the dome is not distributed along the length of the walls but is transmitted to the corners of the structure by means of arches (Fig. 65). The mid-portions of the walls thus freed are extended to form 2.40 m. niches in four directions beyond the limits of the domed-square (Fig. 66). The mosque is narrower on the *kible* axis than it is transversally. For this reason, the dome is slightly elliptical in plan. The diameter of the dome is approximately 9.50 m. The area below it measures 15.30 m. by 14.30 m. on the south-north and east-west axis, respectively. Four arches rest on four massive piers which totally fill the corners of the mosque. The dome sits on an uneven and narrow base, tied to the piers with corbels plastered over to look like a series of overlapping horizontal planes (Fig. 67). The building has one door and seven windows, two flanking and one above the *mihrab* and two on each side wall. Despite the low ratio of window openings to wall surface, the interior is well illuminated.

The Mosque of Orhan Gazi is built of composite stone and brick masonry in the following pattern: one course of stone, one course of brick, another course of stone, and three courses of brick. Under the cornice there is a band of perforations made of hollow, triangular bricks. A similar band is seen below the cornice of the drum (Fig. 68).

The mosque does not have a porch and no traces of an earlier masonry or timber porch are evident.[31] The minarets on either side of the building are new and were probably built during the early years of the present century. A photograph taken in 1882, showing the mosque with no minarets[32] supports this contention. The original minaret, built fifty or sixty years after the erection of the mosque,[33] is in ruins today and is located on a rock some 35 m. from the north wall of the mosque.

68

Mosque of Orhan Gazi, Bilecik
65 *Section*
66 *Plan*
67 *Interior*
68 *Exterior*

67

68

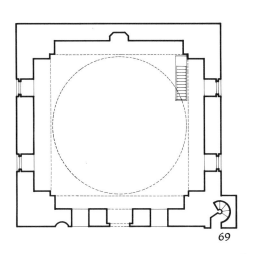

70

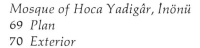

Mosque of Hoca Yadigâr, İnönü
69 *Plan*
70 *Exterior*

Mosque of Hoca Yadigâr in İnönü

Another mosque of the same type built not too long after the Mosque of Orhan Gazi, is the Mosque of Hoca Yadigâr in the town of İnönü. It dates from the period of Murad I, having been erected in 1374 (A.H. 776).

As in the Mosque of Orhan Gazi in Bilecik, the dome is 9.50 m. in diameter, but it sits instead on pendentives. The side extensions are less deep—1.20 m.—and there are nine windows. The interior here is more symmetrical, orderly, and better proportioned than that of Orhan Gazi.

The walls of the Mosque of Hoca Yadigâr are of rubble stone ending in a saw-toothed cornice. The dome is not externally exposed but remains hidden under an octahedral cap covered by terra-cotta roof tiles. A band of triangular perforations, similar to those of the Orhan Gazi encircle the high drum halfway up (Fig. 70). This type of decorative band is peculiar to these two mosques and was not used elsewhere.

Like the Bilecik mosque, the Hoca Yadigâr does not have a porch. Unlike it, the minaret located on the northwest corner of the building is original and dates from the fourteenth century. In the Yeşil Cami of İznik, or the other two mosques with similar interiors, the spatial expansion is only in one direction, along the longitudinal axis. In the Mosques of Orhan Gazi and Hoca Yadigâr, it is in four directions resulting in a modest quadrifoil interior (Fig. 69).

2 The Eyvan Mosque

Mosque of Hamza Bey, Bursa

From the viewpoint of space and form, undoubtedly the most original and interesting type of early Ottoman Turkish mosque is the eyvan mosque, which has been called to date by many names such as the "Bursa Type," the "Reverse T," or the "Multi-Function" mosque. To this nomenclature three more terms have recently been added in attempts to define better the function and the form of these fourteenth- and fifteenth-century Ottoman mosques. Professor Semavi Eyice in a well-documented and learned study showed that the side rooms, where they exist, were used as hostels for the traveling dervishes, and he called these edifices "Convent Mosques" (*zâviyeli cami*).[1] Professor Oktay Aslanapa in his report on the excavations of the Mosque of Orhan Gazi in İznik proposed the term "Mosque with Side Spaces" (*yan mekânlı cami*).[2] The author of this book, searching for the basic architectural concept in this type of mosque, called it the "Cross-Axial Mosque" (*çapraz-mihverli cami*).[3]

In analyzing these three new terms, I find that the "Convent Mosque" refers only to the dual function of the "Bursa Type" mosque and is not suggestive of its architecture. Moreover, where convent rooms do not exist, as in the Mosque of Atik Ali Paşa in Istanbul (see Fig. 212), or where they do occur, but within the context of a different type of mosque, as in the case of the Mosque of Davud Paşa (see Fig. 41), which is a single-unit mosque, the definition ceases to be applicable.

The term "Mosque with Side Spaces" is decidedly a more suitable definition insofar as it relates to the architectural form of the "Bursa Type" mosque. The side spaces, constituting the arms of the T are integral parts of the building, whether as convent rooms or eyvans. But this definition is equally general in nature, going beyond the boundaries of the "Bursa Type" mosque, because it would include such single-unit mosques with convent rooms as side spaces as the Hatuniye Mosque in Tokat (see Fig. 39) or the Mosque of Sultan Bayezid II in Edirne (see Fig. 46).

Similarly, my own term, "Cross-Axial Mosque," in retrospect, falls short of being satisfactory. While the most significant examples of the "Bursa Type" mosque have an interior space developed with respect to the longitudinal and transverse axes, with the main interior space expressed externally by five domes, four at the ends of the axes and the fifth at their intersection in the form of a cross, there are other mosques having interior spaces arranged only along the longitudinal axis with no lateral extensions. They have, of course, their side rooms, but these are sealed off from the central area and do not constitute the second axis, which leaves us with only an axial building.

The two main components of the "Bursa Type" mosque are the central hall and the prayer eyvan. To be sure, neither of these elements or their combined use are novel features of Ottoman architecture. They were borrowed from the Seljuk *medrese*.

Islam scholars generally accept Nizam al-Mulk (d. 1042), the vizier of the Seljuk sultans Alp Arslan (1063–72) and Malik Shah (1072–92) as the founder of the *medrese*. We know today that it existed before Nizam al-Mulk. For instance, there were four *medreses* in Nishapur during the reign of Sultan Mahmud of Gazne (997–1030).[4] His son and successor Mes'ud I (1030–40) also founded a number of *medreses*.[5] But these schools, although founded and protected by the state, were not organized and administered according to a definite educational system. What Nizam al-Mulk did was to establish a policy for Sunnite education and incorporate it with the *medrese* institution. Therefore, the Nizamiyes—or the *medreses* built by Nizam al-Mulk—should not be considered a beginning but rather a turning point in an evolutionary pattern of education. The first Nizamiye was built in Nishapur; the most famous one was that of Baghdad inaugurated in 1066 (A.H. 459). Others were built in the cities of Basra, Mosul, Rayy, Isfahan, Merv, Herat, Tus, Balhk, and Hargird. Unfortunately, none of the *medreses* founded by Nizam al-Mulk has survived. Consequently, we know practically nothing of their architecture. The excavations conducted by André Godard in Hargird may shed a little light on this problem. According to Godard's reconstruction drawing, the Nizamiye of Hargird was a four-eyvan structure arranged around a rectangular courtyard.[6] On the other hand, Creswell does not accept Godard's hypothesis, arguing that the foundations which Godard unearthed could not be those of the Nizamiye but must belong to a mosque.[7] And again, according to Creswell, the first cruciform *medrese* was built in Cairo and the four-eyvan *medrese* originated in Egypt.[8]

Actually the problem of the origin of the four-eyvan *medrese* has been a matter of controversy for a long time. M. van Berchem contended that it must be sought in Syria or, farther east, in Mesopotamia or Chalde.[9]

Pointing out that there exist parts of thirteen *medreses* in Syria built before 1270, and that none of them belongs to the four-eyvan group,[10] Creswell does not agree with van Berchem's thesis. Creswell's point of view is well taken because early Syrian *medreses*, which invariably have a mosque on one side of their courts, can hardly be considered to have been built on the cruciform plan, although they may be accepted as examples of cross-axial planning. On the other hand, the existence of the four-eyvan *medrese* dating from before 1270, when the first Egyptian four-eyvan *medrese* was inaugurated, cannot be accepted; even if one agrees with Creswell, for lack of documentary evidence, that the Hargird structure is not a *medrese*, at least one *medrese* built by the Anatolian Seljuks in the early thirteenth century strongly suggests that the four-eyvan scheme was developed in Iran and brought to Anatolia by the Seljuks. The building I refer to is the Çifte (Double) Medrese in Kayseri, which according to its inscription was dedicated in 1205 (A.H. 602).[11]

Creswell, who argues that the four-eyvan scheme originated in Egypt points to medieval houses of Cairo as a possible source of influence.[12] These houses, which date back to the eleventh century, are composed of two principal parts: the *mak'ad* and the *ka'a*. The former is a veranda looking out to the north; the latter is a skylit hall with two eyvans opening on it. This internal organization

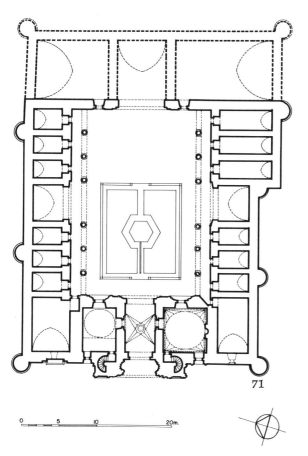

71

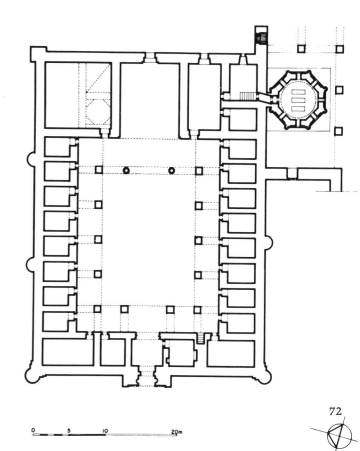

72

Gök Medrese, Sivas
71 *Plan*

Medrese of Hunat Hatun, Kayseri
72 *Plan*

fits well the two-eyvan *medrese* scheme, and Creswell contends that originally the professors gave lessons in their own houses and afterwards the professors' houses were taken as the model for the *medrese*.[13]

A similar argument is put forward by Godard, except that his professors' houses are in Khurasan and date back to the tenth century.[14] Godard's thesis seems to me to have great merit, and the existence of a four-eyvan building, the Gaznavid Palace of Lashkar-i Bazaar (early eleventh century), strongly indicates that the origin of the four-eyvan *medrese* must be sought for in central Asia. Although the idea of eyvans around a court was adapted to other types of buildings, such as mosques or caravanseries, in Iran, the Anatolian Seljuks restricted its use to the *medrese* and *darüşşifa*, the latter being in no way different in its architectural composition from the former.

I have already mentioned Cifte Medrese in Kayseri. Among other examples of the four-eyvan *medrese* in Anatolia one can cite the Sahibiye Medrese in Kayseri (1267) or the Gök (Sky) Medrese in Sivas (1271) (Fig. 71). In all three, a rectangular court with its longer arms arranged along the longitudinal axis of the building occupies the center. The main and the entrance eyvans are placed across from each other at mid-points on the shorter sides of the quadrangle. The other two eyvans are placed, again at mid-points and across from each

74

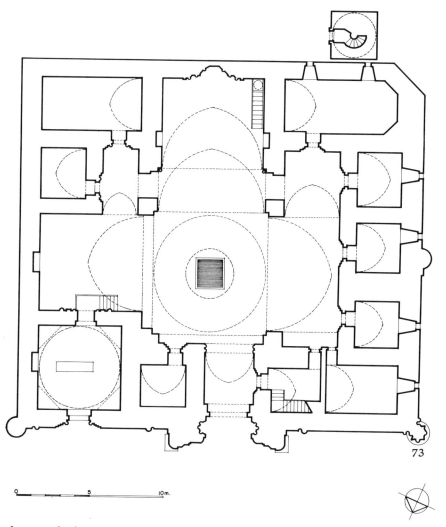

73

other, on the longer sides. Four focal elements are located at the ends of the two axes. Thus the backbone of the four-eyvan *medrese* is a cross-axial system of architecture.

A variation of the four-eyvan *medrese* is the more common two-eyvan type. In these buildings the side eyvans are omitted, and only the longitudinal axis is expressed. A good example of this type is the Medrese of Hunat Hatun in Kayseri (1237) (Fig. 72).

A further variation on the same theme is the "enclosed *medrese.*" In this, the open rectangular court gives way to a domed-square hall, but otherwise the basic interior arrangement remains the same. The enclosed *medrese* may have three eyvans within the framework of a cross-axial scheme, as in the Medrese of Câcâbey in Kırşehir (1272) (Fig. 73) or the Yakutiye Medrese in Erzurum (1310); two eyvans, as in the Çukur (Hollow) Medrese in Tokat (1152?) or the Taş Medrese at Çay in Afyon (1278) (Fig. 74); or simply a single eyvan, as in the Medrese of Karatay in Konya (1251) (Figs. 75, 76).

Except for two examples,[15] however, the Ottomans did not favor the enclosed *medrese* but patterned their *medreses* after the traditional prototype with the open courtyard. They did accept and widely employed the concept of the domed

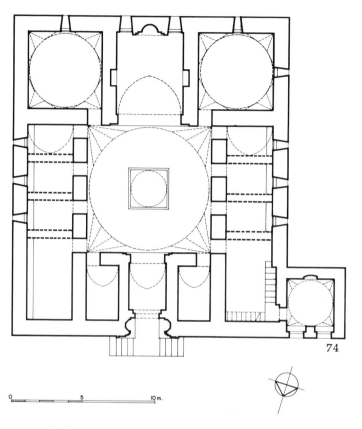

74

Taş Medrese, Çay
74 *Plan*

central hall in other types of buildings, such as the convent (*zâviye*), the public kitchen (*imâret*), and the "Bursa Type" mosque.

In the Seljuk enclosed *medrese*, the square central hall is surmounted by a dome with an unglazed oculus through which light, air, and rainwater are admitted to the interior; the rainwater was collected in a pool placed directly under the oculus at the center of the hall. The main eyvan is generally rectangular in shape and covered by a pointed barrel vault. In the Ottoman buildings using the same elements of the central hall and the eyvan, the former retains the basic Seljuk characteristics, at least until the second half of the fifteenth century. The latter loses them sooner when it is converted into another domed-square unit. In some cases the eyvan is divided in two by an arch and each section is roofed differently. And in a few instances, it is built in the form of a polygon or an oblong rectangle and covered by a halfdome.

Whether barrel-vaulted or domed; whether rectangular, square, or semicircular in shape, the eyvan is the most important space in the "Bursa Type" mosque, since it constitutes the focal point of the edifice. It is the main prayer area in which the *mihrab* and the *minber* are placed. For this reason, I am now proposing a new term to replace my earlier one, the "Cross-Axial Mosque": the eyvan mosque.[16] I feel that this new term is more universal a definition than all the previous ones and is expressive of the mosque and not the auxiliary areas within a multifunction building. In other words, the eyvan mosque is not a building

76

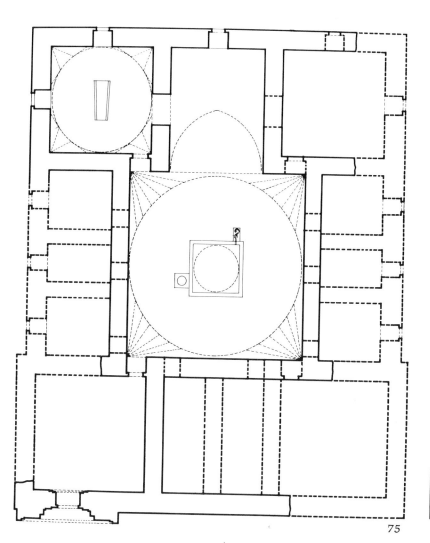

75

76

Medrese of Karatay, Konya
75 *Plan*
76 *Interior*

assigned in its totality to worship. The space that serves as the mosque is the main eyvan in which the *mihrab* and the *minber* are located. In the multi-eyvan schemes the side eyvans also function as auxiliary parts of the general prayer area. But it must be noted that the side eyvans were designed primarily for meditation and private worship between regular daily services. The corner rooms, on the other hand, had a different function, a fact which has led to several hypotheses (guestroom, classroom, court of law, kitchen, etc.).[17] The most convincing is that forwarded by Semavi Eyice, who contends that they were convent rooms for traveling dervishes.[18] Since the objective of this book is to study the architectural form and spatial organization of early Ottoman mosques, I shall not discuss this subject further. One way or another, the function of the corner rooms in the eyvan mosque does not affect its basic architectural concept.

Like the single-unit mosque in chapter 1, I shall consider the eyvan mosques in two groups: "The Axial Eyvan Mosque," and "The Cross-Axial Eyvan Mosque."

AXIAL EYVAN MOSQUE

Mosque of Sultan Orhan in İznik

The earliest of the eyvan mosques, the Mosque of Sultan Orhan in İznik, located approximately 400 m. outside of the Yenişehir Gate to the right of the road as one enters the walled town, was built in 1334 (A.H. 735).[19] It was previously thought that this building was erected prior to the capture of İznik by the Ottoman Turks in 1331. But Aslanapa, who partially recovered the inscription slab during his recent excavations in the area, proved that the mosque could not have been erected before 1334.[20]

The building, as excavated, is composed of two interlocking areas flanked by two rooms and a five-bay porch (Fig. 77). No remains of a minaret were found, but elderly people of İznik remember that forty or fifty years ago a minaret did exist on the left corner of the porch.[21]

The central interior space is divided into two rectangular units, one being two steps higher than the other and both having finished floors. The higher area on the south is surfaced with rectangular terra-cotta tiles, whereas the lower area is covered by large square slabs of stone. The side rooms, whose doors open to the lower central space, are also rectangular and have terra-cotta tile floors similar to the floor of the higher central space.

The five-bay porch is supported by six columns of Byzantine origin that must have been collected from various buildings in the area. Consequently, they are of different size and diameter.

The center bay of the porch is wider than the others, accentuating the entrance to the building. Since the remains of the Mosque of Sultan Orhan consist of low walls, it naturally opens the way for speculation about its original upper structure. Aslanapa contends that owing to the rather clumsy and unsturdy character of the existing walls, neither the main structure nor the porch could have been domed or vaulted and that both must have been covered by either a flat or a pitched roof.[22] I take exception to this view, for, in my opinion, the walls, which are 1.00 m. thick, are sufficiently strong to support a masonry upper structure. The rectangular forms of the southern central space as well as the side rooms suggest that they were surmounted by barrel vaults. The porch, in all probability, was covered by cross-vaults. The northern central space, on the other hand, presents a problem. The central hall

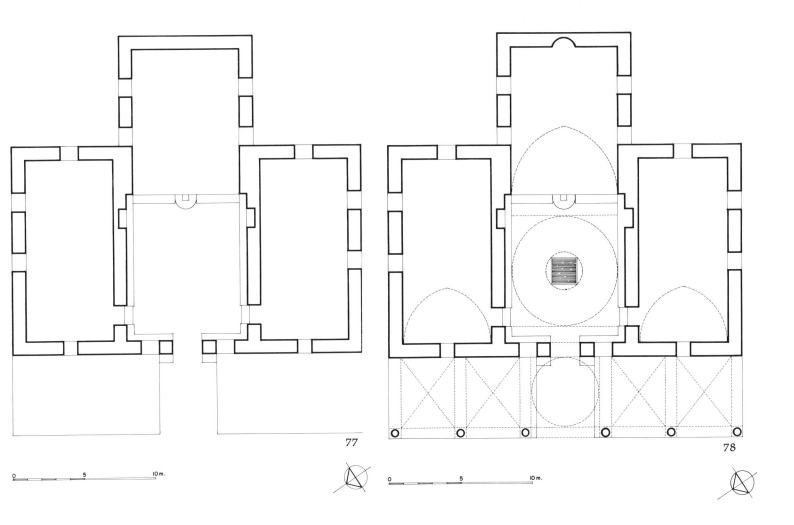

77

78

Mosque of Sultan Orhan, İznik
77 *Plan (after Aslanapa)*
78 *Restored plan (Kuran)*

of the eyvan mosques are covered by domes, although the rectangular shape
of this hall does not immediately bring one to mind. But the existence of
other early Ottoman buildings whose domed units are not square but rectangular,
such as the domed central hall of the Mosque-Medrese of Hüdavendigâr in
Bursa, indicate that here, too, the central hall could have been domed. As is the
Bursa mosque, two arches, approximately 1.00 m. in width and slightly higher
than the arch-opening of the eyvan, placed at the ends of the longer sides of
the rectangle may have converted it into a square, thus providing a suitable
base for the dome to rest upon (Fig. 78). Similar eyvan mosques with domed
central halls immediately following the Mosque of Sultan Orhan in İznik and
preceding examples of Seljuk enclosed *medreses* of the thirteenth century,
and a building even closer in place and time, the Vacidiye Medrese in Kütahya
(1314), lead one to believe that the mosque under discussion does not constitute a
break in the evolutionary pattern of the eyvan buildings with domed central
halls but establishes the crucial link in the transition from the Seljuk and
Germiyan enclosed *medrese* to the Ottoman eyvan mosque.

79

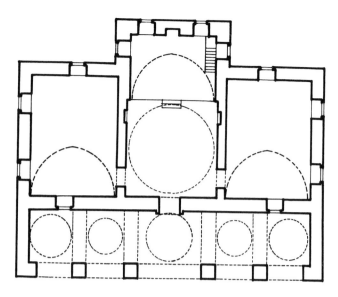

Mosque of Timurtaş in Bursa

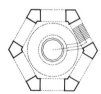

79

Mosque of Timurtaş, Bursa
79 Plan

Built by Kara Timurtaş, an army commander during the reigns of Murad I and Bayezid I, who died in 1403 (A.H. 806) according to the epitaph on his tomb, this uninscribed mosque can safely be accepted as a late fourteenth-century structure, probably dating from the era of Bayezid I.[23] Although the mosque has undergone several restorations in the past and in the process suffered severe alterations, portions of the building, notably the eyvan, still retain their original character. The five-bay porch, on the other hand, is totally reconstructed.

The Mosque of Timurtaş comprises two separate structures: the main building, and the minaret located some 20 m. to the north of the porch (Fig. 79). The cylindrical shaft of the minaret is elevated on a base supported by piers on six corners. At the center of this domed hexagonal structure, which measures 7.20 m. across, stands an ablution fountain. The masonry technique of the hexagonal base and the cylindrical shaft of the minaret is homogeneous, although there is a possibility that this unique structure does not represent an original concept but is merely an expedient solution of erecting a minaret on top of an earlier structure which was a part of a totally different building.[24]

The main structure is composed of a five-bay porch, the central axial area, and the flanking convent rooms. The square central hall is surmounted by a dome that rises above squinches. The stalactite decorations on the squinches probably date from a later restoration.[25] Another element not of the fourteenth century is the lantern covering the oculus. The eyvan is raised from the central hall by three steps and covered by a pointed barrel vault. Unlike Seljuk eyvans, it is wider than it is deep. There is no possibility that the eyvan could have been shortened at a later date, since both the *mihrab* and the exterior masonry work are original. Of the large convent rooms, the western room is barrel-vaulted but its eastern counterpart is covered by a contemporary roof. It is safe to assume, however, that originally the eastern room was also surmounted by a barrel vault.

80

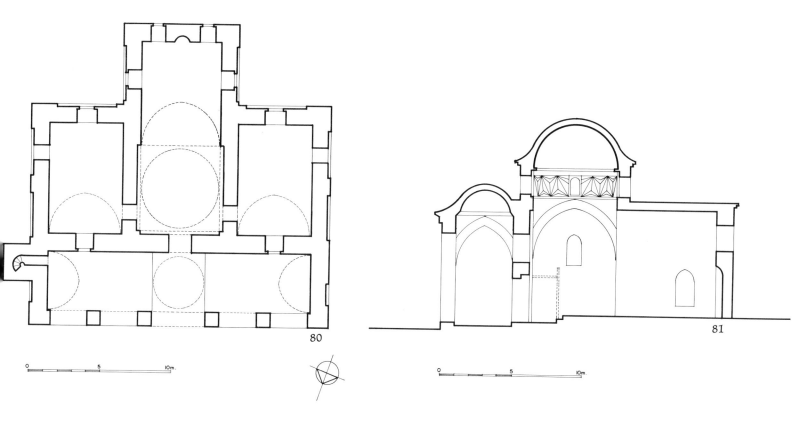

80

81

Mosque of Ebu İshak in Bursa

Mosque of Ebu İshak, Bursa
80 *Plan*
81 *Section*

Another axial eyvan mosque dating from the later fourteenth century is the
Mosque of Ebu İshak, or Baba İshak, in Bursa. The inscription plate above the
door records that it was built by Bayezid I for the Sheik Ebu İshak Kazerûnî, the
founder of the İshaki Order of Dervishes.[26] The mosque was restored in 1479
(A.H. 884) by the order of Mehmed II.[27]

In its basic outline this building is very similar (Fig. 80) to the Mosque of
Timurtaş, with the exception of its minaret, which is located at the east end of
the porch. The square central hall is surmounted by a dome which sits over a belt
of Turkish triangles. In all probability, the present dome is not the original one,
which must have had an oculus. The rectangular eyvan is barrel-vaulted and two
steps higher than the central hall (Fig. 81). The elevated platform extends beyond
the barrel-vaulted upper structure of the eyvan. But again, this peculiarity must
be due to a later innovation to provide more room for prayer, the original prayer
area being confined to the boundaries of the barrel-vaulted eyvan.

Similarly, the convent rooms were without doubt originally barrel-vaulted.
At the present only the western room is covered by a barrel vault, that of the
eastern room having collapsed and been replaced by a timber roof.

Two other axial eyvan mosques dating from the fourteenth century are
the *imâret* Mosques of Sultan Orhan in Bilecik and Yıldırım in Balıkesir. Both
buildings are in ruins. The porch and the side rooms of the first have been

81

completely destroyed. The entire upper structure of the second collapsed, was replaced by a timber roof, and its interior rearranged. But although the fourteenth-century examples of axial eyvan mosques are in poor repair, much altered, or have been totally or partially destroyed, a good number of fifteenth-century examples do exist in fairly good condition. Let us now study the more significant of these in chronological order.

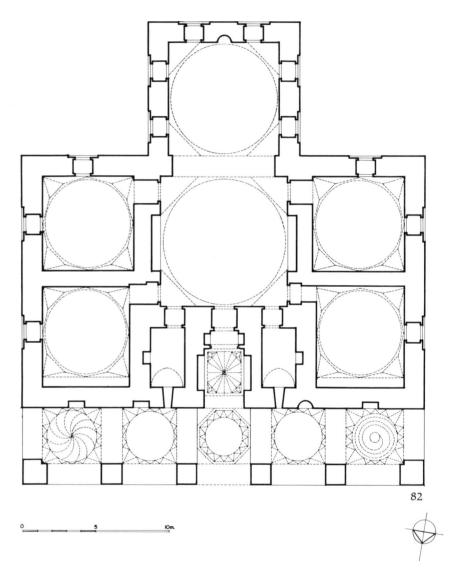

82

Mosque of Bayezid Paşa in Amasya

According to the inscription slab above its portal, this mosque in Amasya was founded during the reign of Mehmed I by his grand vizier Bayezid Paşa (d. 1421). The construction began in 1414 (A.H. 817) and the mosque was completed in 1419 (A.H. 822).[28] It was built by the architect Yakub bin Abdullah, one of the mamelukes of Bayezid Paşa.[29]

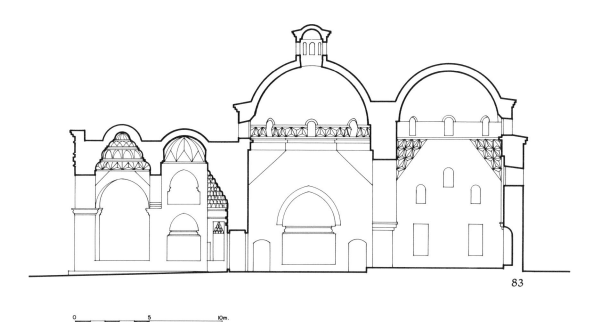

83

Mosque of Bayezid Paşa, Amasya
82 *Plan*
83 *Section*

The mosque comprises a vestibule, a central hall, a prayer area, four large side rooms, two cells, and a five-bay porch (Fig. 82). Except for the two cells, all the spaces are square, or near square, and covered by domes of varying sizes and transition systems. The largest of the domed-square spaces is the central hall, measuring 8.50 m. on each side. Its hemispherical dome rests on a belt of Turkish triangles which, in turn, is supported by four squinches. It is punctured on top by an oculus (Fig. 83). The lantern is of a later date. Originally, the oculus was not covered, and directly under it at the center of the hall was a pool.

Raised by a step from the central hall on the south is the prayer eyvan. It is slightly smaller—7.50 m. across—than the central hall. Consequently its dome is somewhat smaller and lower than the first one. The transition of the second dome is also effected by squinches, but these are decorated with inclined triangular planes in a pattern of stars. Above them, between window openings, a simple curvilinear band converts the octagon created by the squinches into a circular base for the hemispherical dome to sit upon.

The four convent rooms, two each on the east and on the west, as well as the two cells on the north, are arranged around the central hall and are accessible from it. The domes of the square rooms rest on triangular corner panels; the rectangular cells are barrel-vaulted.

The remaining six small domes surmount the five bays of the porch and the vestibule. The elliptical dome of the latter is fluted. Of the four outer domes covering the side bays of the porch, the easternmost is decorated with rotating semicircles, and the westernmost with a fluted spiral. The dome of the center bay rises above the others and is built of four superimposed tiers of Turkish triangles and stalactites.

84

There is a staircase inside the northwest convent room that once gave access to the now nonexistent minaret which rose on top of the northeast corner of the room. This staircase slices the domed room in an awkward manner and is obviously a later addition. In the absence of a more direct approach and because of its rather unusual position, one can conclude that the minaret was not an original component of the mosque. Along with the staircase, it must have been added to the mosque at a later date.

The Mosque of Bayezid Paşa is solidly constructed of finely cut stone and is richly decorated inside and out (Fig. 84). The ornate fireplaces and niches of the convent rooms, the original stained glass panels of the prayer eyvan, and the sculptured portal with its stalactite arch and side niches are all tastefully decorated. The *tour de force* of the mosque is definitely the monumental, boxlike porch (Fig. 85) whose alternating red and yellow stone arches, carved marble frames with geometric designs and shapely moldings, crowning stalactite cornice (Fig. 86), and, of course, profusely decorative domes inside make it one of the most elegant porches in early Ottoman architecture.

85

Mosque of Bayezid Paşa, Amasya
84 Exterior. Rear view
85 Exterior. Front view
86 Porch. Detail

86

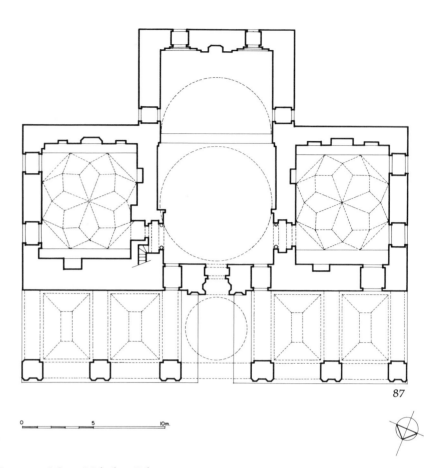

87

Mosque of Gazi Mihal in Edirne

Mosque of Gazi Mihal, Edirne
87 *Plan*
88 *Exterior. Rear view*
89 *Exterior. Front view*

Located on the eastern shore of the River Tunca, a little to the north of the Mosque of Kasım Paşa, in Edirne, the Mosque of Gazi Mihal was built in 1421 (A.H. 825). Although, its five-bay porch is fairly similar in design and character to that of the Bayezid Paşa in Amasya, it is a much simpler mosque comprising only four spaces: the central hall, the prayer eyvan, and two convent rooms (Fig. 87).

The square central hall is surmounted by a dome on pendentives. The two convent rooms, which today are accessible only from the outside but were originally also connected to the central hall, are similarly domed. Unlike the central dome, which is a simple hemisphere, the domes of the side rooms are visually enriched by ribs. The raised prayer eyvan is shallower than it is wide and is covered by a barrel vault protected on the exterior by a pitched roof (Fig. 88).

The domed central bay of the porch is wider and higher (Fig. 89) than the other four, which are all covered by barrel vaults. Earlier photographs of the mosque show a minaret on top of the northwest corner of the western convent room. A portion of its rickety base can still be seen on the roof. But this minaret was not original; one can safely attribute it to the nineteenth century.

88

89

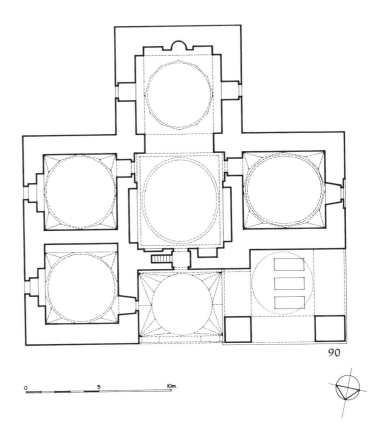

90

Mosque of Yörgüç Paşa in Amasya

According to the inscription plate above its door this mosque in Amasya was built in 1428 (A.H. 832)[30] by Yörgüç Paşa, one of the viziers of Mehmed I, during the reign of Sultan Murad II.

The Mosque of Yörgüç Paşa shows a number of deviations from the typical axial eyvan mosque scheme. It has no porch. But a deep, rectangular vestibule surmounted by a dome on fan-shaped Turkish triangles, serves as an outdoor hall giving access to three different types of spaces. To the east is a domed room which probably was a public kitchen for the poor. Across from it on the west there is an open *türbe*, covered by a dome on pendentives, awkwardly carved out of the main structure. To the south is the portal leading into the four-unit interior composed of the central hall flanked by two rooms and the main eyvan (Fig. 90).

The dome of the central hall sits on a high drum, octagonal on the exterior but circular inside. It is decorated by a band of sixteen arches, four of which, above the corners, are window openings. This dome is mounted on pendentives. Those of the two square side rooms rest on triangular corner panels. Although both are square and have similar upper structures, the two rooms are not symmetrical, the room on the west being larger than the other. The prayer eyvan is raised from the central hall and is surmounted by a small low dome.

Mosque of Yörgüç Paşa, Amasya
90 *Plan*
91 *Exterior. Front view*

A squat timber minaret which gives the impression of being a later addition is mounted on the front wall to the east of the entrance (Fig. 91). The structure is solidly built of rubble stone externally faced with dressed stone and white marble. The interior is enriched by a number of ornamental features. But the exterior is severely designed, the only attempt at decoration being the alternating red and white colored arches.

Beylerbeyi Mosque in Edirne

A second axial eyvan mosque in Edirne is Beylerbeyi Mosque built in 1428 (A.H. 832) by Beylerbeyi (Governor General) Sinaneddin Yusuf Paşa. Left to deteriorate over the years, its prayer eyvan partially destroyed, its porch gone, and its minaret fallen, it has recently been restored and saved.

Beylerbeyi Mosque is composed of a domed central hall flanked by two domed-square convent rooms and a highly ornate prayer eyvan. Except for the latter, the arrangement of the interior is not unlike the Gazi Mihal. But the prayer eyvan is not only deeper, comprising two sections with different roof structures, but also comes to an end in an apse-like polygonal form (Fig. 92).

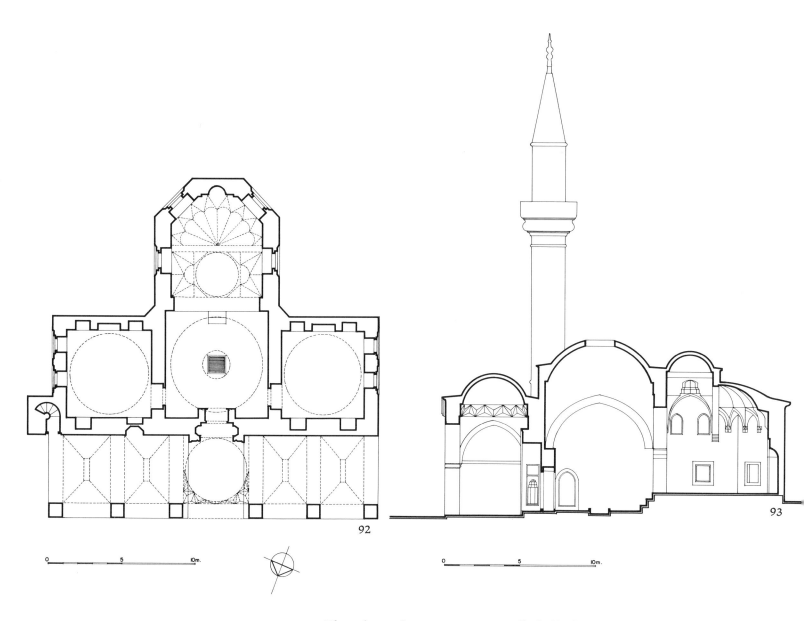

92

93

Beylerbeyi Mosque, Edirne
92 *Plan*
93 *Section*

The polygonal rear section is actually half a hexagon surmounted by a fluted halfdome. The rectangular front section has an octagonal vault covering its center portion with triangular planes filling in the corners (Fig. 93).

The minaret is located at the northwest corner of the mosque. What remained of it before its recent reconstruction dated from the eighteenth century, at which time the building underwent an earlier restoration. Since nothing was left of the five-bay porch before it was reconstructed in 1963 except traces of its arch springs on the north wall and the foundations of its column bases, one must consider it an appropriate but totally conjectural contemporary addition to an otherwise historic monument.

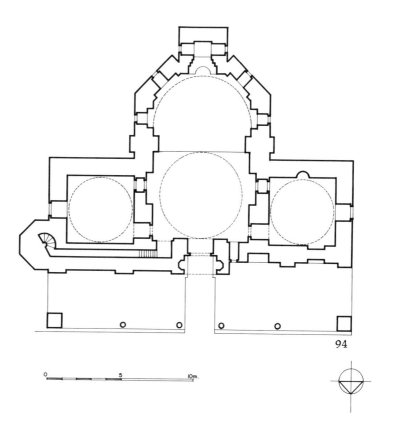

94

Mosque of Yahşi Bey in Tire

Mosque of Yahşi Bey, Tire
94 Plan

Another building which shows a great similarity to the Beylerbeyi Mosque in Edirne is located at Tire near Aydın. It was built by Halil Yahşi Bey in or about 1441 (A.H. 845).[31]

Also known as Yeşil Cami (Green Mosque), it has a five-bay porch, a minaret on the northwest corner, a domed central hall flanked by two domed-square convent rooms, and an apse-like polygonal prayer eyvan. The only major difference between this mosque and the Beylerbeyi is that in the Yahşi Bey the prayer unit is not divided in two by an arch but is a single space covered by a halfdome (Fig. 94).

The prayer eyvan of the Mosque of Yahşi Bey marks an important event in the evolution of Ottoman Turkish architecture, for, so far as we know, it is the first and only occurrence of a halfdome built by a Turkish architect prior to the conquest of Constantinople by the Ottoman Turks.

Mosque of Karacabey in Karacabey

One of the most majestic examples of the axial eyvan mosque is to be found in Karacabey, Bursa. Unfortunately, this important mosque was destroyed during the Turco-Greek War (1920–22). What remains of it is sufficient to give one a good idea of what this monument was like in its day. The mosque was built by Karacabey, or Karaca Paşa, known by the epithet *Dayı* (uncle) because he was the maternal uncle of the crown prince Alâeddin Ali Çelebi (1425–43), the eldest son of Murad II. Karacabey died in the second siege of Belgrade in 1455. His mosque was completed by his heirs the year after his death in 1456 (A.H. 861).[32] There he lies buried under the porch, his grave marked by a modest marble sarcophagus.

The central hall measures 10.20 m. across. Its partially existent upper structure shows that the transition to the dome was effected by an octagonal belt of Turkish triangles sitting on stalactite corbels at the corners (Fig. 95). Nothing is left of the domed-square prayer eyvan except its foundation walls. These indicate that the eyvan was smaller by 1.30 m. on a side than the central hall. The two side rooms are fairly large, both measuring 7.30 m. square. They

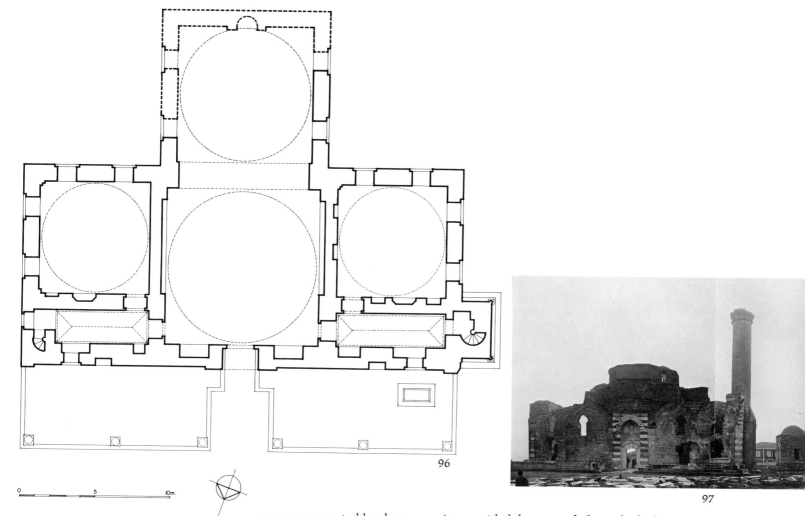

96

97

Mosque of Karacabey, Karacabey
95 Exterior. Rear view
96 Plan
97 Exterior. Front view

were surmounted by domes on sixteen-sided drums, each face of which was decorated by blind pointed arches, on pendentives. The side rooms are not directly accessible from the central hall; they are entered from low passages 2.15 m. wide between the rooms and the porch (Fig. 96). Above these are two cells. The one on the east is reached by a spiral staircase cut into the wall. The staircase of the minaret leads to the other on its way up to the balcony.

The stone minaret is original. It exists, however, only up to the cantilever of the balcony. The five-bay porch is almost totally gone (Fig. 97). The arch springs, pier bases, and a pendentive left on the northwest corner of the façade show that it was covered by five domes of equal size. The walls of the Mosque of Karacabey are constructed of composite stone and brick masonry, the arches and the upper structure of brick alone. The porch, on the other hand, was built of alternating white and dark gray marble, many pieces of which lie on the ground in front of the building. The portal is well preserved and attests to the elegant simplicity which I feel to be a major characteristic of early Ottoman Turkish architecture.

93

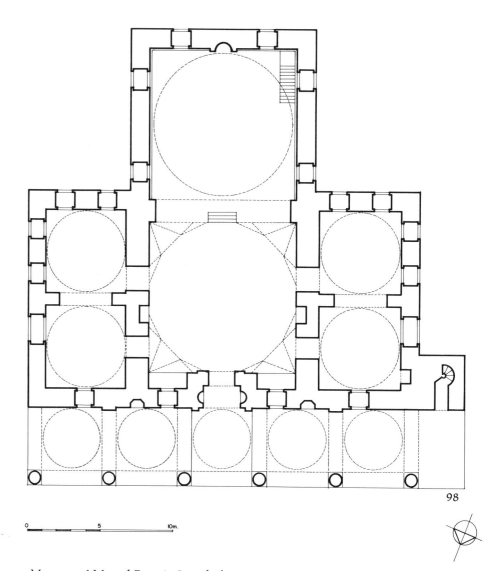

98

Mosque of Murad Paşa in Istanbul

Mosque of Murad Paşa, Istanbul
98 *Plan*
99 *Section*
100 *Exterior*

The Mosque of Has Murad Paşa (d. 1473) which bears the name of one of the governors general (*Rumeli Beylerbeyi*) of Mehmed II is located at Aksaray in Istanbul. According to its inscription, it was built in 1469 (A.H. 874).

In this mosque, from the five-domed porch, one passes into the central hall surmounted by a large dome. The central hall is flanked on either side by smaller domed-square units, each of which is joined spatially by an arch opening (Fig. 98). Despite this interrelationship, however, both rooms, or each coupled unit, have individual doors leading from the central hall, suggesting that originally they were separate rooms. Between the doors of the convent rooms on both side walls there are two tall niches with stalactite arches.

The prayer eyvan is four steps higher than the central hall. Otherwise it is quite similar in size (10.50 m. across) and character to the central hall. The

94

99

100

two big domes are not only of equal diameter but of equal external height
(21.00 m.) as well (Fig. 99). They have, however, slightly different transition
systems: the dome of the central hall rests on triangular panels and that of the
prayer eyvan on a belt, decorated with triangles and lozenges, which is supported
at the corners by corbels. One last point of interest is the unusual spatial quality
of the interior. Owing to the excessive height of the walls—obviously the
outcome of the 1 : 2 ratio between the width (10.50 m.) and the height (21.00 m.)
of the two central spaces—the connecting arch is also placed rather high,
resulting in a volumetric and visual amalgamation of the domed-square units. I
shall have more to say about this development at the end of the present chapter.

95

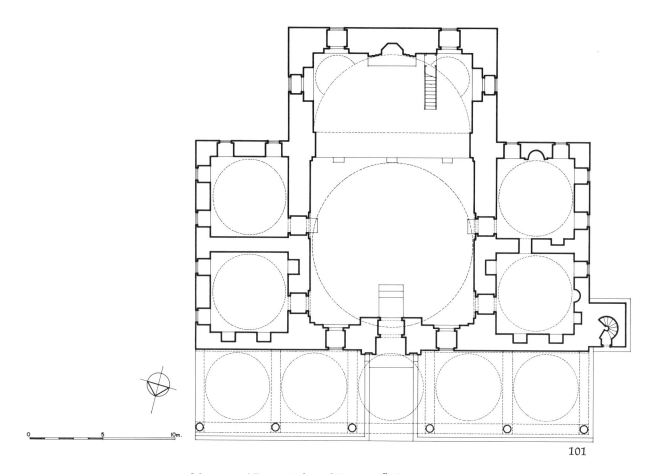

101

Mosque of Rum Mehmed Paşa in Üsküdar, Istanbul

This mosque overlooking the Bosporus on the Anatolian shore of Istanbul was built by the grand vizier (1466–69) of Mehmed II. Its two-line inscription gives the date of construction as 1471 (A.H. 876).

The square central hall is 11.15 m. across and surmounted by a dome on pendentives. The convent rooms, two each on the east and west, measure 5.30 m. across and are also domed. All four have door openings from the central hall. The minaret is located on the northwest corner of the building. The porch is composed of five domed-square units of equal size and height (Fig. 101).

In regard to these components, the Mosque of Rum Mehmed Paşa exhibits a close similarity to the Mosque of Murad Paşa. The difference between the two lies in the prayer eyvan: in the Murad Paşa the prayer eyvan is another domed-square unit; in this mosque it is an oblong rectangular space 10.75 m. by 5.30 m. covered by a halfdome that rests on squinches. The latter are underlined by a row of stalactites which droop on the corners of the walls and at the tips of the squinch arches (Fig. 102).

A more radical difference between the two mosques is their exterior treatment. Although fundamentally Ottoman in plan arrangement and over-all composition, its semicircular window heads, the four big arches that rise above the cornice of the central hall, and the circular drum give the Mosque of Rum Mehmed Paşa a Byzantine character which is not common in Ottoman

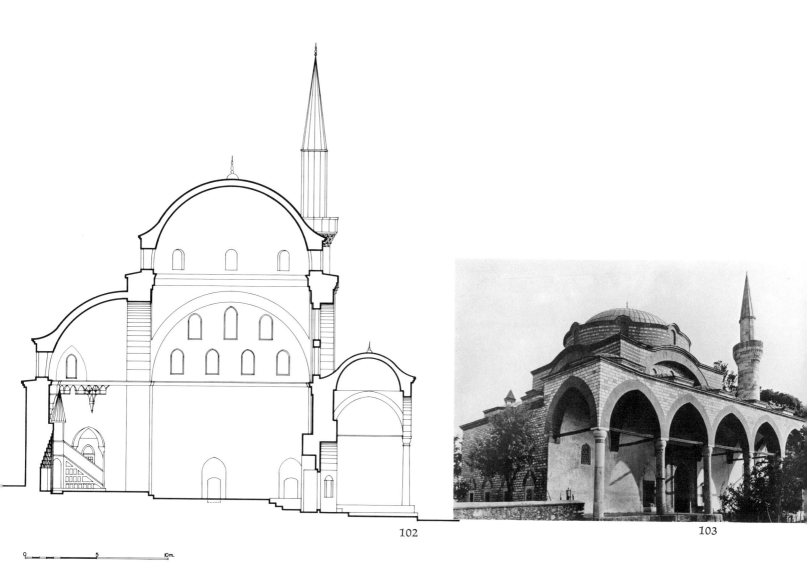

102

103

Mosque of Rum Mehmed Paşa, Istanbul
101 *Plan*
102 *Section*
103 *Exterior*

architecture of the fifteenth century (Fig. 103). These deviations from the basic pattern and rules of early Ottoman architecture have been ascribed to the fact that Rum (Roman) Mehmed Paşa, as his epithet states, was by birth a Byzantine, even possibly a member of the Imperial House of the Palaeologues. It has been suggested that he wanted to revive Byzantine architecture.[33] I rather think that the Byzantine quality of this mosque was due to the particular artistic taste of its founder, who, after all, was brought up in Constantinople and, in all probability, could never totally free himself of Byzantine cultural values.

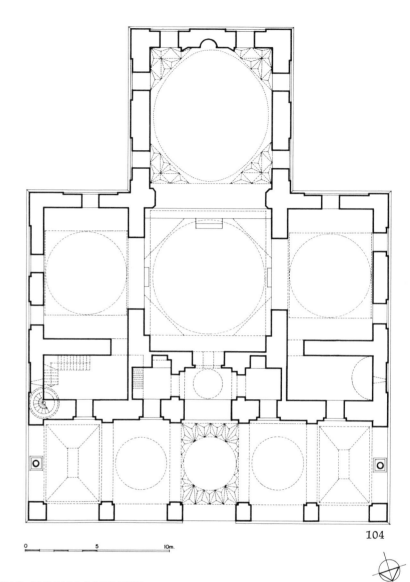

104

CROSS-AXIAL EYVAN MOSQUE

Mosque of Orhan Gazi in Bursa

According to the inscription plate above its door, the construction of the Mosque of Orhan Gazi in Bursa was begun in 1339 (A.H. 740). The building was burned by the Karaman forces at the turn of the fifteenth century, but repaired soon afterwards in 1417 by Bayezid Paşa. Seriously damaged once again in the earthquake of 1855, it underwent a second major restoration in 1864.[34]

    The five-bay porch of the Mosque of Orhan Gazi is supported on the façade by piers. The three center bays are domed, but the outer bays are covered by flat-topped cross-vaults. Slender columns placed at the center of each end of the porch give it scale and lightness. A domed vestibule leads one to the domed

105

Mosque of Orhan Gazi, Bursa
104 *Plan*
105 *Section*

central hall, which is rectangular. But a deep arch on the north converts the rectangular lower structure of the central hall into a square at the upper level to provide a suitable base for the circular dome.

    Raised by two steps from the hall on the south is the main eyvan. This space is a domed rectangle measuring 9.30 m. by 8.65 m. However, here no auxiliary arch to adjust the base of the dome was provided. As a result, the dome of the main eyvan is not circular but elliptical. Two more eyvans flank the central hall. Like the main eyvan these side eyvans are also raised, covered by domes, and rectangular. In these cases the square bases for the domes are furnished by two arches placed on the south and on the north. Two more rectangular spaces are placed between the side eyvans and the porch. One enters these barrel-vaulted rooms from inside the eyvans as well as directly from the vestibule (Fig. 104).

    Among the three eyvans and the central hall there are differences not only in floor levels but also in dome heights and transition systems (Fig. 105). The largest of the domes covers the central hall. It is 8.45 m. in diameter and 16.00 m. in height at the center, and sits on a belt composed of eight fan-shaped panels of triangles placed between tall windows (Fig. 106). This belt, however, does not rest on the walls but is reinforced by pendentives. The elliptical dome of the main eyvan is broader but not as high, measuring 13.50 m. at the center. The transition is effected by squinches decorated inside with broken triangular panels (Fig. 107). The lowest are the domes of the side eyvans, which sit on pendentives. All four major domes are braced on the exterior by octagonal drums.

106

107

Mosque of Orhan Gazi, Bursa
106 *Interior. Central dome*
107 *Interior. Main eyvan*
108 *Exterior. Front view*
109 *Exterior. Side view*

The minaret of the Mosque of Orhan Gazi dates from the nineteenth century. The walls are built of composite brick and stone and are topped by saw-toothed cornices (Fig. 108). The two end columns of the porch are of Byzantine origin. Tall narrow window openings with semicircular arch heads, decorative brick medallions on the walls, and the general character of the masonry work are further indications of Byzantine influence (Fig. 109).

100

108

109

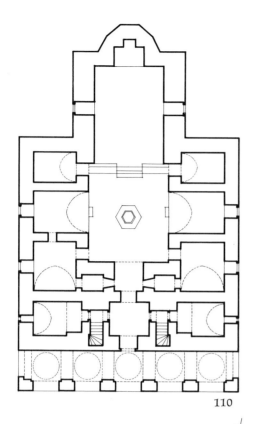

110

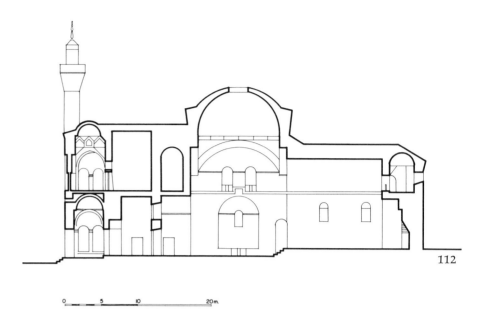

112

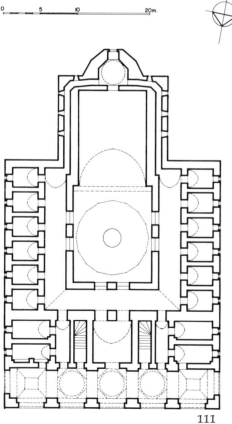

111

Mosque of Hüdavendigâr in Bursa

The Mosque of Hüdavendigâr at Çekirge in Bursa is a two-story building comprising a mosque-convent on the ground floor with a *medrese* on the upper level. Its construction was ordered by Murad I (the Hüdavendigâr) in 1365 (A.H. 767) and, according to foundation records, was completed in 1385 (A.H. 787).[35]

The ground floor is composed of a five-bay porch, a vestibule which gives access to the interior on the south and to staircases on either side, a main interior space of four eyvans around a central hall, and six rooms—three each on the east and the west (Fig. 110). On the upper level, there is a five-bay gallery directly above the porch, a large room between the two staircases, eight *medrese* cells on each side accessible by a corridor that follows the perimeter of the central hall, and a small room above the *mihrab* on the south (Fig. 111). The latter is covered by a dome. The large room, the cells, and the corridors are barrel-vaulted. The three center bays of the gallery are surmounted by domes, the outer ones by flat-topped cross-vaults. All arch-openings of the gallery—five at the front, two at the ends—have a single column at their centers dividing them into two units, each topped by an arch.

On the first floor, the bipartite openings occur only at the two ends of the porch. Here all five of the bays are surmounted by domes. The six rooms, on the other hand, are barrel-vaulted. Two of these are accessible from the vestibule. The other four have doors opening to the central hall. The intermediary rooms are also connected to the entrance eyvan by means of two narrow passages.

In the center of the main hall there is a fountain inside a pool. Owing to the two-story structure, the dome—11.00 m. in diameter—rises to a height of 23.00 m. (Fig. 112). It rests on a simple sixteen-sided belt on pendentives. There

Mosque of Hüdavendigâr, Bursa
110 *Plan. Lower level*
111 *Plan. Upper level*
112 *Section*
113 *Interior. Main eyvan*

are sixteen cantilevered supports around the base of the dome. These look superfluous today because they belonged to the original upper structure, which collapsed in the earthquake of 1855.

To the south of the domed central hall, elevated by five steps from it, is the main eyvan. Like the central hall, the barrel-vaulted main eyvan is also two stories high (Fig. 113). The *mihrab* is placed inside a large niche that forms a pentagonal protrusion at the back of the building. Across from the main eyvan, there is the small, barrel-vaulted entrance eyvan. A timber balcony, obviously the work of a later era, occupies the upper section of this eyvan, dwarfing it. On the sides, two more eyvans, again barrel-vaulted and higher by two steps from the central hall (Fig. 114), complete the cross-axial interior (see Fig. 107).

The exterior walls of the Mosque-Medrese of Hüdavendigâr are constructed of stone and brick. Masonry work is very uniform: the cut stone courses being 50 cm. and the triple brick courses being 20 cm. in height, respectively, throughout the wall surface. Instead of the usual saw-toothed cornice, there is one of small blind arches (Fig. 115). On the side elevations, the decorative arches are bigger than they are on the façade or at the rear. On the square base of the central dome there are two tiers of them. As in most other Ottoman buildings of the fourteenth century, a number of Byzantine pieces are incorporated into the structure of the Hüdavendigâr. All the columns and their capitals, as well as the marble door jambs or heads decorated with acanthus leaves, were taken from Byzantine buildings. The Mosque-Medrese of Hüdavendigâr is an experimental Ottoman building, not as yet embodying Ottoman ideals but in search of an expression of form.

Mosque of Hüdavendigâr, Bursa
114 *Interior. Side eyvan*
115 *Exterior*

114

115

A second mosque designed along the lines of the Mosque of Hüdavendigâr in Bursa is located in Edirne. It is erroneously attributed to the reign of Yıldırım Bayezid and called by the name of that sultan. I am of the opinion that it was built—or, rather, reconstructed as a mosque since its lower structure dates from an earlier period—by Murad Hüdavendigâr, probably not long after the capture of Edirne by the Ottoman Turks in 1361.

The mosque as it exists today comprises a fountain courtyard, a porch, a minaret, and an interior consisting of two side rooms and a general prayer area (Figs. 116, 117). The fountain courtyard is defined by low walls. At the center there is a fountain the upper structure of which no longer exists. The roof of the five-bay porch has also disappeared. Although all of the four column bases are intact, only one column stands in place. Of the minaret, the shaft remains as far as the balcony (Fig. 118).

One enters the interior of the mosque through a wide, barrel-vaulted vestibule that leads into a central hall on which open three similar eyvans (Fig. 119). The central hall is a square area, measuring 8.20 m. per side, surmounted by a dome. The eyvans are also square but they are covered by barrel vaults. The *mihrab* and the *minber* are located at the corners of the southern eyvan. Although the side rooms that flank the vestibule are rectangular (8.05 m. by 6.30 m.) arches were placed on their long sides to create square bases for domes. The transition from the domes of the side rooms, as well as from the central dome, to the walls is carried out by belts of Turkish triangles. Each side room originally had two windows, one opening on the side and the other onto the porch, and a fireplace with gypsum decorations inlaid with turquoise-colored tiles, part of which still exist. Neglected and in poor repair, the mosque is nevertheless open to prayer. The side rooms, however, are in ruinous condition, and their door and window openings have been greatly altered.

The building is plastered on the inside, but the masonry work is exposed externally (Fig. 120). The walls are constructed of alternating stone and brick courses, not unlike those of the Hüdavendigâr in Bursa (Fig. 115). Window arches are decorated with brick designs, each having a different pattern, and the walls are terminated by saw-toothed cornices.

I have already mentioned that this mosque was reconstructed on the remains of an earlier structure. According to Osman Rifat the original building was the Church of Tiris Iye Hares.[36] Gurlitt, noting the resemblance between the mosque and the Mausoleum of Galla Placidia in Ravenna contended that the original structure must have been erected not long after the Mausoleum of Galla Placidia (A.D. 440?) and that it was converted into a mosque round 1400.[37] The plan of the mosque as drawn by Gurlitt does, in fact, exhibit a close relationship to that of the Galla Placidia, if one disregards the scale of the two buildings and the fact that the former is in the form of a Greek cross while the latter is in the form of a Latin cross. Be that as it may, the plan and section drawings published by Gurlitt do not present an accurate picture of the mosque as it stands today—or

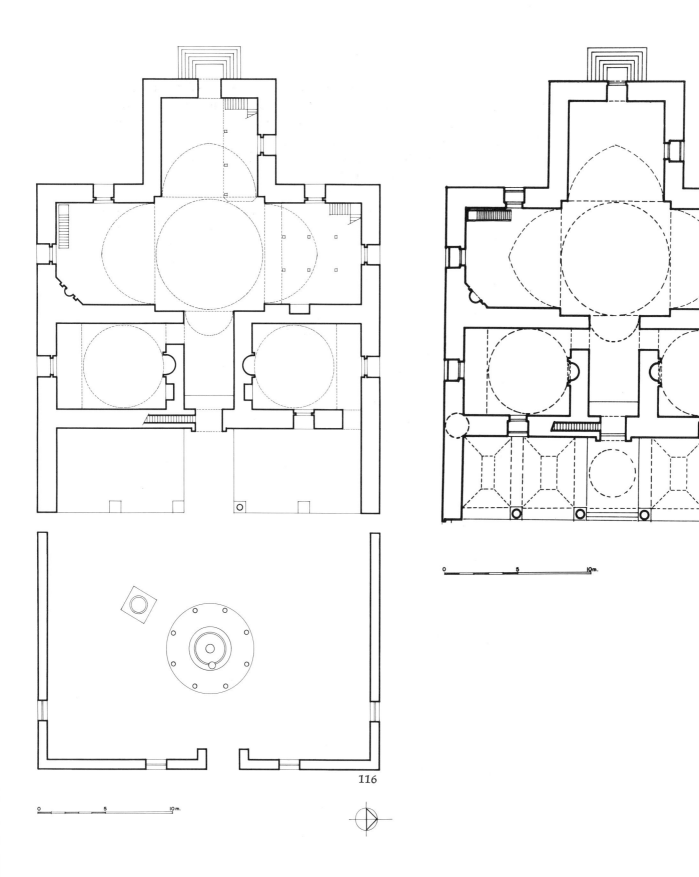

116

117

0   5   10 m.

0   5   10 m.

Mosque of Hüdavendigâr, Edirne
116 *Plan (after Gurlitt)*
117 *Restored plan (Kuran)*
118 *Exterior. Front view*

as it was when Gurlitt studied it—but rather project his opinion pertaining to the original condition of the mosque. Gurlitt himself states that the drawings may be incorrect and that he could not vouch for the accuracy of the barrel-vaulted entrance hall.[38] Indeed, the eastern arm of the cross, which is the vestibule, is narrower and shallower than the other three arms, and, consequently, the mosque is not in the form of a perfect Greek cross. It is not possible to state with any reasonable certainty at this time whether the original building was in the form of a perfect Greek cross as Gurlitt surmised. In my opinion, it was not. Because if it were so, the Turks, when they converted the building into a mosque, would have placed the *zâviye* rooms on either side of the western eyvan and built the porch across from the *mihrab*. Since this logical arrangement was not exploited, it can be deduced that the eastern side of the original building was a more favorable location for the *zâviye* rooms. And this deduction brings to mind the Greek-cross Byzantine church whose apsidal east wing is enriched by two small chapels on either corner.

A close study of the mosque will indicate that the original structure was in

119

ruins when it was taken over by the Ottomans. Since the Ottomans, in converting a church into a mosque imposed on the building a minimal number of changes required by their religion or architectural tradition, the pointed arches, the barrel vaults, and the Turkish triangles all indicate that the upper structure of the church had collapsed before the arrival of the Turks. As can be observed in exterior photographs (Figs. 118, 120), the walls are of rubble stone masonry up to the middle of the windows, then change to regular alternating stone and brick courses. The pointed arches of the windows are further indications that, apart from the foundations and the lower section of the wall which determine the plan of the building, the mosque should be credited to Ottoman architecture.

The problem of determining what the fourteenth-century mosque was like is not easy because the mosque underwent a major restoration during the eighteenth century, when a number of changes and additions were made. Although the side walls of the porch date from the fourteenth century, the columns were subsequently raised on marble bases to support a timber roof (Fig. 118), a feature totally alien to early Ottoman architecture. The original porch was probably a five-bay structure whose columns sat directly on the floor, in which case the tops of the capitals and the arch springs which can still be seen on the wall fall on the same horizontal line. The central bay of the porch was probably surmounted by a dome and the other four bays were covered by either shallower domes or flat-topped cross-vaults.

The stone minaret and the walls of the courtyard must also date from the eighteenth century, because the eyvan mosques did not have fountain courts and the fourteenth-century minarets were built of brick and not stone. Gurlitt contends that the central dome was rebuilt in the eighteenth century.[39] I also think that the existing dome is not the original, which must have had an oculus.

108

120

Mosque of Hüdavendigâr, Edirne
119 *Interior*
120 *Exterior. Side view*

After having studied the architecture of the mosque, let us now try to date it. The generally accepted date of erection, or restitution, of the mosque is 1397 (A.H. 799) or 1400 (A.H. 802).[40] Since this is the first known mosque built by the Ottomans in Edirne and since the city was taken by the Ottomans in 1361, did Edirne have no mosque for thirty-five to forty years after its conquest by the Turks? Why did Murad Hüdevendigâr, who, upon taking Assos (Behramkale), a minor town compared to Edirne, order a mosque built there and not have one erected in Edirne? It seems to me that the answers to both questions are self-evident. Not only the character of the masonry technique (cf. Figs. 115 and 120) but the entire architectural composition and expression of the Edirne mosque which closely resemble those of the Mosque of Hüdavendigâr in Bursa enable us to attribute the Edirne mosque to the third quarter of the fourteenth century. As a matter of fact, it is quite possible that the Edirne mosque was erected before its sister in Bursa and that the spatial features of the latter were inspired by the former. A further, and so far as I am concerned, more conclusive proof that the Edirne mosque was built prior to the reign of Yıldırım Bayezid is that the conversion of the barrel-vaulted eyvans into domed-square units takes place for the first time in the Mosque of Yıldırım in Bursa. Since the construction of the Bursa Yıldırım Mosque began soon after Bayezid's ascension to the throne in 1389, and since after this time, with one exception, no eyvan mosque was erected with barrel-vaulted eyvans, and since the eyvans of the Edirne mosque are barrel-vaulted, it must have been erected before 1390 during the reign of Murad Hüdavendigâr and, therefore, must be named after this sultan and not his son.

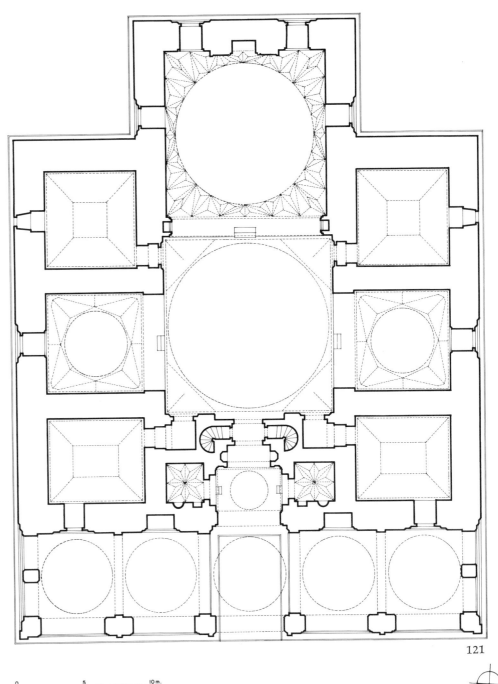

121

0   5   10 m.

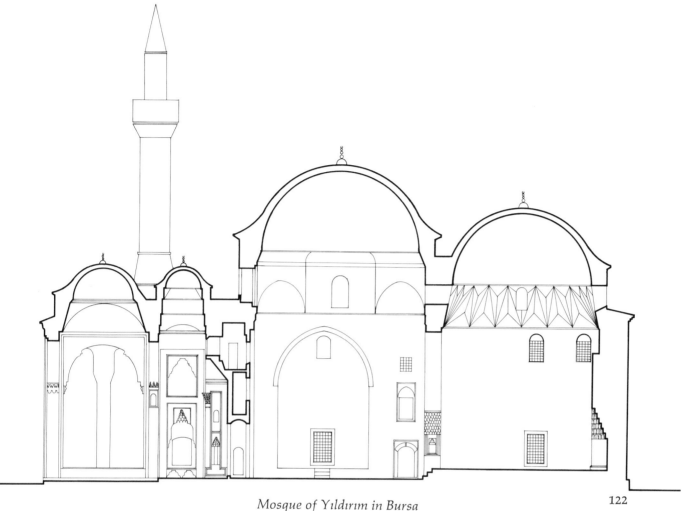

Mosque of Yıldırım in Bursa

Mosque of Yıldırım, Bursa
121 *Plan*
122 *Section*

The complex of Yıldırım located on a hill to the east of the city of Bursa is one of the earliest and largest of the neighborhood centers (*külliye*) built by the Ottoman Turks. It was composed of an eyvan type of mosque-convent, a *medrese*, the *türbe* of its founder, Bayezid I, a *hamam*, an *imâret*, a *darüşşifa*, and a palace. Today only the first four of the original seven buildings are still in existence. The focal building of the complex is the mosque placed at the peak of the hill. The construction of the mosque began in 1390 (A.H. 793). According to Gabriel it was completed by 1395, before the Battle of Nikopolis.[41] Other sources place the date of completion before[42] or after 1395.[43] Severely damaged in the earthquake of 1855, the Mosque of Yıldırım was repaired and its upper structure reconstructed during the second half of the nineteenth century. Although it is an important monument, its architect is not known.

Like the Mosque of Orhan Gazi, all three eyvans of the Mosque of Yıldırım are domed. Unlike it, there are four convent rooms placed on either side of the auxiliary eyvans (Fig. 121). All four of the rooms are covered by flat-topped cross-vaults and are furnished with fireplaces and storage niches. The doors of the two southern rooms open directly onto the central hall. Those of the northern rooms are reached through small passages that also give access to two cells.

Mosque of Yıldırım, Bursa
123 *Interior. Central hall*
124 *Interior. "Bursa arch"*
125 *Exterior*

The high vestibule as well as all the five bays of the porch are also covered by domes. The central bay of the porch is slightly wider (5.10 m.) than the others, which are 4.50 m. in width. All six smaller domes sit on pendentives. The other four of the central hall, the main eyvan, and the two side eyvans are placed on squinches, a belt of Turkish triangles, and on triangular corner panels, respectively (Fig. 122).

As in the Mosque of Orhan Gazi, the eyvans of the Mosque of Yıldırım are raised, all three having been built three steps higher than the central hall. The eyvans are spatially integrated to the central hall by arch openings (Fig. 123). The arches of the side eyvans are typical pointed arches. That of the main eyvan, on the other hand, is shallow and has a slight rectangular nook at its apex. It is known as the "Bursa arch," and generally considered to be an Ottoman invention. This belief has no foundation, since the same type of arch can be seen in a number of Seljuk buildings in Anatolia built during the thirteenth century.[44] It merely makes its first appearance in Ottoman architecture in the Mosque of Yıldırım in Bursa, where the big interior arch (Fig. 124) and the arches of the porch are of this type.

124

The two minarets of the Mosque of Yıldırım have both collapsed and have not been reconstructed. Their stubby bases rise on the northeast and northwest corners of the mosque. Complex and winding staircases and passages lead from the vestibule to the base of the minarets. Unlike the Mosque of Orhan Gazi, the Mosque of Yıldırım is constructed entirely of cut stone (Fig. 125) and except for the frames of two rear windows, which come from a Byzantine building, every part of this mosque was designed and built specifically for it.

125

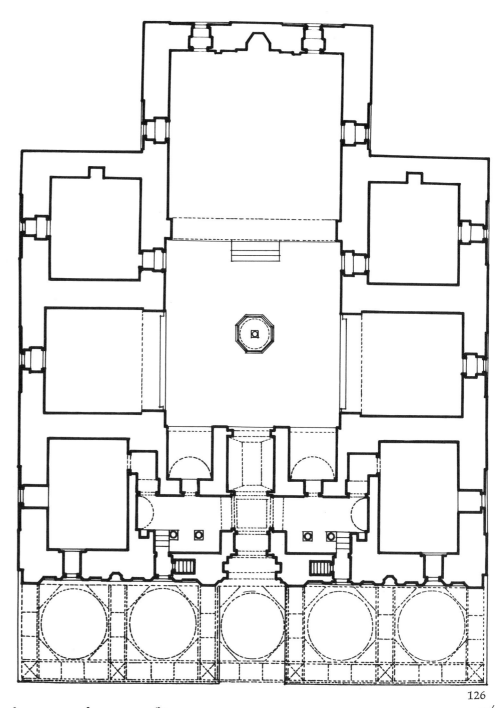

126

The Yeşil Cami in Bursa was built by the architect Hacı İvaz between the years 1412 and 1419 (A.H. 815–822) for Mehmed I. Work on decoration continued for three years after Mehmed I's death (1421) at which time construction was discontinued.[45] The mosque does not have a porch, though arch springs visible on the façade indicate that a five-bay porch was designed but for some reason never built.

The interior plan of the Yeşil Cami shows some similarity to that of the Mosque of Yıldırım. Four eyvans—three large and one small—open to the central hall on four sides and two rooms each on the east and west flank the auxiliary eyvans (Fig. 126). The main eyvan is raised from the central hall by four steps, the side eyvans by one step each. Both major domes sit on belts of Turkish triangles (Fig. 128), whereas the transition to the domes of the side eyvans are effected by squinches decorated with stalactites. The fourth or the small entrance eyvan is covered by a barrel vault. At the center of the hall there is a pool (Fig. 129) and a lantern rises on top of its dome (Fig. 131). This lantern does not date from the fifteenth century but was built in the nineteenth century to cover the original oculus. The pool and the oculus do not constitute important innovations; both are to be found in other eyvan mosques. Originally, eyvan mosques built before the second half of the fifteenth century all had them. What does constitute an important development, however, is the two-story wing on the north, which is unique. It comprises the sultan's private quarters (Fig. 127), thus adding a third function—after mosque and convent—to the building.

From the ornate marble portal one passes into a low, square vestibule. To the south of the vestibule is the barrel-vaulted eyvan that leads to the central hall. And on either side of the vestibule are two stair halls. At the upper level both staircases open onto two antechambers, each with a small water basin at the center of the floor. Located behind deep, unglazed windows, these spaces served as protected balconies for the royal family. Between the two staircases above the vestibule and the entrance eyvan the private pew of the sultan is arranged. This is composed of two sections: a small, domed-square rear chamber and a raised and richly decorated barrel-vaulted eyvan that looks onto the interior of the mosque (Fig. 130). It is interesting to note that this two-unit private pew of the sultan follows the single eyvan–central hall interiors in its basic components. On either side of the royal pew there are two prayer rooms for the sultan's family, and under these, accessible from the central hall, are placed the pews for the courtiers.

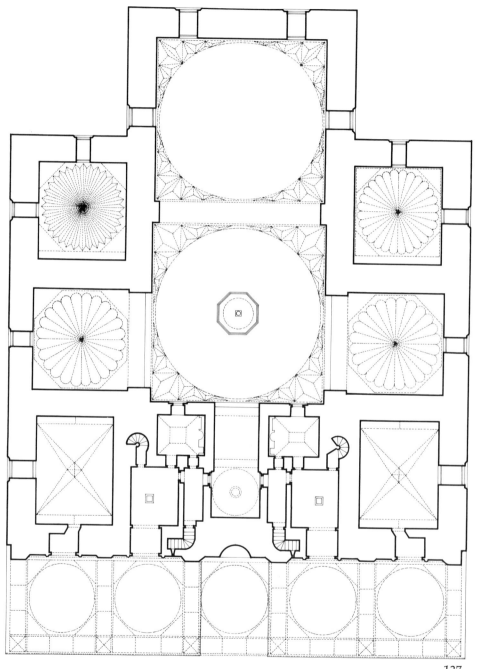

0   5   10 m.

127

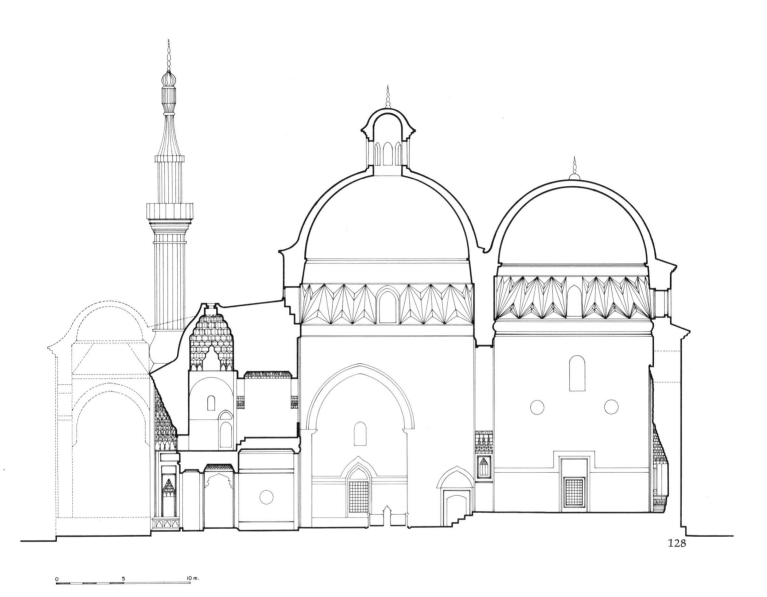

128

0   5   10 m.

Yeşil Cami, Bursa
127 *Plan. Upper Level*
128 *Section*

Both minarets of the Yeşil Cami date from the nineteenth century. Like the Mosque of Yıldırım the building is constructed of cut stone and marble (Fig. 131). The portal as well as the entire façade is of marble (Fig. 132). Window frames are also built of marble inlaid with turquoise ceramic tiles. But the most decorative part of the mosque is its interior, where walls finished with ceramic tiles of blue, yellow, and gold, delicately carved wooden window shutters, and a general atmosphere of exuberance and taste rightfully entitle the Yeşil Cami in Bursa to be considered the most beautiful mosque in early Ottoman architecture.

129

130

Yeşil Cami, Bursa
129 *Interior. Central hall*
130 *Interior. Sultan's pew*
131 *Exterior. Rear view*
132 *Exterior. Front view*

131

132

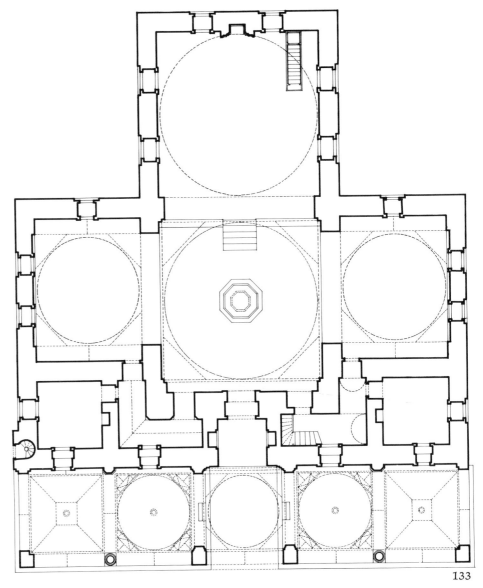

133

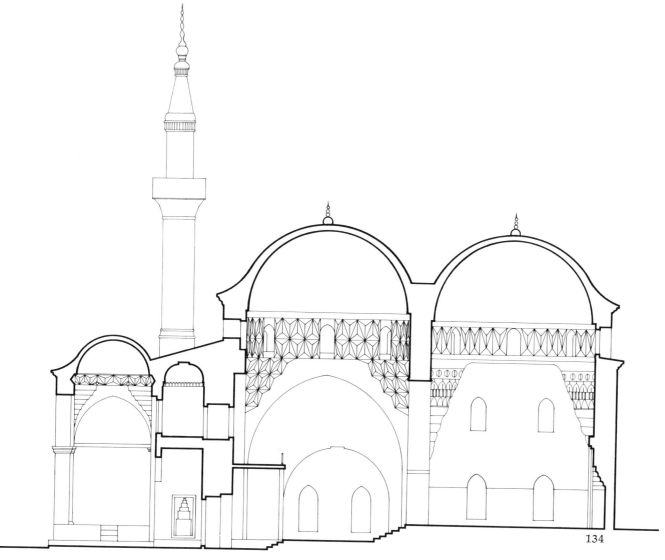

134

Mosque of Murad II in Bursa

Mosque of Murad II, Bursa
133 *Plan*
134 *Section*

The third royal mosque-convent in Bursa is that of Murad II, built between the years 1424 and 1426 (A.H. 828–830). In its basic space organization, this mosque follows the general pattern of the Mosque of Yıldırım and the Yeşil Cami. A closer study, however, shows a number of differences which are of great importance in regard to the evolution of the eyvan mosque (Fig. 133). For one thing, the two major domes of the Mosque of Murad II in Bursa are of equal size (10.60 m. in diameter) and height (Fig. 134). From the exterior they look identical (Fig. 135), but their interior treatment is not. The dome of the central hall sits on an intricate system of triangles springing from the corners (Fig. 136); that of the main eyvan rests on a typical belt of Turkish triangles placed above tiers of bulging corbels much like convex pendentives (Fig. 137). A second innovation worthy of note is that the auxiliary eyvans are not raised from the central hall. In this mosque the side eyvans and the central hall form a continuous lateral space behind the main eyvan, which is elevated from it by six steps (Fig. 136).

121

135

In the Mosque of Murad II in Bursa there are only two convent rooms. Both are small square spaces covered by cross-vaults and are reached by passages which lead from the rear of the central hall. They also give access to side eyvans.

The five-bay porch recalls that of the Mosque of Orhan Gazi with its cross-vaulted end bays. The front elevation is somewhat different, for in this mosque, instead of the usual six-pier façade one finds a composite system of piers and columns, the columns being used between the two outer bays. There are two minarets, both of them new. The staircase of the eastern minaret is accessible from the outside. The western minaret is reached from inside the mosque.

Mosque of Murad II, Bursa
135 *Exterior*
136 *Interior. Central hall*
137 *Interior. Main eyvan*

136

137

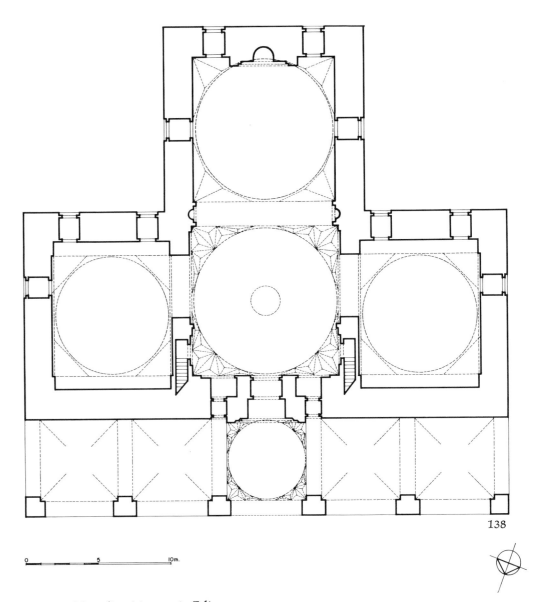

138

Muradiye Mosque in Edirne

The most impressive of the eyvan mosques in Edirne is the Muradiye Mosque, which perches by itself on top of a hill to the northeast of the city. It was built by Murad II in 1435 (A.H. 839) as a convent for the Mevlevî order of dervishes but the conventicle was later converted into a mosque during the reign of the same sultan.[46]

The Muradiye Mosque exhibits the simplicity of organization found in all the eyvan mosques of Edirne. It is composed of a five-bay porch, one minaret, and four interior units (Fig. 138). The largest unit is the central hall, whose dome sits on a belt of Turkish triangles and supports a lantern on top of its original unglazed oculus. Although the traditional pool under the oculus no longer exists,

139

Muradiye Mosque, Edirne
138 *Plan*
139 *Exterior. Rear view*

excavations conducted during the recent restoration of the mosque uncovered its foundations and also showed that the floor of the central hall was originally lower than that of the main eyvan and that it was later built up to the level of the prayer area, presumably to make room for more worshippers.

The main eyvan, which is slightly smaller than the central hall, is richly decorated with frescoes and ceramic tiles. Portions of the fresco work have been ruined by dampness, but the tiles are still in good condition. The ceramic decoration of the *mihrab* is considered to be among the best of the early fifteenth-century Ottoman ceramic art.

The dome of the main eyvan sits on triangular corner panels. Those of the side spaces rest on squinches. The reason I use the term spaces and not eyvans in this connection is that the arch openings of the side spaces in the Muradiye are small and restrictive. This is probably due to the conversion of the convent to a mosque. Originally the side spaces were designed as rooms but were later incorporated into the general prayer area. Since the northern half of the walls between the central hall and the side rooms was built with staircases leading to a gallery at the rear of the hall, the arch-openings of the rooms had to be limited in width.

The center bay of the porch is covered by a dome and the other four bays by cross-vaults. All five upper structures protrude above the cornice. The minaret (Fig. 139), located on the northwest corner of the building, is not original but dates from the nineteenth century.

125

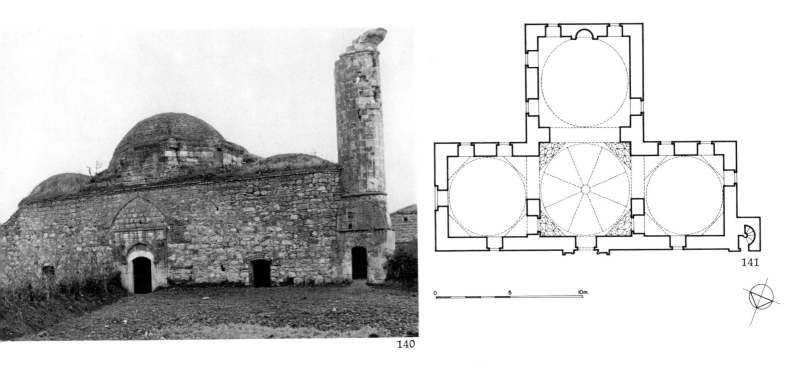

140

141

Mosque of Mezid Bey in Edirne

This modest eyvan mosque in Edirne was built in 1441 (A.H. 845) by Mezid Bey, the governor of Alaca Hisar (Kragujevac) who died in action in Wallachia the following year.[47] Although in poor repair and abandoned, the whole structure is in place and in its original condition, except for the top of its minaret (Fig. 140).

The Mosque of Mezid Bey does not have a porch. Otherwise it is a smaller replica of the Muradiye Mosque in terms of form and plan (Fig. 141). The central hall and the main eyvan are of equal size but the dome of the former rises higher. Actually the first major dome is an eight-sided vault whose alien hemispheric top was obviously added later (Fig. 142). The transition to the angular upper structure, expressed on the outside by an octagonal drum, is effected by six tiers of saw-toothed corbels.

Unlike most eyvan mosques whose main eyvans are fairly dark inside, the small, domed-square prayer unit of the Mezid Bey is exceptionally light (Fig. 143) having two sets of superposed windows (some of which are blocked today) cut into its three exterior walls. On the outside, its hemispherical dome on pendentives is dwarfed by a high octagonal drum.

The domes of the side eyvans also rest on pendentives. As in the Muradiye Mosque, the low arch-openings of the side eyvans do not encompass the length of the wall but puncture a little over half of the surface. In addition to these a door on each side, located to the north of the arch-openings, gives access to the side spaces from the central hall (Fig. 141). This is an innovation which we have not seen elsewhere.

126

142

143

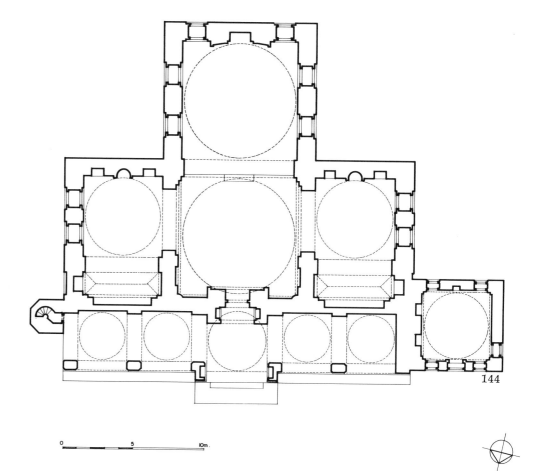

0   5   10m.

Mosque of Hamza Bey in Bursa

Located on a hill to the west of the Muradiye quarter overlooking the Plain of
Bursa, this mosque was founded in the mid-fifteenth century by Hamza Bey, the
brother of Bayezid Paşa, who played an important role during the reigns of
Murad II and Mehmed II and died in 1461.[48]

    The interior of the mosque comprises four units—the central hall, the main
eyvan, and two side eyvans (Fig. 144). Although the two major domes are
similar in diameter—8.50 m.—the first dome is slightly higher than the second
(Fig. 145). The first dome sits on squinches decorated with stalactites, and the
second rests on a belt of Turkish triangles. The main eyvan is raised by two
steps from the central hall and, like the Mosque of Mezid Bey, has two sets of
superposed windows on its three exterior walls. Unlike the Mezid Bey, the side
spaces in this mosque are defined not simply by a dome each but by a double
system of a dome and a vault. To the south, opening to the central hall by means
of "Bursa arches" are the side eyvans surmounted by hemispherical domes. The
western dome sits on stalactite pendentives, the eastern one on Turkish triangles.
Since the side spaces are only 6.00 m. in depth and run the length of the central
hall, two narrow areas are left over to the north. They are separated from the
domed front sections by arches and are covered by long barrel vaults.

128

Mosque of Hamza Bey, Bursa
144 *Plan*
145 *Exterior*

All five bays of the porch are domed, the central dome being larger and higher than the rest. The minaret is located on the northeast corner. Across from it, adjacent to the west end of the porch, is a domed-square *türbe*, which houses the uninscribed sarcophagi of Hamza Bey's wife and two daughters.[49] Hamza Bey's own *türbe* is the octagonal structure placed to the right in front of the mosque.

The Mosque of Hamza Bey is constructed of composite stone and brick. The minaret is completely of brick, with two bands of turquoise ceramic tiles encircling the shaft under its balcony (Fig. 145).

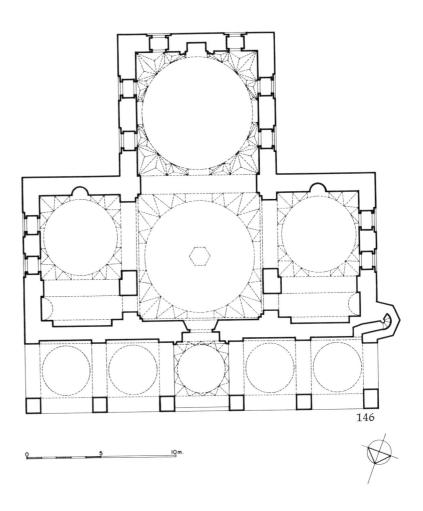

146

Mosque of Ishak Paşa in İnegöl

A mosque similar to the Hamza Bey is located at İnegöl. It was founded by İshak Paşa (d. 1486) who served as the governor of Bosnia and later as grand vizier (1469–72) to Mehmed II and his son Bayezid II. The original inscription plate of the mosque no longer exists; its place above the door is filled by another dated 1877 (A.H. 1294) marking a restoration during the reign of Abdülhamid II. But on the inscription plate of the *medrese*, which is a part of the İshak Paşa complex in İnegöl, the date of A.H. 887 (1482) is given. Ayverdi accepts this as the construction date of the mosque as well.[50] Ülgen thinks that the mosque was built earlier, in A.H. 881 (1476).[51]

The interior arrangement of the Mosque of İshak Paşa is different from that of the Hamza Bey in only the transition systems of its four domes, all of which sit on belts of Turkish triangles, and two additional doors leading from the central hall to the narrow, barrel-vaulted spaces behind the side eyvans (Fig. 146). The major difference in massing is the minaret which, in the İshak Paşa, is placed on the northwest corner of the mosque (Fig. 147).

147

148

As can be observed in the ten examples of the cross-axial eyvan mosques I have given, the side eyvans of some may not have been originally intended as such at all. I feel that the side eyvans of the Mosque of Orhan Gazi in Bursa (Fig. 104) were, in the first building, not eyvans but rooms, as I shall try to prove in the section devoted to the analysis of the eyvan mosque at the end of this chapter. Similarly, what seem to be side eyvans in the Mosque of Mezid Bey in Edirne (Fig. 141) must also have been designed as rooms because the presence of doors next to the arch openings clearly indicate that the latter were opened later. That the Muradiye in Edirne (Fig. 138) was originally built as a convent and that it has narrow arch-openings between its central hall and side spaces also show that the side eyvans are but later innovations.

Because of the passages leading from the rear of the central hall and ending at doors opening to the side eyvans in the Mosque of Murad II in Bursa (Fig. 133) a similar scheme comes to mind. Why have a door when one entire side of a unit is open to a central area? Gabriel answers the question in a straightforward way: because it was not an eyvan opening to the central hall but an enclosed room.[52] If this point of view is to be accepted, then the same argument can be directed to the Mosques of İshak Paşa and Hamza Bey (Figs. 144, 146). The narrow, barrel-vaulted areas behind the domed spaces could have been the antechambers of the side rooms. The doors leading from the central hall to the narrow spaces in the İshak Paşa strengthen the argument. And the plan of the Mosque of Karacabey (Fig. 96), a building not altered by later restorations so far as I know, supplies a prototype.

This argument leads to three possibilities concerning the original interior arrangement of the Mosque of İshak Paşa. Either the side spaces were built as eyvans but the arch between the side eyvan and the narrow space behind it was blocked so that the door leads only to the narrow room. Or the domed side space was actually a room which was entered through the door of the antechamber but the two spaces were not separated by a wall. Or there were two rooms on each side, and one passed through the rear chamber to reach the domed front room. In my opinion, the third alternative is the least likely because it would make the rear room useless. It must be noted that in the Karacabey the similar narrow space is not a room but a passage giving access not only to the domed side room but also to the rooms on the upper level. The first alternative is also not rational in the absence of windows on the north because, cut off from the domed front spaces, the narrow rooms would be completely dark and unventilated. This leaves us with the second alternative, rectangular rooms with antechambers.

The same argument may, of course, also be applied to the Hamza Bey, in which the doors leading to the antechambers were probably filled in when their function was eliminated by the conversion of the side rooms to eyvans.

In the introduction to this chapter I pointed out that the origin of the eyvan mosque lies in the Seljuk enclosed *medrese*. The fourteenth-century mosques of Sultan Orhan in İznik (Fig. 78), Timurtaş (Fig. 79), Ebu İshak (Fig. 80), Hüdavendigâr in Bursa (Fig. 110), Hüdavendigâr in Edirne (Fig. 116), and even the fifteenth-century Gazi Mihal (Fig. 87), with their barrel-vaulted eyvans, constitute architecturally a continuation of the thirteenth-century Seljuk enclosed *medrese*. The only exception is the Mosque of Orhan Gazi in Bursa, where the eyvans are covered by domes instead of barrel vaults. Indeed the domed upper structure of the Orhan Gazi has been a matter of controversy among art historians for a long time. Wilde felt that the mosque was completely reconstructed in the fifteenth century after having been destroyed by the Karamans and that nothing remained from the original building except a few columns.[53] Gabriel more or less accepts this point of view.[54] Eyice goes a step further when he suggests that the first building could have been of timber and that the present mosque was erected after the timber structure burned down in 1414.[55] Çetintaş however, is convinced that the present mosque is the original edifice,[56] and this conviction is shared by Ayverdi.[57] I personally do not see how the lower structure of the Mosque of Orhan Gazi, with its typically fourteenth-century masonry work, rectangular inner compartments, and general architectural character, can be considered to have been built in the fifteenth century. Similarly, the multidomed upper structure is equally alien to the fourteenth century. In the light of these observations I find it more logical to think that the fourteenth-century mosque was not completely but only partially destroyed in the Karaman onslaught and that the collapsed upper structure was reconstructed in the fifteenth century, not according to its original form but along the lines of the more developed Mosque of Yıldırım, which had been completed by 1417.

Judging from earlier Seljuk examples, one can safely assume that the central hall of the fourteenth-century mosque was surmounted by a dome. But were the three eyvans also covered by domes? Çetintaş explains at great length the technical difficulties of placing an "egg shaped" dome over the rectangular main eyvan.[58] The odd shape of this dome could be due to insufficient technical knowledge of the inexperienced early fourteenth-century Ottoman architect. It could also be the natural outcome of having to build a dome on top of a rectangular lower structure. I prefer the second alternative and contend that the rectangular shape of the main eyvan is proof enough that it was originally covered by a barrel vault much like the other eyvan mosques of the early fourteenth century.

The side eyvans of the fourteenth-century building must also have been covered by barrel vaults. But unlike those of the Mosque of Hüdavendigâr in Bursa or the Hüdavendigâr in Edirne, whose barrel-vaulted side eyvans continue the transverse axis, the barrel vaults of Orhan Gazi were probably constructed along the longitudinal axis, as were those of Sultan Orhan in İznik and Timurtaş and Ebu İshak in Bursa. This speculation leads me to believe that the side eyvans of the Mosque of Orhan Gazi are also fifteenth-century innovations, and that the original mosque had only the main eyvan plus two barrel-vaulted rooms flanking the central hall. Thus I conclude that the two eyvan mosques, one in İznik, the other in Bursa, built four years apart by Orhan Gazi were not radically different from each other but in fact were almost identical in scale, form, character, and plan.

The architectural influence of the Seljuk enclosed *medrese* continues in early eyvan mosques through the eras of Orhan Gazi and Murad I. The first important change occurs toward the end of the fourteenth century when in the Mosque of Yıldırım in Bursa the traditional Seljuk pattern is redefined in terms of Ottoman architectural ideals. It is in this mosque that the barrel-vaulted rectangular eyvan is replaced by the domed-square eyvan.

Although the Ottoman substitution of the dome for the barrel vault may at first glance seem to be a mere matter of upper structure, it is in fact a development born out of a different concept of interior space and exterior form. A barrel-vaulted eyvan opening to a central hall tends to become an integral part of that central space because the projection of the arch-opening in depth creates a movement in space. Standing in the central hall of the Mosque of Hüdavendigâr in Bursa, one feels the expansion of space in four directions. The sensation is quite the reverse in the Mosque of Yıldırım, where the interior space is frozen and fragmented. Consequently, one does not readily feel the movement of space from one unit to the other. Not only is there a variation of floor level between the central hall and the main eyvan but the transition systems of their respective domes are also built differently. The dome of the central hall is both larger and higher than that of the main eyvan, the first dome being 11.30 m. in diameter and 22.50 m. in height and the second 10.10 m. in diameter and 18.80 m. in height (Fig. 122). In the central hall the dome sits on squinches, whereas the dome over the main eyvan sits on Turkish triangles.

One observes the same heterogeneous character in the Yeşil Cami in Bursa, decidedly the most complex and monumental of the eyvan mosques. In the Yeşil Cami the diameters of the two domes are 11.80 m. and 10.40 m. and their heights are 24.80 m. and 22.80 m., respectively (Fig. 128). Owing to the similarity of transition systems, a closer tie is established here between the two major units. But the character of the central hall with its marble flooring (now unfortunately carpeted), its fountain and pool, with light pouring down from the lantern above—or from the original oculus—is essentially different from the darkened and reposeful prayer eyvan elevated by four steps from it. The quality of light, acoustics, and ornamentation is not similar in the four interrelated spaces but is deliberately and consciously differentiated. Inside the Yeşil Cami one cannot help feeling that the objective of the architect was not so much to create a unity of space but, on the contrary, to seek different types of spaces, each retaining its identity. Whereas the eyvans of the Hüdavendigâr are integral parts of the total central space, those of the Yıldırım and the Yeşil Cami are independent compartments attached to a central hall to form an articulated interior space in which each unit preserves its individuality and spatial integrity.

The basic approach of this architecture is to create a composition with domed-square units. The space defined by a domed-square unit denotes completeness. Because of this inherent characteristic, even when domed-square units are placed adjacent to one another with their adjoining walls removed, the movement of space from one unit to the other is not strongly felt. The eye is caught by the arches in between and an optical screen hinders the vision while the dome of each unit pulls the space in toward the center.

As for the exterior formation of the eyvan mosque, in the earlier barrel-vaulted eyvan mosques the flat roof is broken only by the single central dome of the hall. The more developed domed eyvan mosques have more enriched upper structures. In the Mosque of Yıldırım, for instance, apart from the domes of the porch, there are three domes covering the vestibule, the central hall, and the main eyvan on the longitudinal axis, and two more domes over the side eyvans flanking the major dome. The same cross-axial pattern is found in the Yeşil Cami. In the Muradiye, the dome of the vestibule is not expressed on the upper structure (Fig. 135), but the dome of the center compartment of the porch, which rises higher than the other four, acts as the focal point of the north end of the longitudinal axis. A similar arrangement is observed in other eyvan mosques with no vestibules, such as the Mosques of Murad II in Edirne, Hamza Bey in Bursa, and İshak Paşa in İnegöl, to name a few. The barrel-vaulted eyvan mosques with eyvans opening to the central hall merely create an articulated interior space. In the domed eyvan mosques, the articulation of the interior space is reflected on the exterior as well. The former echoes the spirit of the severe, box-like Seljuk architecture. The latter promulgates the expressive, architectonic disposition of Ottoman architecture that reached its zenith in the sixteenth century.

If the Mosque of Yıldırım constitutes the first step in the Ottomanization of the eyvan mosque, the Mosque of Murad II in Bursa heralds the second step in its evolution. As I have already shown, the prayer eyvans of the Mosque of Yıldırım or the Yeşil Cami are subordinate spaces to the central hall. Both inside and out, the central hall is the dominant element in these two mosques. The first signs of change in this basic pattern appear in the Mosque of Murad II, where both the major domes are of equal size (Fig. 134). The functions of the two spaces covered by the major domes are still different, one being the prayer area, the other serving as the central hall with the pool. But from the outside, the similarity of the two major domes begins to dilute the expression of two different interior units.

The complete break with the Seljuk tradition took place during the second half of the fifteenth century. In the Mosque of Murad Paşa in Istanbul, although the prayer eyvan and the central hall are still treated somewhat differently, the similarity of the two major units is further stressed and the central hall loses its character (Fig. 99). It is a space to which all doors open and as such retains its function as a central hall. But it is no longer the domed outdoor court. Its dome was not built with an oculus and no fountain or pool ever occupied its center. The central hall of the Mosque of Murad Paşa was designed as another closed, domed-square unit.

The same design approach is observed in the Mosque of Rum Mehmed Paşa. In the two previous mosques of similar type—the Beylerbeyi Mosque in Edirne and the Mosque of Yahşi Bey in Tire—the halfdomed prayer areas serve as eyvans of the open-topped domed central halls, but in the Rum Mehmed Paşa the halfdomed prayer area and the central hall become well integrated and inseparable (Fig. 102).

Actually the degeneration of the eyvan mosque took place before the Mosques of Murad Paşa and Rum Mehmed Paşa, with the erection of the Mosque of Mahmud Paşa in Istanbul. This mosque as well as the Mosque of Gedik Ahmet Paşa in Afyon have always been considered to be "Bursa Type" mosques. Despite the fact that both are flanked by convent rooms, they cannot be included in the eyvan mosque group, because in both the central hall completely disappears, leaving its place to another unit for prayer. For this reason, I shall consider them in the next chapter, dealing with multi-unit mosques, to which group, in my opinion, they belong.

136

3 The Multi-Unit Mosque

Eski Cami, Edirne

As I have shown in the two previous chapters, both the single-unit and the eyvan mosques are basically one-unit mosques. Regardless of how complex their building program or how involved their massing may be, the actual area for prayer in both groups is restricted to one structural unit. Even in the three- or four-eyvan mosques where more than one unit could be employed for prayer, the formal mosque is the unit in which the *mihrab* and the *minber* are located. The side eyvans are not adjacent to the main prayer area but are joined to it by means of a common central hall. Thus in the multi-*eyvan* mosque the various prayer units are fragmented and scattered instead of being integral parts of a unified whole as they are in the multi-*unit* mosques.

To date, the term "multi-domed" has denoted the *ulucami*—or great mosque—as opposed to the small neighborhood mosque. It is true that the Ottoman great mosque is a large structure composed of many domed units all of which are assigned for prayer. On the other hand, there are a number of other early Ottoman mosques whose interiors also comprise two or more adjacent units for prayer and to which the term "multi-unit" is equally applicable. In this book I have accepted the term multi-unit in its literal sense and included in this group not only the monumental great mosques that support many large domes but also all early Ottoman mosques whose prayer areas are composed of two or more units.

In regard to interior space and form, the early Ottoman multi-unit mosques may be divided into two major groups. The first comprises the mosques composed of similar units. The second includes those in which one or two of the units are more pronounced than the others. Repetition of like units gives the interior space a sense of repose. Accentuation of the central area by one or two large and high units gives a sophisticated and dramatic quality to the building.

MULTI-UNIT MOSQUE WITH SIMILAR UNITS

Mosque of Abdal Mehmed in Bursa

The construction date of the mosque bearing the name of the celebrated mystic Abdal Mehmed in Bursa is not definitely known, since there is no inscription plate. But there are records showing that it was founded by Başcı İbrahim (d. 1490), a rich merchant of Bursa, during the second half of the fifteenth century.[1] The *türbe* of Abdal Mehmed is located across the street from the mosque. An inscription in Arabic above its door states that it was constructed in A.H. 854 (1450) upon the order of Sultan Murad II.

The mosque comprises a two-unit prayer hall, one minaret, and a three-bay porch (Fig. 149). Both units are covered by domes on pendentives and are placed adjacent to each other on the transverse axis. The interior is an oblong rectangle measuring 15.20 m. by 7.70 m. and divided by a big, heavy arch. The *mihrab* niche is centrally located, having been cut into the southern leg of the bisecting arch (Fig. 150). On the opposite side, structural considerations

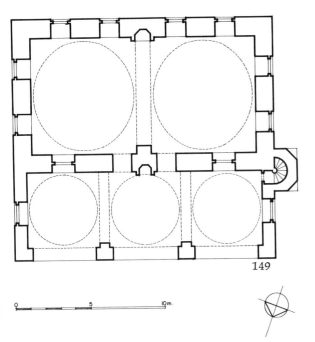

149

0   5   10m.

138

150

151

Mosque of Abdal Mehmed, Bursa
149 *Plan*
150 *Interior*
151 *Exterior. Rear view*

necessitated two doors on either side of the northern leg of the arch, which bears on its exterior face a second *mihrab* niche for the porch.

The domes of both units are slightly elliptical (Fig. 151) because they were built on rectangular bases—7.70 m. by 7.00 m. The porch is also surmounted by hemispherical domes of equal size. The minaret is located on the northwest corner of the main structure, its door accessible from the porch.

152

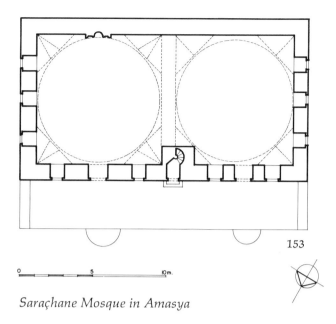

153

Saraçhane Mosque in Amasya

Saraçhane Mosque, Amasya
152 Exterior. Front view
153 Plan

A second mosque of the same type is the Saraçhane Mosque in Amasya. It has no porch, and its single minaret rises on the north between the two domes (Fig. 152). Otherwise the two-unit interior is similar to that of the Mosque of Abdal Mehmed.

Both units of the Saraçhane Mosque are 8.50 m. square and both domes rest on squinches (Fig. 153). The window and door openings are placed in an orderly manner and occupy corresponding positions in their respective units. The base of the minaret juts into the interior at the mid-point of the rear wall, emphasizing the symmetrical arrangement. Despite these features, the two units are not identical in their details. The windows of the western unit are arched; those of the eastern unit have simple lintels. The squinches of the eastern unit have long, pointed triangles at their corners; those of the western unit do not. The drum of the western unit is higher than that of the other. There is only one *mihrab* in the mosque, and it is located in the eastern unit.

As a matter of fact, a crack on the façade running vertically from the cornice down to the floor to the west of the minaret's base indicates that the two units were not built simultaneously. Judging from the more austere character of the eastern unit and from the fact that the *mihrab* is located in this unit, one can safely state that the eastern wing of the mosque was constructed first, probably as a single-unit mosque. There is no inscription. But according to some sources the Saraçhane Mosque was erected in A.H. 802 (1399). Since the Ottoman Turks captured Amasya in 1393, this date seems not an impossibility. As for the western wing, my guess is that it was built not long after the eastern wing, during the second half of the fifteenth century at the latest. In any case, there is no reason to doubt that the Saraçhane Mosque, as it exists today, dates from the fifteenth century and, though built in two stages, is a pertinent example of the early Ottoman multi-unit mosque with similar units.

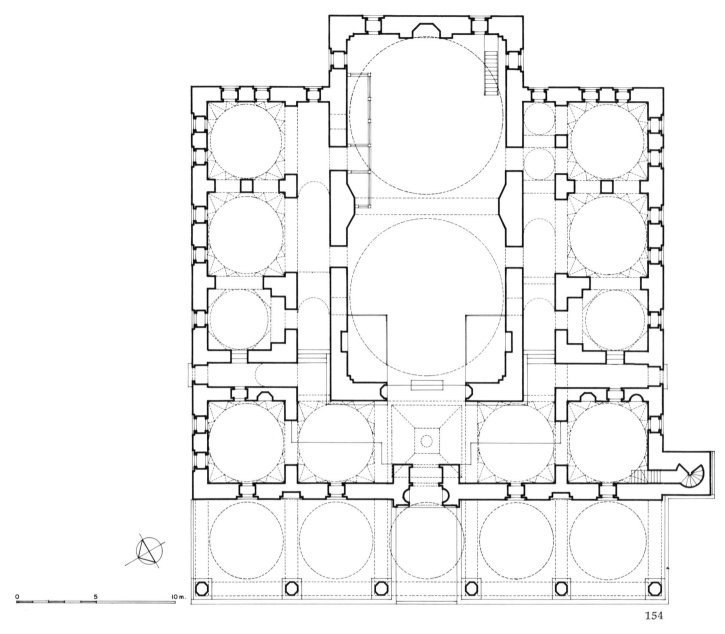

154

Mosque of Mahmud Paşa in Istanbul

The mosque built by Mahmud Paşa, the most famous of Mehmed the Conqueror's grand viziers (1453–66 and 1472–74), and located in the quarter of Istanbul bearing his name, was, according to the inscription above its door, founded in 1462 (A.H. 867).[2]

The porch of the Mosque of Mahmud Paşa is a five-bay structure, all five of the bays being surmounted by domes. The portal is simple in its architectural lines but rich in inscriptions. Above the door is the foundation inscription flanked by two inscribed medallions. On the right and left of the portal are two eight-line inscriptions showing that the mosque was restored in A.H. 1169 (1755).[3] From the portal one passes into a three-bay vestibule which, in turn,

155

Mosque of Mahmud Paşa, Istanbul
154 *Plan*
155 *Section*

gives access to a two-domed prayer hall. Both domes of the prayer hall are of equal size (12.50 m. in diameter and 19.75 m. in height) and both sit on pendentives (Fig. 155). Nor is there a difference in floor level between the two domed units.

Three smaller domed units flank the prayer hall on either side. Unlike the eyvan mosque, these units are not directly accessible from the first major domed unit but open onto barrel-vaulted corridors situated between them and the prayer hall (Fig. 154). Two shorter passages placed at right angles to the corridors lead to the outdoors. Below these, at the northeast and northwest corners of the building, are two eyvan-like domed-square rooms, both of which look onto the three-bay vestibule through arch-openings. The outer bays of the vestibule are also covered by domes, but the center compartment is surmounted by a flat-topped cross-vault. This three-bay vestibule, much like a narthex, as well as the side corridors, are features alien to Ottoman architecture. But with the conversion of what served as a central hall in the typical eyvan mosque into a second unit for prayer in the Mosque of Mahmud Paşa, obviously a different arrangement had to be devised in order to reach the side rooms. The solution, in my opinion, is not a successful one, but it does indicate an important development in early Ottoman architecture. The clear separation of the prayer area from the auxiliary rooms eliminates the Mosque of Mahmud Paşa from the eyvan mosque group and places it among the multi-unit mosques.

143

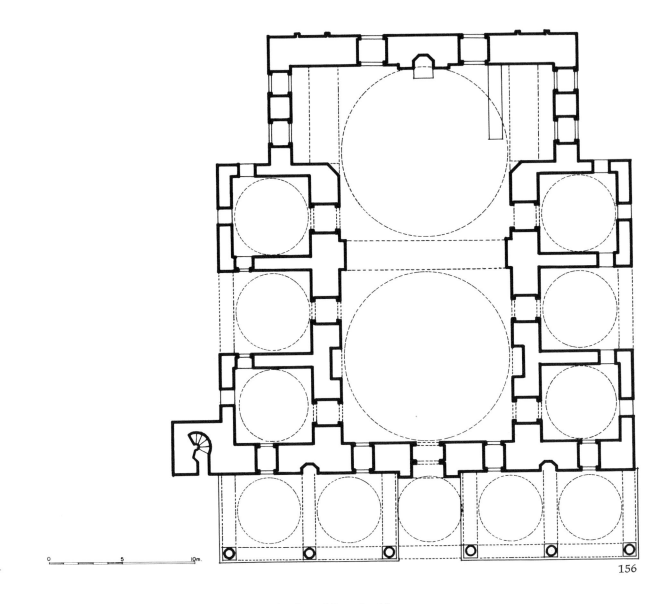

156

Mosque of Gedik Ahmed Paşa in Afyon

A second example of the same type of the two-domed multi-unit mosque is the Mosque of Gedik Ahmed Paşa—the grand vizier of Mehmed II from 1474 to 1477—in Afyon, built in 1472 (A.H. 877). Like the Mosque of Mahmud Paşa, it has a five-bay porch and a prayer hall composed of two similar units both surmounted by 11.50 m. domes on pendentives (Fig. 156). Unlike the Mahmud Paşa, the southern domed unit of this mosque is flanked by shallow niches which are not prominent enough to be considered eyvans. They merely provide the main space with a slight expansion along the transverse axis.

In the Mosque of Mahmud Paşa the problem of integrating the side rooms to the prayer hall was solved by means of corridors. In this mosque the same

144

Mosque of Gedik Ahmed Paşa, Afyon
156 *Plan*
157 *Exterior. Side view*

problem was approached in a far simpler manner. Three domed-square units flank the two-domed prayer hall on either side (Fig. 157). Of these, the central unit acts as an antechamber to the other two, whose doors open onto it. The central units are open on one side and therefore resemble eyvans. But unlike the side eyvans of the eyvan mosques, their arch-openings do not occur inside but look out to the exterior (Fig. 158). In the Mosque of Gedik Ahmed Paşa one finds a superficial kinship to the traditional three-eyvan mosque. In reality, the side eyvans are reversed and as such are not integral parts of the main interior space, and the interior is not separated into two by a central hall–main eyvan arrangement but is an integrated space comprising two units of prayer.

The Mosque of Gedik Ahmed Paşa is a well-proportioned and attractive structure entirely faced with cut stone. In most of its basic features it exhibits the rationality of the mid-sixteenth-century classical Ottoman architecture.

158

Mosque of Gedik Ahmed Paşa, Afyon
158 *Detail of eyvan*
159 *Exterior. Rear view*

Perhaps the only element out of tune with the rest of the building is the minaret built in the more sensational spirit of the pre-Ottoman era (Fig. 159). It is actually a very striking structure. The shaft, which rises from a tall base, spirals up to the stalactite consoles of the balcony. The nodes of the twisting shaft are constructed of stone; the grooves are inlaid with dark purple ceramic tiles.

As can readily be seen, the four two-domed multi-unit mosques which I have discussed fall into two subgroups. In the first group the units are placed side by side; in the second, they are put back to front. I know of no precedent for the oblong two-unit mosques exemplified by the Abdal Mehmed, the Saraçhane, and the now nonexistent Mosque of İvaz Paşa, which was located in front of Pirinç Hanı (The Rice Inn) in Bursa. These simple, modest structures seem to me to be rational attempts to produce with a limited budget, a rather large interior space for prayer. The two mosques of the second group, on the other hand, are neither expedient solutions to a practical problem nor unique examples of an unprecedented burst of creativity. They merely represent a definite stage in the evolutionary pattern of Ottoman mosque architecture—a transitional link between the early Ottoman eyvan mosque and the more sophisticated sixteenth-century sultans' mosques. I shall have more to say about this subject in the next chapter, devoted to the general analysis of early Ottoman mosques as a whole.

If the oblong two-unit mosque is an Ottoman invention and the axial two-unit Mosques of Mahmud Paşa and Gedik Ahmed Paşa represent the degeneration of the traditional eyvan mosque, the many-unit Ottoman great mosques may be said to have roots in the Anatolian Seljuk *ulucami*.

The typical Anatolian Seljuk *ulucami* is a rectangular structure with exterior walls of stone and an interior consisting of rows of masonry piers, marble columns, or wooden posts to eliminate big spans. The roof is generally flat, the ceiling being built of timber joists or shallow cross-vaults, but it is not uncommon to find one or more sections of the mosque raised and thus emphasized by a dome or groups of domes.

It would be difficult to place all Anatolian Seljuk great mosques in one large group with respect to their interior arrangement. Where the internal vertical supports are slender and rise all the way up to the ceiling, as in the Ulucami of Afyon (late thirteenth century) or the Ulucami of Sivrihisar (mid-eighteenth century), the flat ceiling acts as a unifier of space. But in most cases the piers or columns are tied by arches in one or in both directions. In the first instance, where the arches are arranged in parallel rows, the interior is divided into strips of space and there appears to be a sense of movement along the aisles. In the latter instance, where internal vertical supports are tied by arches in both directions, the space is compartmented and the sense of movement is reduced.

One of the earliest great mosques built by the Seljuk Turks in Anatolia, the Ulucami of Sivas,[4] has a rectangular interior 54 m. wide and 31 m. deep (Fig. 160). It has a flat earth roof—now protected by a timber structure covered with corrugated sheet iron—supported by ten rows of five stone piers each that

159

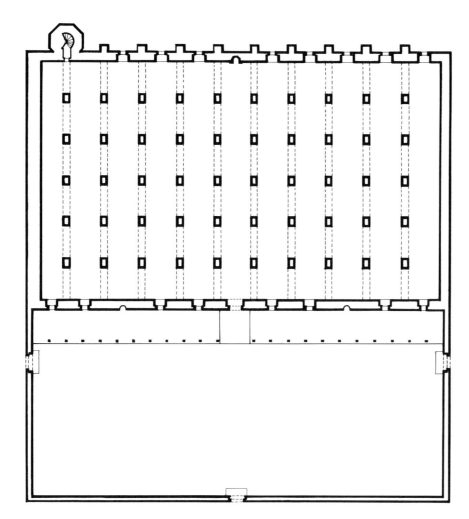

Ulucami, Sivas
160 *Plan*
161 *Interior*

run perpendicular to the south wall. These rows of piers, more than a series of individual vertical elements, resemble walls into which low, arched holes have been cut (Fig. 161). This arrangement critically hinders the transverse expansion of space, and the significant spatial movement within the mosque therefore occurs between the aisles along the north-south axis.

In the eastern wing of the Mosque of Alâeddin in Konya (twelfth century) the interior is planned in five rows of seven columns each. The rows of columns are tied by arches that run parallel to the south wall (Fig. 162) resulting in a transverse movement of space. Timber joists and tie beams accentuate the spatial movement by creating a rhythm. The eastern wing of the Mosque of Alâeddin has a flat roof. In the central section, the compartment in front of the *mihrab*, which is the largest bay in the building, is surmounted by a dome.

In the Ulucami of Sivas the piers are designed longitudinally and transversally with equal spans between them. The masonry work is uniform and elegant. In the central and western sections of the Mosque of Alâeddin the spans are uneven, and the organization of space is irregular. Even in the eastern

wing, which has a fairly orderly plan, different sized column shafts and capitals give the interior an air of irrationality. Except for the *maksure* dome of the latter, both buildings have flat roofs. The particular features of these two twelfth-century Seljuk great mosques are amalgamated in the Mosque of Hunat Hatun in Kayseri (1237, or A.H. 635).

The interior of the Mosque of Hunat Hatun is composed of ten longitudinal and eight transverse strips of space. Most of the compartments are square and have flat roofs. A square section, two bays wide and two deep, occupies the center of the building. Today it is surmounted by a dome but originally it was uncovered and served as a fountain court. The two bays directly to the north of the court are covered by cross-vaults; the two rectangular bays across from these, as well as the other two rectangular bays to the east and west of the domed compartment in front of the *mihrab*, are barrel-vaulted. If we disregard the section at the entrance, which is nine bays square and which is cut off from the main space and serves as an enclosed garden for the *türbe* of Hunat Hatun, the mosque exhibits a symmetrical and rational architecture. Unlike the dynamic aisled spaces of the Alâeddin and Sivas great mosques, the sense of space that one experiences in the interior of Hunat Hatun is of static nature. But the *maksure* dome, the central court, varying roof formations, and different qualities of light soften the severity of this interior, which would otherwise be gloomy and monotonous.

Mosque of Alâeddin, Konya
162 *Interior*

162

As can be seen from the three examples briefly considered above, the Anatolian Seljuk great mosques, in terms of space and form, do not follow a definite architectural pattern or show similarities beyond having interiors punctured by piers, columns, or posts. The early Ottoman great mosque, on the other hand, does have one specific and concise characteristic: it is composed of recurrent structural units of domed squares. Also, in the early Ottoman *ulucami* where internal supports do occur they are always piers and never columns or posts. The piers are tied in both directions by arches and the unit is covered by a dome. The transition to the dome is generally effected by pendentives.

The common denominator in the early Ottoman *ulucami*, seems to be the domed-square unit. This element points to a most significant difference between the Ottoman and the Anatolian Seljuk great mosques. The Anatolian Seljuk great mosque is defined by four walls. The space so contained is broken up by vertical supports and a flat upper structure enlivened at times by one or more domes or vaults, or a combination of these is built over the base. The Ottoman *ulucami* is conceived in recurrent units that are joined together, with their adjacent walls removed. The square and the circle are perfect geometric shapes. A three-dimensional unit composed of these shapes results in a complete, finished, and independent form. Each domed-square unit of the Ottoman *ulucami* possesses an architectural definition and expression—a characteristic not applicable to the Seljuk great mosques in Anatolia.

Although it is probably a legend, the story of Bayezid I, who vowed to build twenty mosques in Bursa should he return victorious from the Battle of Nikopolis (Niğbolu) and fulfilled his costly promise upon the advice of his wise seer Emir Sultan by building one mosque with twenty domes (the Ulucami),[5] well expresses the repetitive character of the Ottoman *ulucami*. It is not possible to apprehend the interior space of the Ulucami in Bursa, for instance, by standing on a single spot inside the building. Among the piers and the arches only a section of the interior can be seen at one time. Nor is the total space meant to be fully appreciated. The only strongly felt spatial sensation is the totality of the domed unit under which the onlooker is standing.

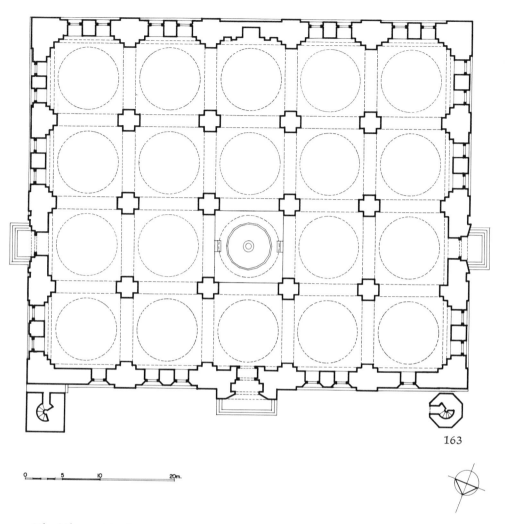

163

The Ulucami in Bursa

Ulucami, Bursa
163 *Plan*

The Ulucami in Bursa was begun in the fall of 1396 during the reign of Bayezid I, and according to the inscription above the door of its *minber* it was completed in 1399.[6]

The Ulucami of Bursa is a large rectangular building whose exterior dimensions are 68 m. by 56 m. Twelve square piers divide the interior into twenty equal units, each of which is surmounted by a dome (Fig. 163). Nineteen of these domes are full shells, but the twentieth dome, the second from the main portal in the center row, is open on top and was originally unglazed (Fig. 164). This unit has a pool in the center and is lower by two steps than the other units. Its floor, unlike the rest of the carpeted interior, is finished with white marble slabs. From the fountain at the center of the pool, water pours down in three stages from bowl to bowl. It is not similar to the other units, which form the prayer area (Fig. 165), but resembles an interior court. The longitudinal and transverse axes are established by the main portal and the *mihrab* and by

151

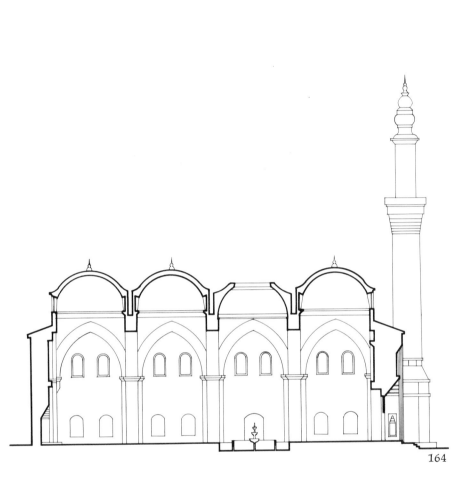

164

the two side entrances, respectively; they intersect at the center of the interior court, establishing a cross-axial design.

The domes of the Ulucami rest on pendentives and are girdled on the exterior by octagonal drums. All the domes have the same diameter but are not the same height. The center row on the north-south axis has the highest domes; the two side rows diminish in height in two stages (Fig. 166). But the difference is slight and can hardly be noticed from the inside. There are eight windows on each drum and generally two tiers of superposed windows on each exterior bay.

The Ulucami of Bursa does not have a porch. The two minarets are placed on the northeast and the northwest corners of the building. The northwest minaret, which is attached to the main structure, was built along with the mosque.[7] An inscription plate on its base states that it was erected by order of Bayezid I. The independent northeastern minaret probably dates from the reign of Mehmed I.[8]

152

165

Ulucami, Bursa
164 Section
165 Interior
166 Exterior. Rear view

166

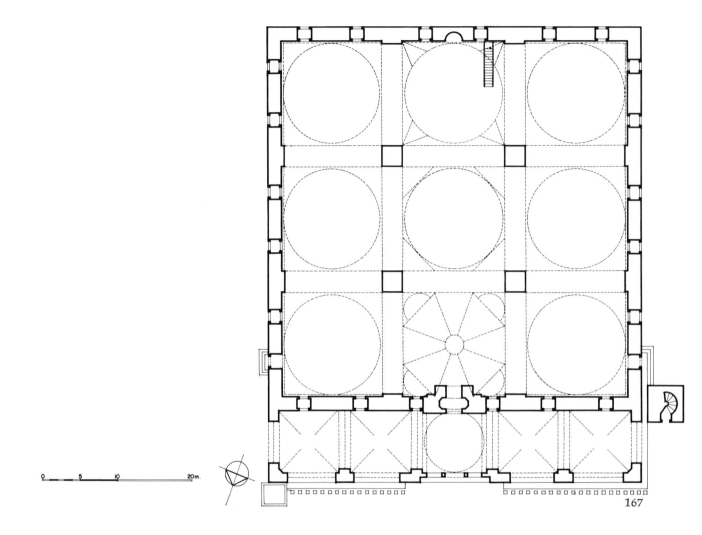

167

The Eski Cami in Edirne

The Eski Cami (Old Mosque) in Edirne dates from the early part of the fifteenth century. It was begun in 1402 (A.H. 815) upon the order of Emir Süleyman and was completed by his brother Çelebi Mehmed in 1413 (A.H. 816). The mosque suffered a fire in 1749 and an earthquake in 1752, but was repaired during the reign of Mahmud I (1730–54). It underwent another major restoration between the years 1924 and 1934.[9] The inscription plate above the western side entrance informs us that its architect was Hacı Alâeddin of Konya and its builder Ömer ibn İbrahim.

The Eski Cami is a perfect square building measuring 49.50 m. per side. It is divided into nine equal sections covered by nine domes (Fig. 167). In other words, the building comprises three domed units in each direction. Four massive masonry piers 2.80 m. square act as the inner supports for the nine domes. The transition to the domes of the center row is effected by three different

154

168

Eski Cami, Edirne
167 *Plan*
168 *Section*

systems: the first dome, where it enters the mosque, sits on simple squinches, the center dome on stalactites, and the dome in front of the *mihrab* on Turkish triangles (Fig. 168). Pendentives support the other six. The difference in transition between the center and the side rows of domes is also visible on the exterior of the mosque. Where pendentives are employed, the drums are circular. In the center row they are octagonal, and, as in the Ulucami of Bursa, slightly higher than those of the side rows (Fig. 169).

Gurlitt quotes von Hammer, who wrote that construction continued during the reign of Fâtih Mehmed (the Conquerer)and that the center dome, which originally had an oculus, was closed at that time.[10] It is, perhaps, not unreasonable to suppose that an interior court similar to that of the Ulucami of Bursa was also built in the Eski Cami, since the two mosques date from the same period and are of the same type. The space serving as the inner court was, in all probability, not the center unit, as von Hammer supposed, but the first bay at the entrance. This first unit has an open topped dome. Today the oculus is covered by a lantern, but one can safely assume that, like all the other lanterns placed on the oculi of early Ottoman buildings, it is a later addition. The side doors of the mosque are located on the first side bays.

The main portal and the *mihrab* define the longitudinal axis; the side doors determine the transverse axis. As we have already observed in the multi-eyvan

155

169

Eski Cami, Edirne
169 *Exterior. Front view*
170 *Interior*

mosques or in the Ulucami of Bursa, where there is an inner court in early Ottoman architecture it occurs at the intersection of the axes. Since the longitudinal and transverse axes intersect at the first center unit in the Eski Cami, it would be more logical to suppose that the inner court was located here. What misled von Hammer may have been the nine-unit hospices of the Mosque of Sultan Bayezid in Edirne (Fig. 46). In exterior form these hospices look like smaller versions of the Eski Cami but their interiors are different. The nine units are broken up into four individual rooms at the corners and a five-unit Greek-cross central space. The unit with the lantern is located at the center where the two axes, defined by the arms of the cross, intersect. Although in a completely symmetrical building it might be more logical to have the inner court right at the center, the placing of the inner court next to the main entrance in the Eski Cami would not be altogether unreasonable. In the Ulucami of Bursa the inner court occupies the second bay from the main entrance. But this mosque is four bays deep and the location of the inner court at the second unit from the entrance still permits a prayer area two bays deep in front of the *mihrab*. Since the Eski Cami is only three bays deep, the location of the inner court at the center of the

156

170

mosque would leave too narrow a prayer area in front of the *mihrab*. I am of the opinion that the inner court of the Eski Cami occupied the first center unit much like the central halls of the eyvan mosques. It probably was a step or two lower than the rest of the interior and had marble flooring and a fountain pool at its center directly under the unglazed oculus.

The interior of the Eski Cami is more spacious than the Ulucami of Bursa owing to fewer internal supports and bigger spans (Fig. 170). The domes of the Ulucami are 10.60 m. in diameter; those of the Eski Cami are 13.50 m. A significant difference between the two great mosques is the five-bay porch of the latter. The central unit of the porch is higher than the other four cross-vaulted units and is covered by a dome. The prayer hall is constructed completely of stone but the porch is a combination of stone and brick. This, plus a very weak connection of the two structures,[11] leads one to suspect that the porch is a later addition to the mosque; the original design probably did not include one. The two minarets are also of different periods: the eastern minaret was built along with the mosque, and the taller and independent western minaret came later. Söylemezoğlu, pointing to the close resemblance between this minaret and the

171

main minaret of the Üç Şerefeli Mosque (Fig. 202) located across from the plaza, concludes that "we can accept it as the work of the same architect,"[12] an opinion which I share.

During the late fourteenth and the first half of the fifteenth centuries quite a number of *ulucamis* were built by Ottoman rulers in the major cities of their state. Unfortunately, apart from the Ulucami in Bursa and the Eski Cami in Edirne, they have either disappeared or completely lost their original character. Among the latter one can mention the *ulucamis* of Bolu, Çankırı, Kütahya, and Söğüt, all of which were rebuilt during the nineteenth century in the architectural style of the period on the foundations of the early Ottoman structure.

Before terminating the discussion on the multi-unit mosques with similar units, I would like to consider one more mosque which shows all the characteristics of a *ulucami* but, in fact, is only a large neighborhood mosque.

158

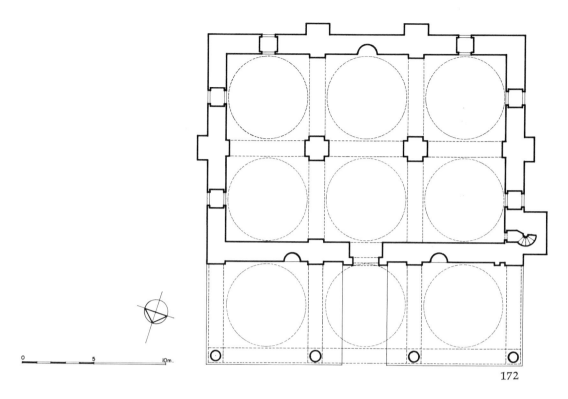

172

Zincirlikuyu Mosque in Istanbul

The Zincirlikuyu Mosque in Istanbul was built by Atik Ali Paşa, the grand vizier of Bayezid II, toward the end of the fifteenth century. Today it consists of a prayer hall and a minaret (Fig. 171), but originally it had a three-bay porch as well. The six-unit interior, whose 5.60 m. domes sit on pendentives, is three bays wide and two bays deep (Fig. 172). The exterior walls of the mosque are of brick and stone. To the south, east, and west they are buttressed against the outward thrust of the arches. The stone minaret is of a later period.

The Zincirlikuyu is the only fifteenth-century example of a six-unit mosque known to be in existence. The Mosque of Emir Sultan in Bursa, which was rebuilt in 1804 as a single-unit mosque, may also have been a multi-unit mosque originally,[13] but this is inconclusive. As a matter of fact, the small neighborhood multi-unit mosque with similar units was not much favored by the Ottoman Turkish architects, who seem to have preferred to build bigger and bigger domes and to achieve articulated spatial expressions instead of dull, repetitive interiors. With the advance in structural techniques and their accumulated technical experience, they rarely chose to build this type of mosque. The only multi-unit mosques with similar units built during the sixteenth century or later that I know of are the nine-unit Mosque of Molla Arab (d. 1531) in Bursa, the six-unit Mosque of Piyalê Paşa in Kasımpaşa, Istanbul (1573), the eight-unit Yeni Cami (New Mosque) in Adana (1724), and the nine-unit Mosque of Alâeddin Bey in Muş (1748).

159

MULTI-UNIT MOSQUE WITH DISSIMILAR UNITS

As we have observed, the Ottomans in their multi-unit mosques with similar units strove to achieve an undramatic, reposeful, and dignified interior space for meditation and prayer. We have also observed the slight emphasis of the central aisle in the two early Ottoman great mosques with similar units—the Ulucami of Bursa and the Eski Cami in Edirne. This tendency can be traced back to the Great Mosques of Damascus (A.D. 706–15) or Kairawan (A.D. 670–726). In the former, the three-bay central aisle is wider and higher than the side bays. It is further accentuated by a dome that surmounts the middle bay. In the latter, the wider central aisle is eight bays deep and the dome occurs on the southeasternmost bay in front of the *mihrab*. Among the later mosques of similar pattern, one can mention the Ayyubid Great Mosque of Diyarıbakır (twelfth century), the Anatolian Seljuk Kale Mescidi (Fortress Mosque) (Fig. 173) in Erzurum (twelfth century), the Ulucami of Divriği (1230 or A.H. 628), or the Mosque of İsa Bey (Fig. 174) at Selçuk near Ephesus dedicated in 1375 (A.H. 777).

Kale Mescidi, Erzurum
173 *Plan*

Mosque of İsa Bey, Selçuk
174 *Plan*

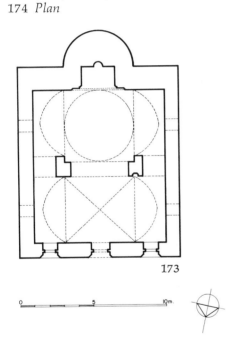

173

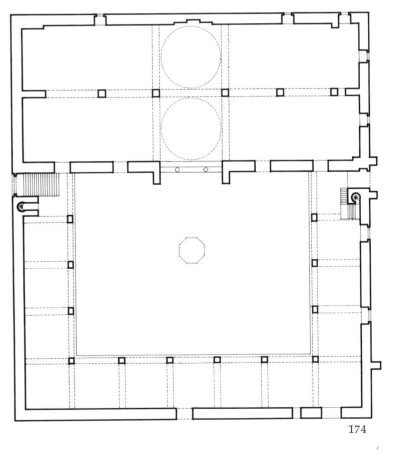

174

160

It was, I suppose, inevitable that the tendency to emphasize the main axis of the Ulucami of Bursa and the Eski Cami would lead to clearly accentuated central aisles in early Ottoman mosque architecture. Although of a different type, the evolution of the early barrel-vaulted eyvan mosque into the structure with two central domes was in all probability due to the desire to accentuate the main axis defined by the portal and the *mihrab*. Or, perhaps, both the eyvan Mosque of Bayezid and the Ulucami in Bursa were influenced by an earlier *ulucami* type of mosque, the central aisle of which was more pronounced than its side spaces. This last observation is not conclusive, however, since the mosque in question was rebuilt in the second half of the nineteenth century after it had been destroyed in the earthquake of 1855. The hypothesis about its original form, though reasonable and convincing, must await corroboration by archaeological findings before it can be fully accepted.

Şehadet Mosque in Bursa

The Şehadet (Martyrdom) Mosque in Bursa, as it stands today, is composed of an axial interior of two large domed units (Fig. 175). Evidence shows, however, that the original structure was not a simple two-domed mosque. Gabriel thinks that it could have been either an *ulucami* (multi-unit) or a "Bursa type" (eyvan) mosque.[14] Baykal believes that it was a nine-domed mosque but fails to mention the source of this information.[15] Anhegger, pointing to old photographs and drawings, also suggests that it was a multi-unit mosque, with a central aisle covered by three successive domes and side bays narrower than the width of the domed central compartments.[16] Pursuing further Anhegger's hypothesis, Sedat Hakkı Eldem, in a recent study,[17] argues that the original Şehadet Mosque had a squarish interior (28 m. by 26 m.) comprising two—and not three—units, each 11.00 m. square, along the longitudinal axis, both flanked by barrel-vaulted side bays (Fig. 176).

Eldem's argument is based on four photographs of the mosque taken before it was repaired in 1892 by Celâleddin Paşa, the governor of Bursa. The photographs show two major domes and the remains of the now nonexistent four-bay porch and minaret. He further strengthens his contention by arguing that the *kible* wall and the two buttresses (Fig. 177), which take the lateral thrust of the second dome on the south, are parts of the original structure. The three exterior walls of the mosque were plastered in the 1892 restoration, but the south wall, which is not visible from the street, was left untouched (Fig. 178). The composite stone and brick masonry of this wall is clearly in the character of early Ottoman architecture. On the basis of these findings Eldem concludes that in 1892 the two major domes and their supports were restored; but, probably owing to shortage of funds, the collapsed side spaces and porch were eliminated. By the exclusion of the porch, the original minaret was detached from the main structure. For this reason, it was also removed and a new but smaller minaret was erected farther back at the northeast corner of the mosque (Fig. 179).

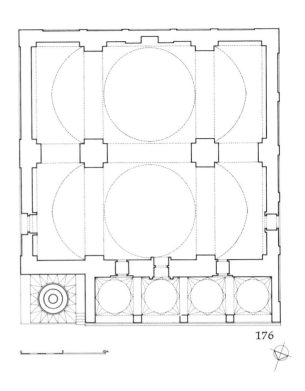

176

175

Şehadet Mosque, Bursa
175 *Interior*
176 *Restored plan (after Eldem)*
177 *Buttresses*

As for the construction date of the Şehadet Mosque: Gabriel, establishing that its Mecca orientation is the same and as incorrect (34° south-southwest) as those of the Mosques of Orhan Gazi and Alâeddin Bey in Bursa, suggests that it could have been built during the first half of the fourteenth century.[18] An inscription plate dated A.H. 738 (1337) placed above the side door of the earlier structure was read by Baykal. The text mentions a *"mescid"* founded by Orhan Gazi. Baykal justifiably points out that a large mosque such as the Şehadet could not possibly be considered a *mescid*, and that the Şehadet Mosque does not date from the reign of Orhan Gazi but from that of Murad Hüdavendigâr, having been built in 1365.[19]

The inscription plate in question must actually have belonged to the earlier Hisar (Citadel) Mosque built by Orhan Gazi, on the site of which the Şehadet Mosque was later erected. This would explain the presence of the Orhan Gazi inscription above the side door. For, obviously, if this inscription plate belonged to the latter mosque, it would have been put above the main entrance, where, according to Eldem, his old photographs show that one did exist.[20] The name of the mosque does not necessarily bring to mind Orhan Gazi, who died of old age, but Murad Hüdavendigâr, who was stabbed to death by a Serbian nobleman in the Battle of Kosova.

We may accept with reservation the conclusion that the Şehadet Mosque dates from the reign of Murad Hüdavendigâr. But the slight possibility of its having been built by Orhan Gazi—because of its orientation—or even by Bayezid I, who may have built it in memory of his martyred father, remains until

162

177

178

179

Şehadet Mosque, Bursa
178 *Exterior. Rear wall*
179 *Exterior. Front view*

additional documentary or archaeological evidence is produced. Whatever its precise construction date, we may assume that the Şehadet Mosque is a fourteenth-century structure. If we are to accept Eldem's reconstruction drawings, it would be the first great mosque built by the Ottoman Turks.

So far as I know there is no other mosque in early Ottoman architecture built on the exact design scheme of the Şehadet Mosque as shown by Eldem. On the other hand, I can point to two existing mosques in Anatolia—one dating from the mid-fifteenth century and the other from the sixteenth century—which bear a close similarity to it. The Mosque of Akşemseddin in Küre, Kastamonu, falls outside the scope of this book, because it was not built by the Ottomans but their neighbors, the İsfendiyaroğulları. Despite this, I shall include it since it may throw some light on the evolutionary pattern of the early Ottoman mosque and provide us with a more complete over-all picture.

164

Mosque of Akşemseddin, Küre
180 *Exterior*
181 *Plan*

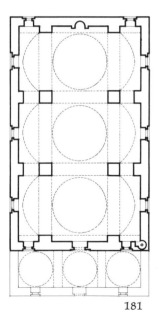

181

The great mosque of Küre was built by Cendirici Zâde Akşemseddin of the House of İsfendiyar in 1455 (A.H. 860). It is a composite stone and brick structure which has undergone numerous restorations. The enclosed porch is obviously a recent addition. So is the minaret that rises on the northwest corner of the building (Fig. 180). The awkward and tight manner in which the stair shaft of the minaret is cut into the thickness of the wall suggests that the original minaret was not where the new one is located. It probably was an independent structure which totally collapsed and was abandoned.

The interior comprises three adjacent domed-square units on the longitudinal axis, each one of which is flanked by smaller, barrel-vaulted compartments (Fig. 181). What one finds in the Mosque of Akşemseddin is a three-unit-deep replica of the Şehadet Mosque as reconstructed by Eldem. The three small—7.80 m. in diameter—domes sit on narrow octagonal bands of Turkish triangles supported at the corners by pendentive-like flat triangular planes decorated with star-shaped moldings (Fig. 182). These ornamental features, the masonry technique, and the unplastered north wall of the mosque, which has been preserved in its original condition (Fig. 183), clearly indicate that there existed a close kinship between this mosque—and indeed many other fifteenth-century buildings in the Kastamonu region—and early Ottoman mosques. The former was greatly influenced by the latter and this influence may be stretched to include form and spatial organization—an observation that would strengthen Eldem's hypothesis about the Şehadet Mosque.

Mosque of Akşemseddin, Küre
182 *Interior*
183 *Original north wall*

182

183

184

Mosque of Lala Sinan Paşa in Sincanlı

Mosque of Lala Sinan Paşa, Sincanlı
184 *Exterior. Front view*

A closer example, barring one structural innovation which must be accepted as a natural outcome of architectural evolution, is the Mosque of Lala Sinan Paşa in the town of Sincanlı in Afyon dating from 1524 (A.H. 931). The original external form of the mosque was much altered in 1876 (A.H. 1293) when the mosque underwent a major restoration. All the domes were covered by prismatic, terra-cotta tile roofs (Fig. 184), some of the original window arches were replaced by pedimental heads, an uncharacteristic circular window was opened above the *mihrab* (Fig. 185), and the proportions of the porch were changed, resulting in a strange and un-Ottoman architectural expression. The interior, however, more

Mosque of Lala Sinan Paşa, Sincanlı
185 *Exterior. Rear wall*
186 *Interior*
187 *Plan*

or less retains its original character (Fig. 186). Not considering the two convent cells on the sides—one of the last applications of a traditional early Ottoman feature—the interior comprises two domed-square central units flanked by halfdomed side compartments (Fig. 187). In plan, this interior arrangement is no different from that of the Şehadet Mosque. In volumetric expression, it is an improvement over the earlier mosque in that the halfdomed upper structure suggests a unified and integrated space.

The three examples of the multi-unit mosque with accentuated central aisles which I have discussed all possess one common design element: their side spaces are not complete square units. In the Şehadet Mosque and the Mosque of Akşemseddin, they are barrel-vaulted and comparatively shallow transversal expansions of space. In the Mosque of Lala Sinan Paşa, they are half-square units surmounted by semidomes. I shall now consider two more mosques of the same general type, in which the side spaces are complete units, but smaller than the domed-square central bays, or less distinct spatial entities.

186

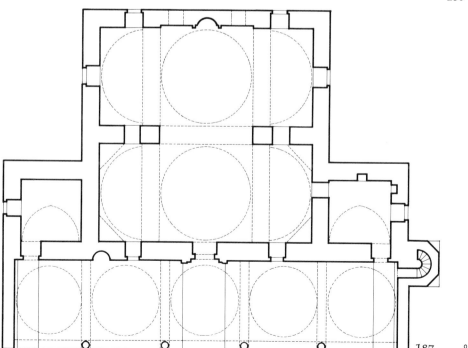

187

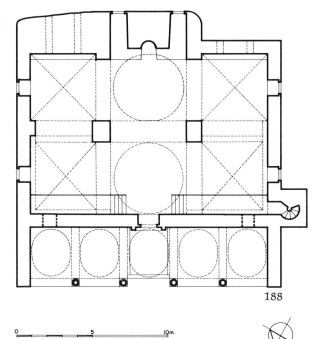

188

Mosque of Bülbül Hatun in Amasya

The Mosque of Bülbül Hatun in Amasya is perhaps the most unimpressive mosque in that city. Located on the sparsely inhabited and seldom visited north bank of the River Yeşilırmak, which flows through the city, it escapes the attention of most visitors. In any case, it is hardly ever mentioned by art historians. To be sure, the Mosque of Bülbül Hatun is neither a significant structure nor a monumental example of Ottoman architecture. It is only a simple, modest, and somewhat irregular building. But I feel that it is historically important, for not only does one find in it a variation of the typical six-unit mosque, such as the Zincirlikuyu in Istanbul, but it is also an early Ottoman mosque which has not been much altered since it was erected and therefore retains much of its original character and looks.

Bülbül Hatun, the founder of the mosque, was one of the wives of Bayezid II,[21] who served as the governor of Amasya before ascending the Ottoman throne in 1481. The construction date of the mosque is not definitely known because there is no inscription.[22] The foundation charter of the mosque is dated A.H. 915 (1509).[23] We can attribute it to the early sixteenth century, or possibly the late fifteenth century.

The oblong rectangular interior of the Mosque of Bülbül Hatun is composed of six near-square units (Fig. 188). The two units of the central aisle are surmounted by domes on pendentives, those of the sides by low, shallow cross-vaults (Fig. 189). On the south, the central and eastern aisles project out externally. This slight protrusion is caused by the thickening of the wall to buttress the building against the slope and does not form a depression on the inside.

All five bays of the porch (Fig. 190) are covered by domes. Like the interior, where the central aisle is higher than the side aisles, the center dome of the porch is also higher than the others. It sits on squinches and is further emphasized by an octagonal drum. The other four domes rest on pendentives and only the upper portions of their hemispherical shells rise above the cornice on top of the roof.

Although the south wall of the mosque overlooking the river was later plastered (Fig. 191), the side walls of rubble stone remain more or less in their original condition. The façade with its marble columns, brick arches and spandrels, timber tie beams and decorative brick frieze under the saw-toothed cornice presents us with an excellent example of early Ottoman architecture (Fig. 190). It was undoubtedly repaired at a later time, but the restoration work was so well executed that it does not seem to have lost its original character.

The minaret was decidedly rebuilt recently. The original timber steps inside the shaft are still intact, however, and were not replaced when the exterior of the minaret was renewed.

170

189

Mosque of Bülbül Hatun, Amasya
188 *Plan*
189 *Interior*
190 *Porch*
191 *Exterior. Rear view*

190

191

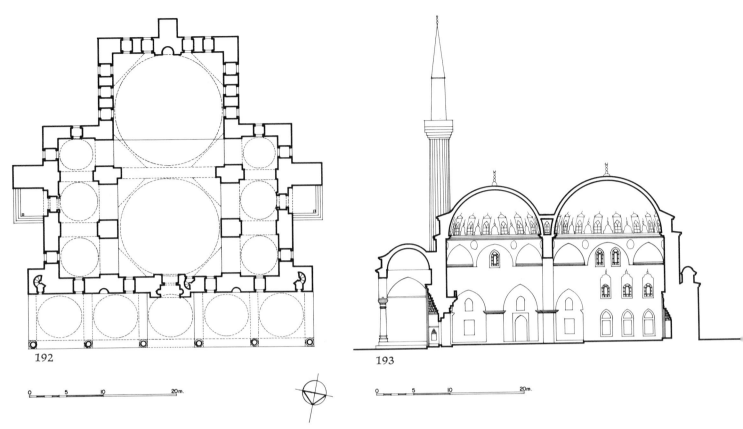

192 193

Mosque of Sultan Bayezid in Amasya

The Mosque of Sultan Bayezid (II), which is flanked by a *medrese* and an *imâret* to form one of the most impressive early Ottoman building complexes, is located on the southern bank of the Yeşilırmak across from the Bülbül Hatun in Amasya. It was inaugurated in 1486 (A.H. 891); but documents do not record when it was begun.[24]

The Mosque of Sultan Bayezid in Amasya comprises a five-bay porch, two minarets, and a large interior surmounted by two big and six small domes (Fig. 192). The first major dome covers a near-square (14.00 m. by 13.15 m.) unit. The second major unit on the south is slightly larger than the first, measuring 15.15 m. square (Fig. 193). Both domes rest on similar squinches and their octagonal drums are of equal height and character and each has sixteen windows. Because of the difference in their diameter, however, the second dome in front of the *mihrab* is a little higher than the other. Two massive square piers are placed at mid-points on either side of the first major unit. Behind the piers are two small domed-square units. To the south of these there exist a third unit on each side, which, unlike the two rear units opening onto the first central unit, open onto the second central unit. The southern side units are supported at the inner corners by a second set of piers from which the thick arch between the central units springs. Two massive external buttresses take the lateral thrust of

172

Mosque of Sultan Bayezid, Amasya
192 Plan
193 Section
194 Exterior. Side view
195 Interior

194

195

Mosque of Sultan Bayezid, Amasya
196 Exterior. Front view

the transverse arch. A third buttress placed behind the *mihrab* reinforces the structure on the south. All three buttresses are marked by small domed caps on high, octagonal drums (Fig. 194). Four more similar dome-capped weight towers rise on the four corners of the tall, two-domed rectangular central structure.

The interior space defined by the first major dome is rather dark, being illuminated only by the sixteen windows cut into the dome's drum. The second central unit is much lighter; besides the sixteen windows of the drum, twenty-six additional windows on three walls are arranged in three tiers which provide the interior with an abundance of natural light (Fig. 195).

The Mosque of Sultan Bayezid in Amasya is enriched by a delightful white marble porch and two superb minarets (Fig. 196). The five-unit porch is covered by five domes of equal size, which are externally supported by six marble columns with stalactite capitals. Slightly recessed exterior arches built of alternating white and red marble provide a rhythmic play and, along with the ceramic decorations on the façade, add a touch of color to the otherwise severe structure. The ornamental *tour de force* of the mosque is the minarets. They rise on gray cut-stone bases and both have similar finely carved balconies which are in the best Ottoman tradition. But their shafts are different: the circular eastern minaret is fluted and the polygonal one on the west is constructed of white and red stone in a zigzag pattern (Figs. 194 and 196)—a carry-over from an earlier era.

As can readily be observed there is a kinship between the Mosque of Sultan Bayezid in Amasya and the Mosque of Gedik Ahmed Paşa in Afyon. Both mosques have an axial, two-domed central space flanked by three-unit side sections. In the latter mosque, the side units are independent of the central prayer hall and are not even accessible from it (Fig. 156), whereas in the Amasya mosque the side units are integrated with the main central space (Fig. 192). Consequently, despite the close similarity of their exterior form, the internal spatial quality of the two mosques is quite different. Whereas the Mosque of Gedik Ahmed Paşa represents the first stage of degeneration of the traditional eyvan mosque, that is, the elimination of the central fountain hall and the incorporation of the first domed unit with the prayer area, the Mosque of Sultan Bayezid represents the second stage in which not only the central hall but also the side rooms have been integrated with the central space. One may consider the Mosque of Sultan Bayezid in Amasya to be the last link in the evolutionary chain of the Ottoman eyvan mosque—a schizophrenic mosque that still superficially reflects the exterior form of the eyvan type, but in reality is a multi-unit mosque whose interior space shows a closer affinity to the Eski Cami than to the Green Mosque in Bursa.

In my discussion of the multi-unit mosque with dissimilar units so far, I have studied those mosques whose central sections are accentuated by two—or three—large domes. Although this type of mosque is of utmost importance in our understanding of the evolutionary process of Ottoman mosque architecture, it represents merely an intermediary stage and not the final goal. As the grand sixteenth-century examples prove, the objective of the early Ottoman architects seems to have been the well-integrated, centrally planned mosque or the type of multi-unit mosque with a huge dome rising at the center of its structure.

The most important fifteenth-century example of the multi-unit mosque with one central dome is the Üç Şerefeli Cami (Mosque with Three Balconies) in Edirne. The Üç Şerefeli is generally considered to be the first important step in the development of the fifteenth-century sultans' mosques. Actually it represents a continuation of the *ulucami* type, but with one significant difference. Owing to a large dome in front of the *mihrab*, it exhibits a more decorative architecture than the previous Ottoman *ulucamis*. We have seen examples of the *maksure* dome in the Mosque of Alâeddin in Konya and the Hunat Hatun in Kayseri. In these two mosques the area covered by the *maksure* dome is rather small with respect to the total area of the interior. In the Hunat Hatun the ratio is 1:20. In the Mosque of Alâeddin it is even lower than that. A more dominant *maksure* dome occurs in the Ulucami of Manisa, in which the dome in front of the *mihrab* covers almost a third of the interior space.

Ulucami, Manisa
197 *Plan*

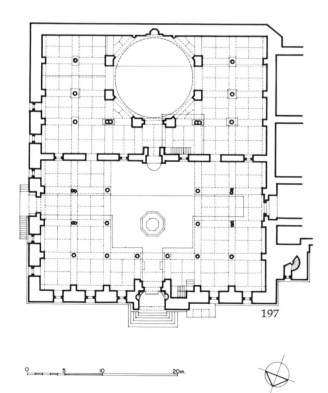

197

The Ulucami of Manisa was built by İshak Çelebi of the House of Saruhan in 1376 (A.H. 778). It is composed of two approximately equal spaces—one serving as the prayer hall and the other as the fountain court—and a minaret. The prayer hall measures 29.90 m. by 15.30 m., and the court is 29.90 m. by 16.90 m. (Fig. 197). Both are composed of twenty-eight units, being seven bays wide and four bays deep. In both, nine of the units have been left free of vertical supports. The larger unit of the court is left open. In the prayer hall it is surmounted by a 10.80 m. dome that sits on pendentives upon an octagonal base. Triangular corners left over from this octagonal base circumscribed in a square area are covered by tripartite vaults. Apart from the domed area and the open section of the court, all the square units inside and out are defined by single or double columns and are surmounted by domical vaults.

In terms of the evolution of early Ottoman architecture the fountain court of the Manisa Ulucami is also of great interest. Most Anatolian Seljuk great mosques do not have a fountain court. The Ulucami of Sivas with its unarcaded court must be accepted as a rare exception. The early Ottoman *ulucami* is also a building without a fountain court. For this reason the Ulucami of Manisa, as well as the Mosque of İsa Bey near Seljuk, built a year earlier, are of additional importance. It may be that the appearance of the fountain courts in Ottoman architecture in the mid-fifteenth century was directly influenced by these two mosques and not by earlier Seljuk or Byzantine courtyards.

176

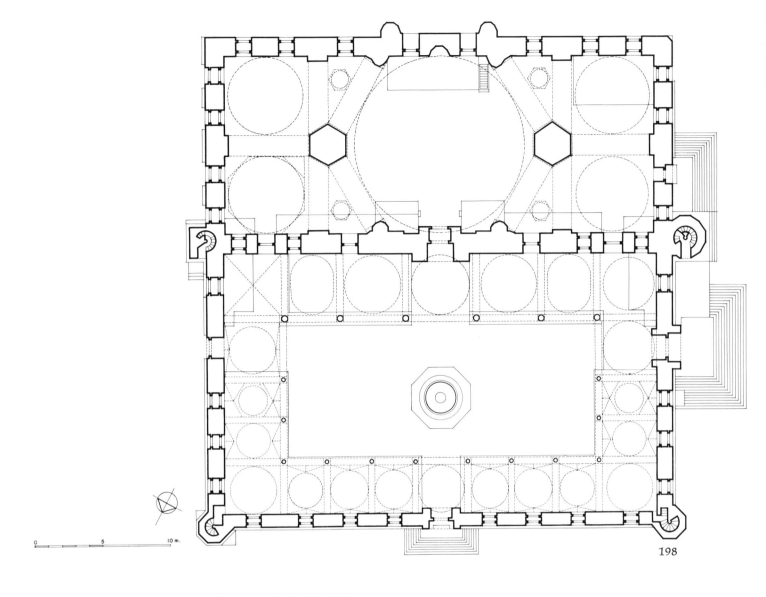

198

Üç Şerefeli Cami in Edirne

The Üç Şerefeli Cami in Edirne was built by Murad II. According to its inscription the construction was begun in 1437 (A.H. 841) and was completed in 1447 (A.H. 851). We do not know who the architect of this important work was.

The Üç Şerefeli is a monumental building composed of an oblong prayer hall, an arcaded fountain court and four minarets. It covers a nearly square area 66.50 m. by 64.50 m. The prayer hall is approximately two-thirds as deep as the fountain court: their inner dimensions being 60.00 m. by 24.25 m. and 60.00 m. by 35.50 m., respectively (Fig. 198).

The central dome of the Üç Şerefeli Cami completely dominates the mosque (Fig. 199). It measures 24.10 m. in diameter and is supported on the south and

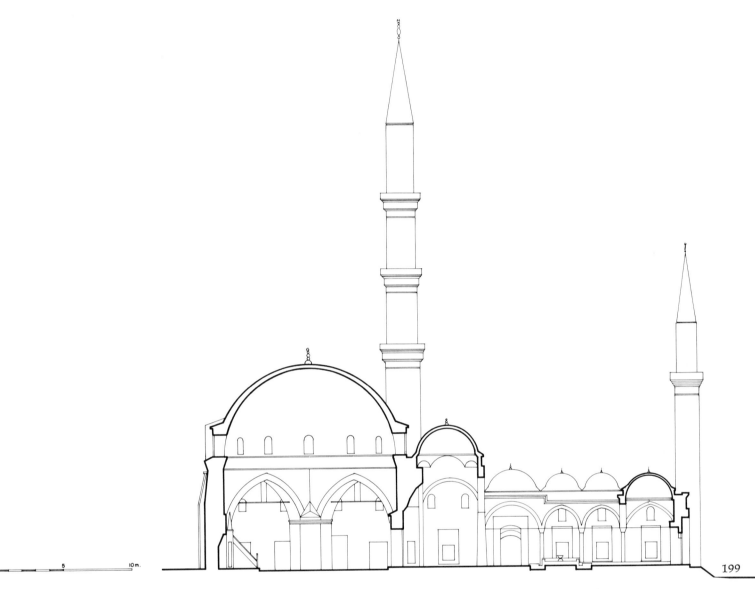

north by the exterior walls, on the east and west by two huge—6 m. across—
hexagonal piers. A belt of Turkish triangles on pendentives encircles the rim
of the large dome. On the exterior, it is girdled by a dodecagonal drum, which in
turn, is reinforced by eight small arched buttresses (Fig. 200). So far as I know,
this is the first time drum buttresses were employed in Ottoman architecture.
The portions of the outer walls on which the major dome presses down are built
thicker than the rest of the walls and they are further strengthened against the
lateral thrust of the dome by buttresses.

The smaller domed square units flank the central domed space on either
side. The side domes are 10.50 m. in diameter. The four triangular spaces left
over at the junction of the central hexagonal area and the square side units are
covered by tiny domes that occupy the center of stalactite-decorated tripartite
vaults.[25] These intermediary domes give the impression of being forced on the

Üç Şerefeli Cami, Edirne
199 *Section*
200 *Roof structure of prayer hall*

upper structure. Although they possess some identity on the exterior (Fig. 200), they get completely lost inside between the heavy arches and deep, wedge-like hollows in which they are set.

The fountain court of the Üç Şerefeli Cami is not symmetrical. Excluding the corners, its southern arcade has five units, its northern arcade seven, and the east and west arcades three units each. On the south, the central unit is 10.10 m. square. Units adjacent to it are equally deep but less wide. Consequently, the domes of the rectangular side units are elliptical. Although the southwest corner of the court is covered by a dome, its counterpart on the southeast is

covered by a cross-vault (Fig. 201). The rest of the units around the open court are more regular, surmounted by hemispheric domes of three sizes. As in the Ulucami of Manisa, the portals occur at the ends of the longitudinal and transverse axes, but in the Üç Şerefeli Cami the axes do not intersect at the center of the court. The fountain, too, is located neither at the intersection of the axes nor at the geometric center of the court. It is shifted slightly to the north on the north-south axis.

The four minarets of the Üç Şerefeli Cami rise on the four corners of the fountain court (Fig. 202). The tallest, occupying the southwestern corner, has

202

three balconies (*şerefe*) which give the mosque its name. This minaret is 67.65 m. high and, after the minarets of the nearby Mosque of Selimiye (1569–75) which are 70.90 m. high, it is the second tallest minaret in Ottoman architecture. The southeast minaret is shorter by a fifth and has two *şerefes*. Those occupying the north corners of the court are shorter still and have only one *şerefe* each.

The Üç Şerefeli Cami is an important work which brought many novel ideas into Ottoman architecture and, structurally, took a bold leap. The mere size of its dome alone represents a most significant achievement. Doğan Kuban, in discussing the mosque, comments: "An interesting development here is to cover with a dome a rectangular area which is wider than the diameter of the dome: the most advantageous aspect of a hexagonal scheme."[26] It is true that in the Üç Şerefeli Cami the base of the major dome is larger than the volume defined by it. But it is also true that the four pie-shaped sections of the upper structure squeezed between low, double arches which span the area from the hexagonal piers to the outer walls at 90° and 60° constitute the weakest elements in this mosque. Even the inexperienced eye can readily see the technical difficulties which the architect of the Üç Şerefeli faced in constructing a 24.00 m. dome in the mid-fifteenth century.

Structurally the Üç Şerefeli Cami may not be a perfect example. The same cannot be said of its spatial organization. In the Ulucami of Manisa, the central dome covers about one-third of the prayer hall. In the Üç Şerefeli, it spreads over one-half of the total interior, if one is to disregard the area taken up by the various arches. This last point is, I think, significant; because, although the Üç Şerefeli Cami is a five-unit great mosque with a central unit approximately four times as large as the other units, it could also be considered an eight-unit mosque four bays wide and two bays deep, with its four central units integrated under one big dome. Despite its structural and aesthetic deficiencies, this mosque stands as a significant turning point in Ottoman architecture, for it is in the Üç Şerefeli Cami that the initial experiment of the centrally planned sixteenth-century mosques was conducted.

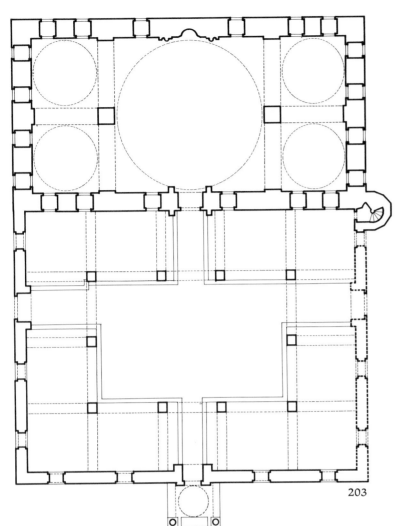

203

204

Mosque of Güzelce Hasan Bey in Hayrabolu

The Mosque of Güzelce Hasan Bey in Hayrabolu, Tekirdağ, built in 1406 (A.H. 809),[27] predates the Üç Şerefeli. Like the Üç Şerefeli, the oblong prayer hall is covered by five domes (Fig. 203). The large, high central dome on pendentives spans the depth of the prayer hall from wall to wall. It is reinforced by a dodecagonal drum unperforated by window openings. On the east and west of the central unit, separated by arches which spring from square piers, there are two smaller square units, each surmounted by hemispherical domes on Turkish triangles.

Like the Üç Şerefeli again, the Mosque of Güzelce Hasan Bey has a fountain court. This court, which is the earliest Ottoman mosque court in existence, is tight and ill proportioned. The upper structure of its arcade has collapsed and it is difficult to ascertain whether it was covered by domes or vaults. But it was supported by piers, some of which are still in place (Fig. 204), instead of the usual columns. A feature of great interest is the domed canopy in front of the

182

205

Mosque of Güzelce Hasan Bey, Hayrabolu
203 *Plan*
204 *Exterior. Front view*
205 *Exterior. Rear view*

north portal of the court, since, so far as I know, this is the only occurrence of such a canopy in early Ottoman architecture.

The minaret is to the west, situated at the intersection of the prayer hall and the court. Whereas the entire structure is built of horizontal courses of stone and brick (Fig. 205), the minaret is constructed of stone alone. It is obviously a product of a later time.

There exist in early Ottoman architecture a number of other mosques with prayer halls built more or less on the same pattern as the Mosque of Güzelce Hasan Bey. Among these one can cite the Mosque of Çaşnigir (1474) and İvaz Paşa (1484) in Manisa, the Ulucami of Akhisar (second half of the fifteenth century) or the Mosque of Fâtih İbrahim Bey in Urla, İzmir (second half of the fifteenth century).

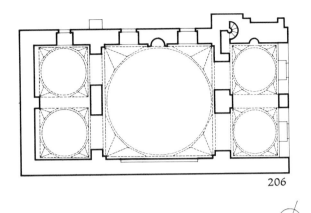

206

Mosque of Rüstem Çelebi, Tokat
206 *Plan*
207 *Exterior*

Mosque of Rüstem Çelebi in Tokat

207

Another building which shows a similarity to the Üç Şerefeli pattern, but in effect has a unique plan, is the Mosque of Rüstem Çelebi—also called Güdük Minare (Docked Minaret)—in Tokat. In terms of massing, the Rüstem Çelebi is a five-unit mosque which is no different from the Güzelce Hasan Bey. It is a rectangular structure composed of four small domed-square units flanking a larger one, two on each side (Fig. 206). In the Rüstem Çelebi not five but three of the units make up the prayer hall, the two small units on the west being a two-bay porch.

This unusual plan arrangement is explained by the fact that the two-unit eastern section of the mosque was later added onto the building. Different masonry work and window sizes tell the story at first glance (Fig. 207). One can easily see that the original mosque was a single-unit mosque whose two-bay porch was located not on the north but on the west, like that of the Hacı Özbek in İznik (Fig. 6). Later on, to make room for an increased congregation, the mosque must have been enlarged by adding the two-unit eastern section, blocking off the exterior arches of the porch and opening arches between the large central section and the side units.

The Mosque of Rüstem Çelebi is in poor repair. Apart from the various additions mentioned above, a protective tiled timber roof was placed upon its domed upper structure (Fig. 207). This improvisation may help keep the rainwater from seeping into the building, but it also alters the architectural character of the mosque. The brick minaret is placed on a stone base. Its balcony consoles and parapet are also of brick and, unlike the prayer hall, it retains much of its original character.

The mosque does not have an inscription, but the masonry work, decorative patterns in brick, and the Turkish triangles of the domes all point to the early Ottoman period. I am inclined to place the Mosque of Rüstem Çelebi in the first half of the fifteenth century. The possibility remains, of course, that it was built during the latter part of that century; but certainly no later than that.

184

208

Mosque of Ağalar in Istanbul

Mosque of Ağalar, Istanbul
208 *Exterior*

Another example of the same type is Küçük Oda Camii (Small Room Mosque), or the Mosque of Ağalar, inside the third court of the Topkapı Palace in Istanbul. It was built during the latter part of the fifteenth century, probably by Mehmed II.

As its name implies it was founded to serve the pages of the court (*enderun ağaları*). Unfortunately, the building has undergone several restorations through the years—the last one being in 1925[28]—and suffered a great many alterations. A smaller mosque was joined to its southeast corner in 1723 (A.H. 1136),[29] its walls were elevated by 2.00 m., its two rows of windows were made larger, and its upper structure completely reconstructed (Fig. 208). What remains of the original structure are the foundations and a portion of the exterior walls. But these, coupled with the information we have of a similar but now nonexistent Mosque of Şeyh Vefa (Fig. 209),[30] show what the original mosque may have been like.

The Mosque of Ağalar is a rectangular structure 27.70 m. by 14.40 m. It comprises a fairly large rectangular prayer hall measuring 21.00 m. by 12.10 m.

185

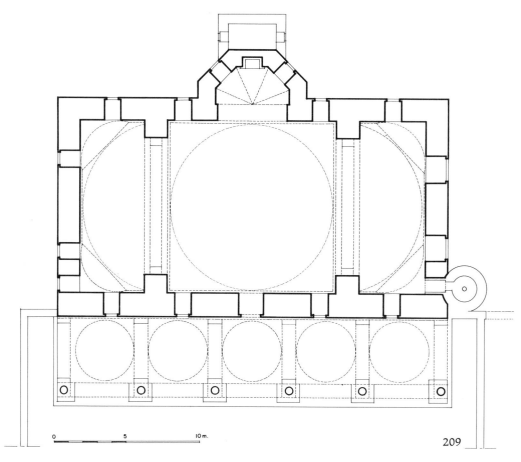

209

Mosque of Şeyh Vefa, Istanbul
209 *Plan*

and a long, narrow room on the west (Fig. 210). The thin—45 cm.—partition wall between the two spaces is obviously a later addition. The prayer hall is covered today by a huge vault which is uncharacteristic of the fifteenth century. In any case, since we know that the walls were elevated in the eighteenth century the present upper structure cannot be original. Ayverdi suggests that the fifteenth-century mosque must have been surmounted by a dome at the center flanked by halfdomes on the east and west, like the Mosque of Şeyh Vefa.[31] His reconstruction plan has great merit, except that it omits the narrow room on the west in order to portray a symmetrical building with the *mihrab* placed at mid-point of the south wall. To achieve this he retains the east wall but disregards the wall on the west by re-creating a new one equidistant from the center of the room. The character of the masonry work on the exterior shows that the west end of the building is not a later addition. Thus the present narrow room could originally have been a part of the prayer hall and the interior not symmetrically designed with respect to the *mihrab*, or the east wall could have been later rebuilt closer to the center line of the structure. In the former case, the unsymmetrical side spaces would have had to be covered by barrel vaults. In the latter, the dome could have been flanked by full halfdomes, or two small domes, instead of the compressed halfdomes shown in Ayverdi's reconstruction. In any case, on the basis of the seventeenth-century French traveler Tavernier's description of the mosque, I am inclined to think that it was a far more involved

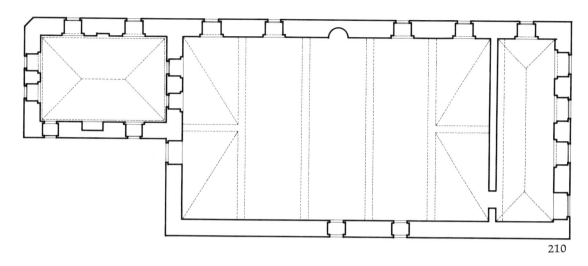

Mosque of Ağalar, Istanbul
210 Plan

structure than that portrayed by Ayverdi. According to Tavernier, who acquired his information from one of the pages of the court,

> . . . there is a Mosquey, of the middle fort, as to the largeness, the length of it somewhat exceeding its breadth, and it stands North and South, a situation the *Turks* observe in all their Mosqueys, which are always turn'd towards *Mecha*, which place is Meridional to all the Provinces of the Empire. There is the wall, opposite to the South, a kind of Neech, which they call *Mihrab*, into which the *Iman* [imam], who is their Priest, gets up to say Prayers at the accustomed hours, and the Grand Seignor [the Sultan] is present thereat, with the forty Pages of the *Haz-Oda*, in a little Room, the Window whereof is opposite to the Neech. On both sides of the said Neech, there is a Gallery sustain'd by five Pillars, some whereof are of green Marble, and the rest of Porphyry. . . . The Window of the Chamber, into which the Grand Seignor comes to do his Devotions is six foot in length, and three foot high, and has a Lattice, with a Curtain behind it, as it is in several Chappels, which our Christian Princes have in their Palaces. There is also opposite to the same Neech, before-mentioned, such another Window, and such another Chamber, for the Sultanesses, and when the *Muezim* [muezzin], whose station is of one side of the *Iman* [imam], and who is as it were his Clerk, hears the drawing of the Curtains, he immediately rings a small Bell; which is the signal, that the Grand Seignor and the Sultanesses are come into their several Rooms.[32]

One gathers from this description that the prayer hall of the Mosque of Ağalar was indeed composed of a central space flanked by two aisles. The side spaces could have been surmounted by halfdomes; but it is also possible that they were covered by two small domes, or cross-vaults, like many other multi-unit mosques of the time. In the former instance, the colonnades of five columns on both sides, mentioned by Tavernier, would only carry the galleries. In the latter, the central columns would rise the full height of the lower structure to support the arches between the two side domes—or vaults—while the other four would bear the

187

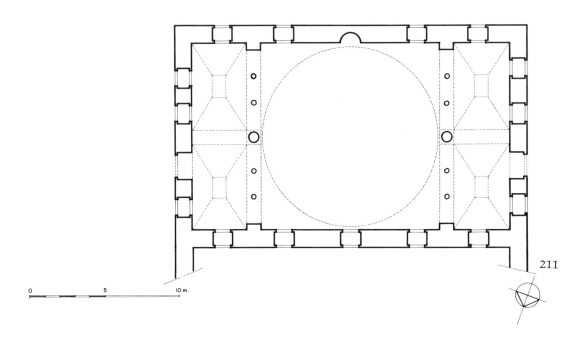

211

Mosque of Ağalar, Istanbul
211 Restored plan (Kuran)

load of the gallery (Fig. 211). The problem of the pews of the sultan and the women of the court is perhaps less difficult to solve. According to Tavernier, the pews were "opposite to the Neech," or at the back of the mosque. This arrangement is not impossible. In the Yeşil Cami of Bursa the sultan's private pew occupies the central position across from the *mihrab* with two pews for women on either side (Figs. 127, 130). During the second half of the fifteenth century, however, the position of the sultan's pew is changed. It is brought forward and placed adjacent to the *kible* wall to the east or west of the *mihrab*, generally the former. Therefore, it could be suggested that Tavernier made a mistake when he placed the pews at the back of the mosque and not on the sides. If the pews were placed at the back, then what were the side galleries used for? The Mosque of Ağalar is located at the second court of the Topkapı Palace close to the harem quarters, with its rear wall facing the Golden Passage (Altın Yol), one of the main arteries of the labyrinthine inner section of the palace. Since it was to the Mosque of Ağalar that the sultan and the women of the harem came for their prayers, it would be logical to assume that it was not an independent structure but was linked to the harem probably by an elevated passage that led directly to the galleries of the mosque. Or, alternatively, there was a walled-in courtyard between the Golden Passage and the mosque from which one reached the galleries by stairs. The pages of the court, on the other hand, entered the mosque through side doors from under the galleries.

Whether covered by a central dome flanked by two smaller domes—or cross-vaults—on either side, an arrangement which I find more probable, or by one full and two halfdomes, it is evident that the Mosque of Ağalar was designed as a multi-unit mosque. Being the largest and most centrally located mosque of the Ottoman palace, it was only natural that it should have been so.

188

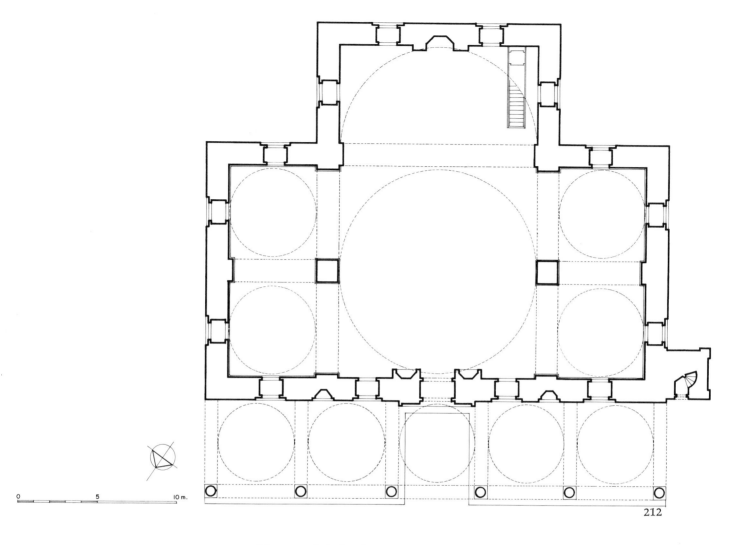

Mosque of Atik Ali Paşa in Istanbul

Mosque of Atik Ali Paşa, Istanbul
212 Plan

A fourth, and far more developed, version of the same type of mosque is that of Atik Ali Paşa in Istanbul, which dates from 1496 (A.H. 902). Like the Güzelce Hasan Bey, the Mosque of Atik Ali Paşa comprises a five-bay porch, a minaret that occupies the northeast corner of the main structure, and a prayer hall with a large central dome. In addition to the two-unit side sections, there is a rectangular area surmounted by a halfdome in front of the domed central unit (Fig. 212). The two corners of the halfdome rest on stalactite corbels (Fig. 214). The full domes of the prayer hall sit on pendentives. Above its pendentives the central dome is encircled by a drum, which is perforated by sixteen windows and reinforced from the outside by eight buttresses, two on each corner (Fig. 215).

Until recently the Mosque of Atik Ali Paşa has generally been considered among the "Bursa Type" group. In the two previous chapters, I have already

189

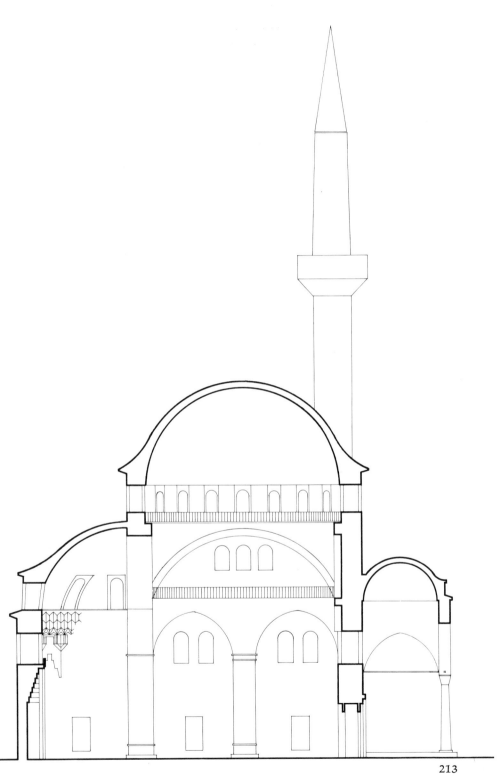

213

214

0 _____ 5 _____ 10 m.

215

Mosque of Atik Ali Paşa, Istanbul
213 *Section*
214 *Interior*
215 *Exterior*

shown how it would not be logical to include all mosques whose central sections project out on the south in any one group. I shall not undertake to expound further on this important subject at this time but defer it to chapter 4. What I would like to comment on instead is the halfdomed rear section in the Mosque of Atik Ali Paşa.

The halfdome in the Atik Ali Paşa does not mark the first occasion of its use in Ottoman-Turkish architecture. We have arleady seen the halfdomed forward sections of the eyvan mosques of Rum Mehmed Paşa (Fig. 101) and the earlier Yahşi Bey in Tire (Fig. 94). But, in the Atik Ali Paşa, one observes the halfdome within the context of the multi-unit mosque. What is the significance of the halfdome as an architectural element? The domed-square structure, whether it be defined by four walls or by piers on four corners, connotes a complete unit and is an entity in itself. Can one say the same for a space surmounted by a halfdome? In my opinion, no. The halfdome is a structural roof cover that by itself does not have an architectural value, nor can it be used alone. It is fitted onto an arch on which a dome sits and probably serves the

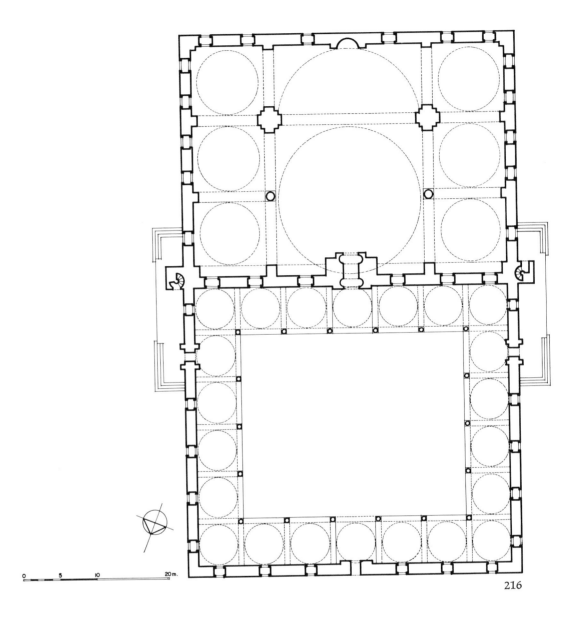

216

Mosque of Fâtih, Istanbul
216 Restored plan (after Ülgen)

dual purpose of allowing the central space to expand while also buttressing the central domed structure.[33] In other words, the halfdome is merely an auxiliary element which acts as the intermediary between the central dome and the exterior walls of the total structure and, in so doing, extends the interior space beyond the immediate boundaries of the dome of which it is a part (Fig. 213).

In the Mosque of Atik Ali Paşa the halfdome occurs on the south of the major dome. Thus the central unit is extended toward the *kıble* and becomes a rectangular area one and a half times as deep as it is wide. The situation differs on the sides: four independent domes rise on square bases provided by longitudinal and transverse arches which sit on one side on the square piers. The Mosque of Atik Ali Paşa is a variation of the five-unit mosque composed

192

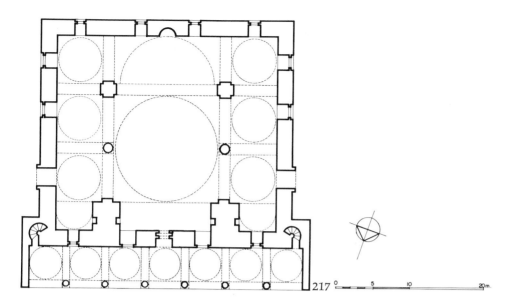

217

Mosque of Selim II, Konya
217 Plan

of a large domed-square central section, enlarged by a halfdomed extension, flanked by four smaller domed-square units.

In terms of plan arrangement and spatial organization there are two other mosques that may be grouped with the Atik Ali Paşa. These are the old Fâtih Mosque (1463–71) in Istanbul, which was rebuilt on a different plan by Mustafa III (1757–74) after the first mosque collapsed in the earthquake of 1765,[34] and the Mosque of Selim II (1566–74) in Konya. In both mosques the two sides of the halfdomed forward section are filled in with two more domed-square units. The exterior walls of both the Fâtih and the Selimiye define a rectangular prayer hall and reflect better the continuation of the traditional Ottoman *ulucami* pattern. Spatially or in terms of architectural form the integration of the halfdomed section with the whole is weak in the Atik Ali Paşa. In the first Mosque of Fâtih, there existed a stronger expression, not only because of the more geometric, rectangular lower structure but also because the halfdomed forward section was incorporated with the rest of the interior on three sides (Fig. 216). Excluding the additional rear piers that were obviously required to counterbalance the protruding front section and the deep niches that resulted from their inclusion in the main space, the general plan organization of the Mosque of Selimiye in Konya is also the same (Fig. 217).

The Üç Şerefeli Mosque is two units deep and its central dome spans the prayer hall from one outer wall to the other on the longitudinal axis. The Mosque of Fâtih and the Selimiye are three units deep and, as a result, their central domes rest on the outer walls only on one side, or at the rear. A third and final stage in this development takes place in the Mosque of Bayezid (II) in Istanbul, which is four units deep with its central dome detached altogether from the exterior walls. The major dome rising at the center of a square structure whose outer walls encompass a bigger area than that covered by the central dome is the inevitable rational solution that the Ottoman-Turkish architect was bound to reach.

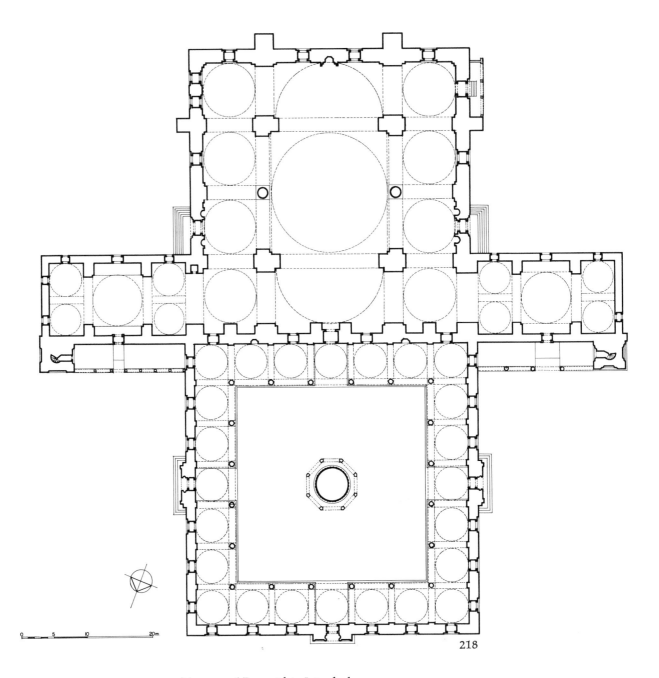

218

Mosque of Bayezid in Istanbul

The Mosque of Bayezid (II) in Instanbul was completed in 1505 (A.H. 911). It
was designed by Yakub Şah bin Sultan Şah,[35] one of the court architects during
the reign of Bayezid II.

The prayer hall and the fountain court of the Mosque of Bayezid in Istanbul
form two adjacent and equal squares, each measuring 42.50 m. per side. The
former comprises a centrally located domed unit enhanced by two halfdomed
units on the longitudinal axis and flanked on the east and the west by four-unit

194

Mosque of Bayezid, Istanbul
218 *Plan*
219 *Exterior*

aisles surmounted by four smaller domes (Fig. 218). The 18 m. central dome rises on pendentives atop four piers. Between these on either side is a porphyry column to support the inner two of the smaller domes. To the rear of the prayer hall, attached to the northernmost corner units, there are two wings which protrude from the main structure at right angles (Fig. 219). These auxiliary wings are like small five-unit mosques of the Güzelce Hasan Bey type. They have separate entrances of their own; but unlike the nine-unit side structures of the Mosque of Bayezid in Edirne, they are not convents but parts of the main prayer area and are directly accessible from it. The two minarets are located as

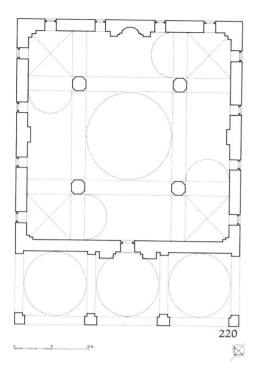

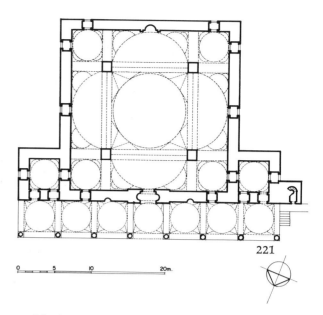

Mosque of Çelebi Sultan Mehmed, Dimetoka
220 *Plan*

Mosque of Bıyıklı Mehmed Paşa, Istanbul
221 *Plan*

far away as possible from the central dome, at the tips of the side wings.

The well-proportioned fountain court is completely symmetrical. Its twenty-four-bay arcade is surmounted by twenty-four hemispheric domes of equal size. The three portals occur at the mid-points of each side and the ornate fountain is placed at the intersection of the axes which pass through the centers of the portals.

The Mosque of Bayezid in Istanbul, of course, is neither the first nor the most developed example of the centrally planned Ottoman or pre-Ottoman mosque. The Ulucami at Elbistan[36] has an interior composed of a domed-square central space surrounded by four rectangular units on each side surmounted by shallow halfdomes and four smaller domed units at the four corners. A second example is the Mosque of Çelebi Sultan Mehmed in Dimetoka, Greece, designed by the architect İvaz Paşa in 1421 (A.H. 825). It comprises a main structure, measuring 30.00 m. square on the exterior, and a three-unit porch (Fig. 220). The 12.00 m. central dome sits on four piers. The space around the central unit and the exterior walls is covered by cross-vaults at the corners and barrel vaults on the sides.

In the two-, three-, or four-bay-deep multi-unit mosques with axial central sections, the interior space is divided into three, and this spatial organization is reflected on their exterior form. The spatial integration is not very strong in the Mosque of Çelebi Sultan Mehmed; although the structure follows a uniform, hierarchical progression from the four walls to the peak of the central dome, the combination of the spherical dome and the two types of vaults results in a compartmentation of interior space. The same plan arrangement was developed into a more integrated and rational scheme in the Mosque of Fâtih Paşa in Diyarbakır (Fig. 221) built by Bıyıklı Mehmed Paşa (d. 1521), and found its ultimate expression in geometric and volumetric finesse in the Şehzade Mosque in Istanbul (1543–48).

196

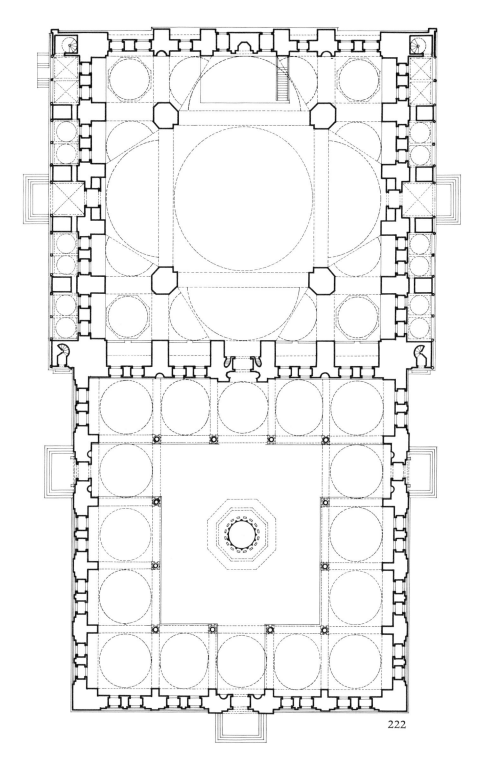

Şehzade Mosque, Istanbul
222 Plan

222

0   5   10   20 m.

223

Şehzade Mosque, Istanbul
223 *Section*
224 *Exterior*

The Şehzade Mosque, which is the first major work of the architect Sinan, like the Bayezid comprises two equal squares as courtyard and prayer hall plus two graceful minarets, which adorn the corners where the two squares overlap (Fig. 222). The prayer hall is crowned by a 19.00 m. dome that rises to a height of 38.00 m. at the center (Fig. 223). Four halfdomes, augmented by two exedrae each, distend the central dome to rest on the outer walls. Smaller domes on the four corners complete the general composition of the upper structure. It must be observed that the piers to which the direct load of the central dome is transmitted through pendentives are treated in the Şehzade Mosque as lightly as possible to allow the space to move around them without visual obstruction. The objective of the sixteenth-century Ottoman architecture was no longer a compartmented, rigid mosque composed of recurrent domed-square units, but a spatially articulated and structurally complex mosque highlighted by a major dome descending through halfdomes, exedrae, and smaller domes (Fig. 224). It reached for a rational architectonic expression which was achieved by the mid-sixteenth century through the genius of Sinan.

198

224

4 Analysis and Conclusion

General view of Edirne

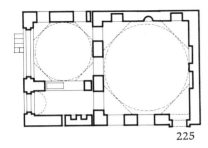

225

After having considered the fourteenth- and fifteenth-century Ottoman mosques in three major groups and discussed the most significant examples of each, I shall now attempt to view the subject from a larger perspective. I have repeatedly drawn attention to the fact that the main architectural theme of early Ottoman architecture is the domed-square—or near square—unit. This basic unit is used in a variety of ways in all three types of mosques. In the single-unit mosque, the prayer hall is defined by only one domed-square unit. In the multi-unit mosque, the domed-square unit is repeated transversally, longitudinally, or both. In the eyvan mosque, it occurs at predetermined locations within an axial or cross-axial scheme. The units are generally of similar dimensions in the multi-unit mosque with the exception that the central unit may be larger than the others. On the other hand, except for the two side units—where they exist—the various units of eyvan mosques are, more often than not, different in size, height, and even structural and decorative details.

As I pointed out in chapter 1, single domed-square mosques existed in Anatolia before the Ottomans. The *mescid* of the Taş Medrese in Akşehir (Figs. 11 and 26), or that of the İnce Minareli Medrese in Konya (1258) may be shown as examples of the single-unit mosques preceding those built by the Ottomans. These two are not independent structures but are attached to larger buildings. But independent single-unit mosques in Anatolia dating from the thirteenth century may also be cited. Among these I shall mention the tiny Mosque of Erdemşah in Konya (1220), the Mosque of Akşebe Sultan inside the Fortress of Alanya, and the Karasi Mosque of Yusuf Sinan in Edremit, Balıkesir. The Mosque of Erdemşah is a small domed-square building without a porch or a minaret. The Mosque of Akşebe Sultan is a brick structure to which a *türbe* was later added adjacent to its eastern wall. There is no porch; but the remains of a large brick minaret stand a few meters to the northwest of the prayer hall (Fig. 225). The Mosque of Yusuf Sinan is as close an example as one can find in the pre-Ottoman era featuring Ottoman architectural traits, so much so that were it not for the inscription on its founder's tombstone which records the date of his death as A.H. 700 (1300), the mosque could very easily be credited to Ottoman architecture (Fig. 226). The composite stone and brick structure (Fig. 227), flat, triangular corner panels decorated with lozenges (Fig. 228), and the three-bay porch supported by Byzantine columns are features not alien to early Ottoman architecture.

The earliest single-unit Ottoman mosques still in existence are the Mosques of Alâeddin Bey in Bursa and Hacı Özbek in İznik, both dating from the first half of the fourteenth century. In terms of the basic domed-square unit, these mosques present us with a simple and unaccentuated spatial expression. But two other fourteenth-century single-unit mosques, the Yeşil Cami in İznik and the Mosque of Orhan Gazi in Bilecik, forecast the direction of development that the Ottoman mosque was to take during the next two centuries.

In the Yeşil Cami, the three-bay vestibule placed between the prayer room and the porch stretches the interior space along the longitudinal axis (Fig. 54). But the main dome so completely dominates the interior that one fails to perceive

226

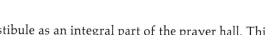

227

Mosque of Akşebe Sultan, Alanya
225 *Plan*

Mosque of Yusuf Sinan, Edremit
226 *Plan*
227 *Exterior*

the vestibule as an integral part of the prayer hall. This intermediary element evolved into a second single-domed unit during the latter part of the fifteenth century in the Mosques of Mahmud Paşa in Istanbul (Fig. 154), Gedik Ahmed Paşa in Afyon (Fig. 156), and Bayezid in Amasya (Fig. 192), in which the longitudinal expansion of interior space is fully realized.

In the Mosque of Orhan Gazi, the extension of internal space occurs in four directions (Fig. 66). But again, owing to the shallowness of the eyvan-like niches, the sense of movement along the axes is not felt. As in the previous mosque, the dome completely dominates the prayer hall. Later, when the axial

Mosque of Yusuf Sinan, Edremit
228 *Interior. Turkish triangles*

Mosque of Orhan Gazi, Bilecik
229a *Plan*

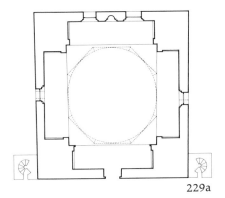

229a

expansions become separate units, Ottoman mosque architecture will reach its architectonic peak.

The cross-axial plan, as I pointed out in chapter 2, was not a scheme that the early Ottomans developed in Anatolia. Having come from the Horasan region, they were familiar with it. On the other hand, the similarity between the Mosque of Orhan Gazi in Bilecik and the centrally planned Greek-cross Byzantine or Armenian churches suggests a possible source of influence. To understand better the basic design concept of the cross-axial Ottoman mosque, I should like to compare the Greek-cross Armenian Church of Mastara (*c* 650)[1] with the Mosque of Orhan Gazi. In both buildings, the central space defined by the dome is expanded on four sides (Fig. 229 *a* and *b*). That this expansion takes a barrel-vaulted rectangular form in one and a halfdomed semicircular form in the other is, in my opinion, of small significance. The important conceptual difference is that expansions in the Mastara church project out from the central domed-cube but that they do not in the Bilecik mosque. In terms of interior space the expression of the extensions are similar. But in terms of exterior form it is not, for, whereas the internal volume of the former is clearly expressed on the

204

outside, the rigid cubic mass of the latter fails to express the spatial richness of the interior. The articulation of form and space of the Mastara church may also be seen in the late Byzantine Church of Panaghia in Heybeliada, Istanbul (first half of the fifteenth century) (Fig. 229 c). Obviously, the architectural quality of both churches is superior to that of the Mosque of Orhan Gazi. In them the cross-axial scheme is fully expressed within and without, from top to bottom, because the substance of this architecture is the exploitation of the Greek-cross form. Although it may seem like an artistic weakness to those not familiar with Islamic architecture, the essential reality of a mosque is its simple, serene, static prayer hall. Even in the most dramatic, pyramidal centrally planned mosques, such as the Şehzade Mosque (Figs. 222, 224) or the other sultans' mosques of the seventeenth and eighteenth centuries, the upper structure composed of a central dome augmented by four halfdomes does not reflect a Greek-cross lower structure but covers a square interior. In other words, the unvariable element in Ottoman mosque architecture is not so much the roof system, which was expressed in a great number of forms throughout six centuries, but the simple square—or rectangular—cube of the lower structure.

The statement that the essence of Ottoman mosque architecture is its cubic lower structure may seem to be contradicted by eyvan mosques, since in these buildings the purity of the cube is destroyed by the protruding eyvans on their southern walls. We observe the same destruction of the cube in the Ottoman *medrese*, where the classroom projects out from the main mass of the building. Thus the focal element in the *medrese* is architecturally emphasized. The most important space—or the prayer area—in eyvan mosques is similarly accentuated. If one is to examine the main eyvans in these mosques, it becomes evident that they are but single-unit mosques. The similarities of scale, lighting, and system of transition, between the Yeşil Cami of İznik and that of Bursa (Fig. 230), for instance, clearly indicate the kinship of the two types of mosques.

This assumption, however, immediately brings the following question to mind: since in eyvan mosques only the main eyvan serves as the mosque, why were the other areas included in the building? To put it differently, why, in early Ottoman architecture, was the *zâviye* combined with the single-unit mosque when the two could easily have been built separately?

The eyvan mosque, up to the second quarter of the fifteenth century, was often built not as an individual building but as the most imposing edifice of a *külliye*, or a complex of buildings. This was especially true of the royal eyvan mosques. During the same period the average diameter of Ottoman domes was 10–12 m. One can readily imagine that a single-unit mosque supporting a 10–12 m. dome is not very imposing even when it is enlarged by the inclusion of a vestibule as in the Yeşil Cami of İznik. This being the case, I propose the following hypothesis: the integration of the single-unit mosque with the *zâviye* was not merely the outcome of a subtle political move to show that the order of traveling dervishes was under the protection of the Ottoman State[2] but was also forced by the aesthetic necessity of making the focal building of a *külliye* the tallest and the most monumental. It could be argued that the Ottomans did

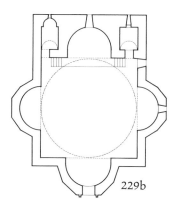

229b

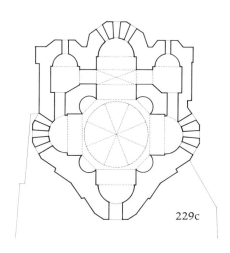

229c

Church of Mastara
229b *Plan (after Khatchatrian)*

Church of Panaghia, Heybeliada, Istanbul
229c *Plan (after Brounov)*

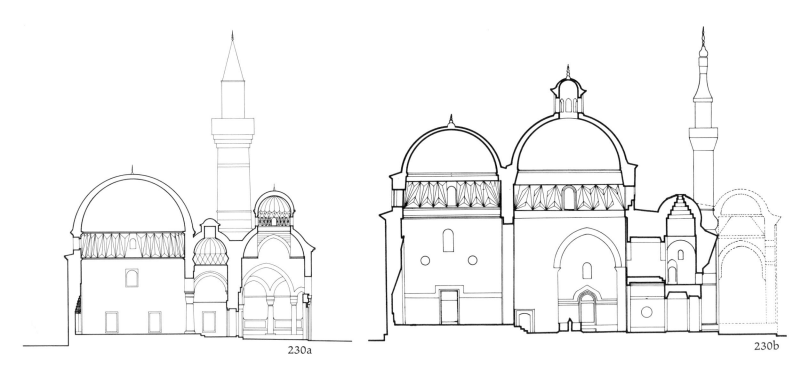

230a

230b

Yeşil Cami, İznik
230a Section

Yeşil Cami, Bursa
230b Section

have the technical knowledge in the fourteenth century to construct domes larger than 10–12 m. in diameter, and the Mosque of Yıldırım Bayezid in Mudurnu with its 19.65 m. dome (Fig. 20) may be cited as a pertinent example. But it must be remembered that a gigantic masonry dome resting on four walls creates structural difficulties and is not architecturally graceful. The great lateral thrust of the Mudurnu mosque necessitated extremely thick and squat walls. Thus its proportions lack balance: the lower structure is too low for the height of the dome (Fig. 22). The fact that such an experiment was never again repeated is proof enough that the Ottomans did not consider it a success. In time the Ottoman architects did develop the technique to erect 20 m. domes and place them on high walls, and they were able to build graceful mosques dominated by large central domes. The development of the dome eliminated the need for eyvan mosques; by the end of the fifteenth century they disappeared from the repertory of the Ottoman architect.

In the eyvan mosque, the single-unit mosque is represented in a new type of composite building directly derived from the traditional enclosed *medrese* of the Anatolian Seljuks. The main eyvan which serves as the classroom in the Seljuk *medrese* is eliminated and replaced by the single-unit mosque. This exchange of the two elements, however, does not take place in a straightforward manner. Whereas the classroom eyvan in the Seljuk *medrese* is arranged within the main square mass of the building,[3] the prayer hall of the Ottoman eyvan mosque projects out from the basic cubic form (Fig. 231). The only explanation that I can find for this innovation is that while the Ottoman architect wanted to create an imposing building as the focal element of his complexes, he nevertheless

206

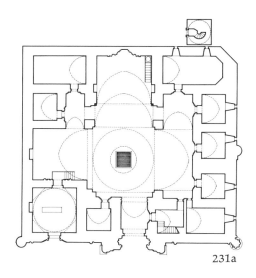

231a

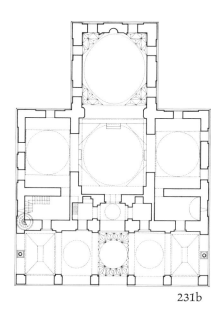

231b

Medrese of Câcâbey, Kırşehir
231a *Plan*

Mosque of Orhan Gazi, Bursa
231b *Plan*

did not wish to destroy the identity of the single-unit mosque. Instead of wrapping the *zâviye* around the mosque, he kept the two separate and retained the formal integrity of the latter both from within and without.

So far as I know, the first experiment of the eyvan mosque is conducted in the Mosque of Sultan Orhan in İznik (Fig. 78). In this mosque, as well as in the Mosque of Orhan Gazi in Bursa (Fig. 104), one observes that the eyvan arch and the rear wall of the mosque fall on the same plane. Both these mosques are modest buildings. The first eyvan mosque of monumental dimensions is that of Murad Hüdavendigâr in Bursa. Located on top of a hill in Çekirge overlooking the plains below, the mosque is further accentuated as an important building by the inclusion of a *medrese* within its mass. This composite mosque-*zâviye*-*medrese* structure is surrounded by an *imâret*, a *türbe*, a primary school, a small, domed building containing public toilets, and a bath (Eski Kaplıca) a little further down the complex.[4] The barrel-vaulted prayer eyvan is projected out of the main structure of the mosque. But, in this case, the convent rooms embrace it on both sides by approximately 4 m. (Fig. 110).

A barrel-vaulted eyvan creates a visual movement in the interior, because the directional vault tends to extend the central space along the axis of the eyvan. Thus the barrel-vaulted eyvans act as parts of the central space. This is the traditional Seljuk concept. The Ottoman ideal based on recurrent domed cubes, on the other hand, gives way to an architectural organization that goes far beyond a mere difference of upper structure. Whether it be a room or an eyvan a domed unit represents unity and completeness. Therefore a domed-square structure, despite its spatial relationship with the central hall, does not represent a continuation of the central space but acts as its satellite.

The crystallization of the eyvan mosque takes place in the Mosque of Yıldırım in Bursa, in which not only is the *medrese* separated from the mosque but also the traditional barrel-vaulted eyvan is replaced by one with a dome. The complex of Yıldırım is composed of a *medrese*, a *hamam*, the *türbe* of Yıldırım Bayezid, the now nonexistent *saray*, *darüşşifa*, *imâret*, and the mosque,[5] which is located on the peak of a hill and clearly stands out as the dominant building of the complex. With one minor deviation, the same is true for the Yeşil *külliye*.[6] Here the *türbe* occupies the paramount position, being situated on higher ground, surmounted by a larger dome, and faced with eye-catching turquoise ceramic tiles. In spite of these, however, the mosque is still the dominant element of the complex because of its two domes and larger size.

The development of the eyvan mosque continued through the 1450's but began to deteriorate during the latter part of the fifteenth century. The first signs of the change become apparent in the Mosque of Murad Paşa in Istanbul. For one thing, unlike typical eyvan mosques in which the dome of the central hall is larger and higher than the dome surmounting the prayer eyvan, in this mosque the domes of the central hall and the eyvan are of equal size and height. For another, the first dome does not and did not have an oculus. But even more important is the number of domes shown on the exterior. In the typical eyvan mosque, regardless of how many side rooms there may be, only the central hall and the eyvans are expressed externally by domes. Although all four of the side rooms are covered by domes in the Yeşil Cami of Bursa, the only domes that show on the roof are the domes of the central hall and the four eyvans (Figs. 131, 132)—or those that define the cross-axial patterns. But in the Murad Paşa both rooms on either side are covered by domes. The side rooms of the typical eyvan mosque rise to the height of the lower structure (Fig. 125). The domed side rooms of the Murad Paşa, however, are reduced in height so that their cornices run at a much lower level than that of the two-domed central unit (Fig. 100). Obviously the diminished height of the side rooms was necessitated by the problem of illumination, since in the absence of an oculus the light of the central hall had to be provided by high windows at the sides. But the lowering of the side rooms accentuates the length of the two-domed central unit, creating the false impression that it is a rectangular room surmounted by two domes rather than two different spaces each covered by a dome.

In fact, the deterioration, or the elimination, of the central hall occurs earlier in the Mosque of Mahmud Paşa, where the central hall becomes a part of the prayer area twice as deep as it is wide. Whereas the first domed space still serves as a central hall in the Mosque of Murad Paşa, the corridor which encircles the prayer hall in the Mosque of Mahmud Paşa completely eliminates the need for one (Fig. 154). And the exclusion of the central hall brings the cycle of the eyvan mosque to an end, since an eyvan can only exist in the context of a central hall on which it must open. It is for this reason that I do not consider the Mosques of Mahmud Paşa, Gedik Ahmed Paşa in Afyon, and Sultan Bayezid in Amasya among the eyvan mosques—although so far they have been classified as "Bursa Type" mosques—but place them in the multi-unit group. It must be remembered, however, that these three mosques do not fall within the development pattern of the multi-unit mosque, but represent stages of transition from the eyvan mosque, which had served its purpose and was no longer favored, to the multi-unit mosque which was still to evolve into the monumental sultans' mosques of the sixteenth century.

The same elongation of the central hall is observed in the Mosque of Gedik Ahmed Paşa in Afyon. Like the Mosque of Murad Paşa, the side rooms are lower than the two-domed central unit (Fig. 157), the first dome does not have an oculus, and the rear section of the prayer hall is illuminated by high windows placed over the side units. The hesitation and irrationality caused by the transition is even more marked in the Gedik Ammed Paşa, which is built with side eyvans. Yet for lack of a central hall, these are not part of the interior space of the mosque but open to the outside (Fig. 156). Nor are the side rooms accessible from the inside. Thus, although the domed side units are structurally integrated into the mosque, they are spatially independent of it.

In the Mosque of Sultan Bayezid in Amasya, the transition from the eyvan to the multi-unit mosque reaches its final stage. Spatially superfluous side wings of the Gedik Ahmed Paşa are integrated in the Sultan Bayezid to the main space, forming an eight-unit interior space (Fig. 192). To my mind the most significant aspect of the Sultan Bayezid is the difference in size of its two major domes. In the traditional eyvan mosque, the first central dome is larger and higher than the second. But in the Sultan Bayezid we observe the reverse, the larger dome being the one in front of the *mihrab*. Similarly, in the typical eyvan mosque it is the central hall, or the first domed space, which is full of light pouring in from the oculus. The light in the central hall increases the feeling of tranquillity in the eyvans and also makes them satellites of the central unit. In the Sultan Bayezid, the well-lit unit is the second domed central space, illuminated by a great many windows (Figs. 194, 195), creating a visual movement from the dim first domed space to the light second domed space. To put it differently, whereas the typical eyvan mosque has a centralized and compartmented organization, the interior of the Mosque of Sultan Bayezid is endowed with a dynamic space that moves toward the *mihrab* and attracts the eye to it.

A second important innovation worthy of comment is that in the Mosque of Sultan Bayezid the side wings push forward and the southernmost units open into the second central unit. In the eyvan mosques, regardless of how many side rooms there may be, they all open into the first central unit, or the central hall, and are never accessible from the second central unit, or the prayer area. Thus the integrity of the latter is always retained. In the Sultan Bayezid there is no longer any reason to preserve the integrity of the second central unit, since both the central units and the side wings have the same function and what needs to be expressed is not compartmentation but the unity of space.

In short, what the plan of the Mosque of Sultan Bayezid in Amasya reminds one of is not so much that of the Mosque of Yıldırım in Bursa, but that of the Mosque of Atik Ali Paşa in Istanbul. In the Amasya mosque the central section of the interior is surmounted by two domes; in the Atik Ali Paşa by one and a half domes (Fig. 212). As in the former mosque, the halfdomed southern portion of the central section protrudes from the rectangular mass, creating a superficial kinship between this mosque and the eyvan mosque. The Mosque of Atik Ali Paşa, however, does not play a part in the evolution of the eyvan type but of the multi-unit mosque with the large central dome. In other words, it represents a link between the two-bay-deep multi-unit mosque, such as the Güzelce Hasan Bey in Hayrabolu (Fig. 203) and the four-bay-deep multi-unit Mosque of Bayezid in Istanbul (Fig. 218).

To understand better the design concept of the multi-unit mosques with large central domes, one must begin with the simplest *ulucami* composed of similar units. The Ulucami of Bursa is five bays wide and four bays deep (Fig. 163). The Eski Cami of Edirne is three bays wide and three bays deep (Fig. 167). In other words, the first is composed of twenty units and the second of nine units. The Mosque of Güzelce Hasan Bey, on the other hand, is two bays deep and three bays wide, containing five units. It must be observed that the central unit of the Güzelce Hasan Bey covers an area four times that of the side units. Thus, in basic geometric terms, it could be considered an eight-unit mosque whose four central units are integrated under one large dome. If the central dome covers four units, then the halfdome covers two units. When we look at the problem in this light, the Mosque of Atik Ali Paşa becomes a ten-unit mosque

232a

whose six central units are integrated under the large central dome enhanced by a halfdome on the south. Similarly, the old Mosque of Fâtih in Istanbul (Fig. 216) was a twelve-unit mosque with three units on each side and a large section covered by one and a half domes at the center.

According to this arrangement, both the Mosque of Güzelce Hasan Bey and the Mosque of Fâtih are four bays wide, but the former is two and the latter is three bays deep. The next step in the evolution of the multi-unit mosque came during the first decade of the sixteenth century, in the Mosque of Bayezid in Istanbul (Fig. 218). In this monumental mosque the central section is covered by an upper structure consisting of a dome and two halfdomes, which reminds one of the upper structure of Hagia Sophia. It stands to reason that the Ottoman architects did learn the use of the halfdome from Byzantine architecture and that the upper structure of the Mosque of Bayezid was possibly inspired by that of Hagia Sophia. It would be unrealistic, however, to assume that this mosque is a variation on the Hagia Sophia theme in its architectural totality, because, although both are centrally planned buildings, one is a basilica and the other is not: one is composed of two shells—a high rectangular nave placed within a low square structure—and the other comprises only a square prayer hall.

In Hagia Sophia the main central space defined by the dome and the two halfdomes is an entity in itself. It is deliberately restrained from expanding laterally by columnar screens that mark the outline of the inner shell. The colonnades on either side running from one pier to the other and along the periphery of the exedrae follow the inner surface of the piers, "effectively screening their thickness and substance,"[7] giving the interior a baroque feeling of lightness, and spatially separating the nave from the aisles and the galleries (Fig. 232a). To put it simply, in Hagia Sophia, piers and columns serve to create an axial space. The structural elements are employed in the creation of a basilica form within a square mass.

Unlike those of Hagia Sophia, the massive piers that carry the central dome in the Mosque of Bayezid are exposed. There are no colonnades to form visual barriers, for the basic idea is to create a unity of space (Fig. 232b). And in this respect, one can say that there is a kinship between the simple single-unit mosques of Iznik and Bursa and the Mosque of Bayezid in Istanbul. The major difference is the scale. As the Ottoman Empire grew in power and stature, so did the works of architecture. The units increased in size but the essence of the *ulucami* remained the same. For in basic terms, the Mosque of Bayezid in Istanbul is nothing but a sixteen-unit *ulucami* whose central section is covered by a large dome extended on the longitudinal axis by two halfdomes.

The Ottoman ideal is perhaps best expressed in the Mosque of Şehzade, which I consider the zenith of the evolutionary pattern of the Ottoman multi-unit mosque. Four halfdomes, augmented by two exedrae each, distend the central dome to rest on the outer walls, and smaller domes on the four corners complete the square upper structure (Fig. 222). In other words, the Mosque of Şehzade is also essentially a sixteen-unit *ulucami* in which the quadrifoil central roof formation surmounts twelve of the units.

Hagia Sophia, Istanbul
232a *Interior*

Mosque of Bayezid, Istanbul
232b Interior

232b

232c

Mosque of Şehzade, Istanbul
232c Interior

To sum up: the basic unit of the early Ottoman architecture is the domed-square structure. This basic unit is used by itself or in recurrent successive rows. The domed-square units of the fourteenth century are generally of modest size. As the technical knowledge of Ottoman architects increased and the function of the halfdome as a structural and spatial element was realized, the evolution of the Ottoman mosque took a more subtle and sophisticated path (Fig. 233). The objective was not to discover the ideal upper structure, but to create the largest single uninterrupted space disturbed by as few vertical structural elements inside the main prayer hall as possible. In other words, the common denominator in early Ottoman mosques is not the form of the interior, such as the Greek-cross or the Latin-cross form of a church, but the nondirectional containment of the inner space by four walls. And despite the many influences throughout its evolution this characteristic feature of the Ottoman mosque architecture remains unchanged.

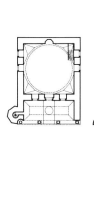

a

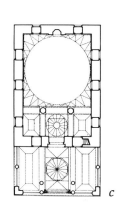

b

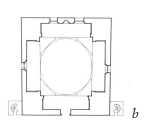

c

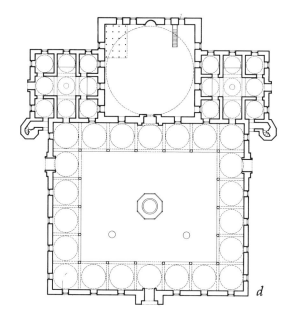

d

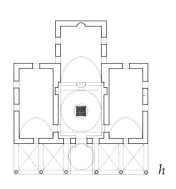

h

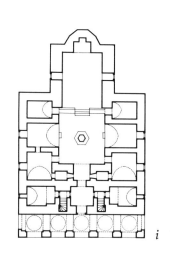

i

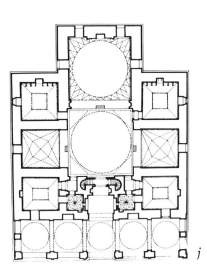

j

214

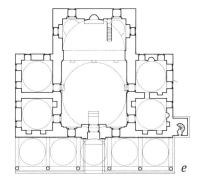
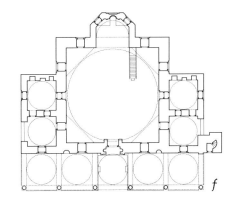
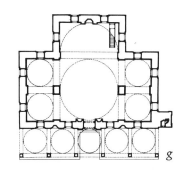

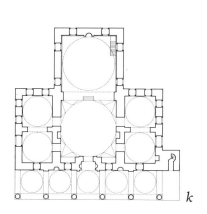
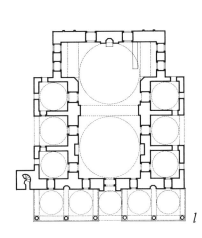
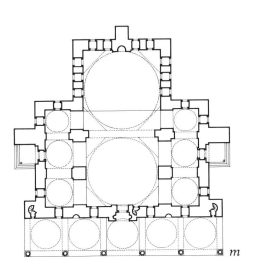

Evolutionary pattern of the early Ottoman mosque
233 *Plans.* a *Mosque of Alâeddin Bey, Bursa*
        b *Mosque of Orhan Gazi, Bilecik*
        c *Yeşil Cami, Iznik*
        d *Mosque of Sultan Bayezid, Edirne*
        e *Mosque of Rum Mehmed Paşa, Istanbul*
        f *Mosque of Davud Paşa, Istanbul*
        g *Mosque of Atik Ali Paşa, Istanbul*

        h *Mosque of Sultan Orhan, İznik*
        i *Mosque of Hüdavendigâr, Bursa*
        j *Mosque of Yıldırım, Bursa*
        k *Mosque of Murad Paşa, Istanbul*
        l *Mosque of Gedik Ahmed Paşa, Afyon*
       m *Mosque of Sultan Bayezid, Amasya*

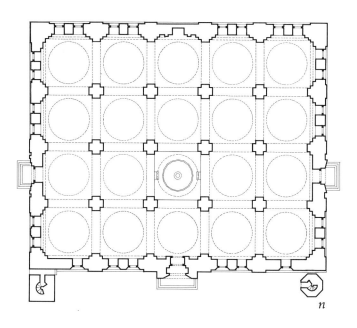

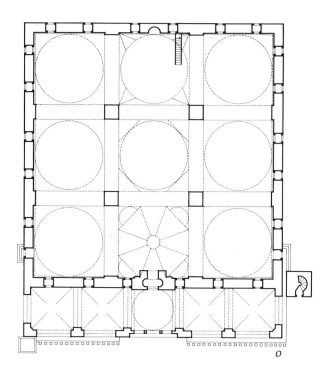

n Ulucami, Bursa
o Eski Cami, Edirne
p Mosque of Güzelce Hasan Bey, Hayrabolu
q Mosque of Fâtih, Istanbul

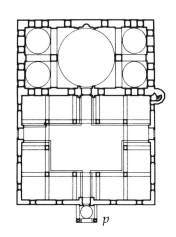

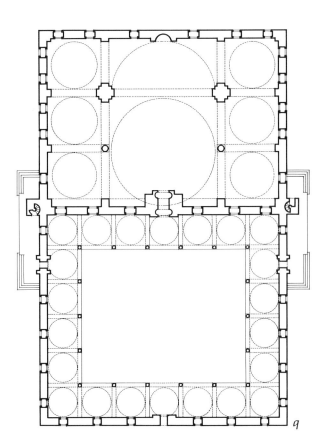

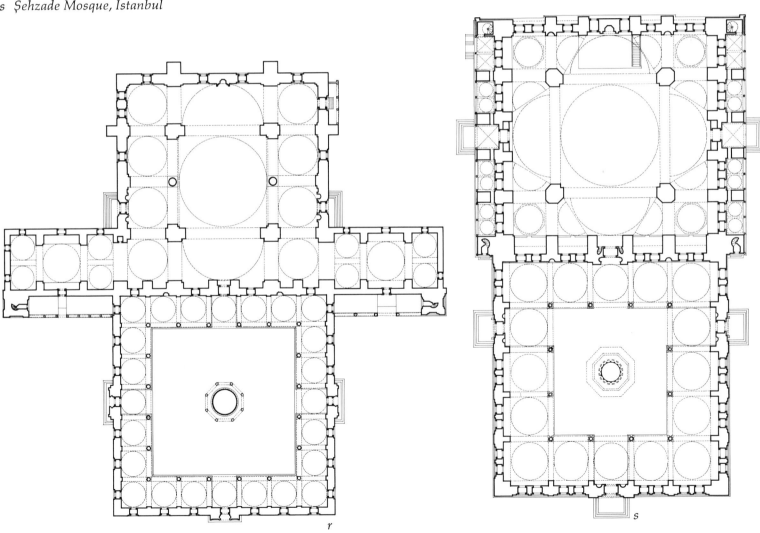

r *Mosque of Bayezid, Istanbul*
s *Şehzade Mosque, Istanbul*

r

s

Notes

1   Ismail Hakkı Uşaklıgil, "Gazi Orhan Bey'in Hükümdar Olduğu Tarih ve İlk Sikkesi," *Belleten* (Ankara), No. 34, p. 207.

2   Albert Gabriel, *Une capitale turque: Brousse*, p. 66, Fig. 26.

3   *Constantinople Ancient and Modern*, p. 174.

4   *Narrative of Travels in Europe, Asia, and Africa in the Seventeenth Century, by Evliya Efendi*, trans. Joseph von Hammer (London, 1834), p. 80.

1   In the town of Söğüt there is a tiny single-unit mosque called the Mosque of Ertuğrul Gazi. Although in form it looks like an early Ottoman building and is located near the tomb of Ertuğrul Gazi, it dates from the nineteenth century. It is possible, of course, that there was a mosque on that location built by Ertuğrul Gazi which later collapsed and was rebuilt in the nineteenth century on the foundations of the original structure. Unfortuately, there are no records to confirm this contention.

2   Ayverdi thinks that the mosque may have been built before 1335. He quotes religious foundation records according to which the mosque was in existence in 1332 (A.H. 733) and points to other sources that set the date of the building as 1326 (A.H. 726), the year Bursa was taken by the Ottoman Turks. (Ekrem Hakkı Ayverdi, "Orhan Gazi Devrinde Mi'mari," *Yıllık Araştırmalar Dergisi*, No. 1: 124). Certainly, if this mosque was built by, and not for, Alâeddin Bey, it must have been erected between 1326, the year the Ottoman Turks captured Bursa, and 1331, when Alâeddin Bey died.

3   *Ibid.*, p. 167; Sedat Çetintaş *Türk Mimari Anıtları—Bursa'da İlk Eserler*, Pl. 15; H. Kemâli Söylemezoğlu, *İslâm Dini, İlk Camiler ve Osmanlı Camileri*, p. 87, Pl. 53; Albert Gabriel, *Une capitale turque: Brousse*, p. 50, Pl. 18; Ali Kızıltan, *Anadolu Beyliklerinde Cami ve Mescitler*, Pl. 60.

4   Ayverdi, "Orhan Gazi Devrinde Mi'mari," p. 125.

5   For the text of the inscription, see Katharina Otto-Dorn, *Das islamische Iznik*, p. 17.

6   Ayverdi, "Orhan Gazi Devrinde Mi'mari," p. 119.

7   Gabriel, *Une capitale turque*, p. 50.

8   *Ibid.*, p. 148.

9   *Ibid.*

10 For example, Hagia Sophia in İznik; and Hagia Sophia, SS. Sergius and Bacchus (Küçük Aya Sofya), St. John of Studion (İmrahor Camii), St. Savior in Chora (Kariye), St. Theodosia (Gül Camii), the Virgin Pammakaristos (Fethiye Camii), all in Istanbul.

11 For the text of the inscription, see Ekrem Ayverdi, "Mudurnu'da Yıldırım Bayezid Manzûmesi ve Taş Vakfiyesi," *Vakıflar Dergisi*, 5: 79–86.

12 Domes over 10.00 m. in diameter were not often built in the fourteenth century. Apart from the three mentioned so far, the most notable example is the dome of the Green Mosque in İznik (1378–92).

13 Ayverdi, "Mudurnu'da Yıldırım Bayezid Manzûmesi ve Taş Vakfiyesi," p. 82.

14 *Ibid*, pp. 82–83.

15 For the Arabic and Turkish text of the inscription, see Tahsin Öz, *Istanbul Camileri*, 1: 61.

16 For the text of the inscription, see Ekrem Hakkı Ayverdi, *Fâtih Devri Mimarisi*, p. 241, Pls. 196, 197.

17 Gabriel, *Une capitale turque*, p. 143.

18 Ayverdi, *Fâtih Devri Mimarisi*, p. 237. I disagree with Ayverdi, who contends that the existing minaret is the original.

19 Ali Saim Ülgen, "İnegöl'ün Kurşunlu Abideleri," *Türk San'atı Tarihi Araştırma ve İncelemeleri*, 1: 198.

20 The subject of the combined mosque-convent will be discussed at length in chapter 2.

21 Albert Gabriel, *Monuments turcs d'Anatolie*, 2: 90–91.

22 Semavi Eyice, "İlk Osmanlı Devrinin Dinî—İçtimaî bir Müessesesi: Zâviyeler ve Zâviyeli-Camiler," *Istanbul Üniversitesi İktisat Fakültesi Mecmuası*, 23: 46, Pl. 47.

23 *Ibid.*, p. 44, Pl. 40.

24 Ayverdi, *Fâtih Devri Mimarisi*, pp. 114–19.

25 İsmail Hakkı (Uzunçarşılı), *Kitâbeler*, p. 127.

26 Gabriel, *Une capitale turque*, p. 137; Ayverdi, *Fâtih Devri Mimarisi*, p. 225.

27 Ayverdi, *Fâtih Devri Mimarisi*, p. 225.

28 This mosque has a twin in Istanbul: the Mosque of Sultan Selim, dedicated in 1522.

29 In the Mosque of Mahmud Çelebi in İznik (1442, A.H. 846), which closely resembles the Yeşil Cami, the porch is also deeper than is customary. It is half as deep as the length of the prayer room. But the Mahmud Çelebi has no vestibule and thus is a typical single-unit mosque.

30 Ayverdi, "Orhan Gazi Devrinde Mi'mârî," pp. 140–41.

31 *Ibid.*, p. 143.

32 *Ibid.*, p. 185, Pl. 44.

33 *Ibid.*, p. 143.

Chapter 2
The Eyvan Mosque

1 Semavi Eyice, "İlk Osmanlı Devrinin Dinî—İçtimaî bir Müessesesi: Zâviyeler ve Zâviyeli-Camiler," *Istanbul Üniversitesi İktisat Fakültesi Mecmuası*, 23: 1–80.

2 Oktay Aslanapa, "İznik'te Sultan Orhan İmaret Camii Kazısı," *Sanat Tariki Araştırmaları*, 1: 16–38.

3 Aptullah Kuran, *İlk Devir Osmanlı Mimarisinde Cami*.

4 K. A. C. Creswell, *The Muslim Architecture of Egypt*, p. 105.

5 Adnan Sayılı, "Higher Education in Medieval Islam," *Ankara Üniversitesi Yıllığı*, 2: 55.

6 *The Art of Iran*, pp. 287–91.

7 Creswell, *Muslim Architecture*, p. 133.

8 *Ibid.*, p. 128.

9 M. van Berchem, *Corpus Inscriptionum Arabicarum: Egypte*, 1: 265–66.

10 Creswell, *Muslim Architecture*, p. 120.

11 For the Çifte Medrese's plan and photographs, see Albert Gabriel, *Monuments turcs d'Anatolie*, Vol. 1, Fig. 36, Pls. XVII (1, 2), XVIII (1). The building has since been restored.

12 Creswell, *Muslim Architecture*, p. 132.

13 *Ibid.*, p. 129.

14 André Godard, "Origine de la madrasa, de la mosquée et du caravansérail à quatre iwans," *Ars Islamica*, 15–16: 1–9.

15 The Medrese of Lala Şahin Paşa in Bursa (fourteenth century) and the Medrese of Murad Hüdavendigâr (1366–85). The latter is built at the second level of an eyvan mosque.

16 I am indebted to Professor Katharina Otto-Dorn for suggesting this new term.

17 For a résumé of the various hypotheses on this subject, see Eyice, "Zâviyeler ve Zâviyeli-Camiler," pp. 11–14.

18 *Ibid.*, pp. 25–29.

19 Aslanapa, "İznik'te Sultan Orhan İmaret Camii Kazısı," p. 25.

20   *Ibid.*, pp. 23–25.

21   *Ibid.*, p. 23.

22   *Ibid.*, p. 25.

23   Albert Gabriel, *Une capitale turque: Brousse*, p. 139.

24   *Ibid.*, p. 139.

25   *Ibid.*, p. 159.

26   Kâzım Baykal, *Bursa ve Anıtları*, pp. 129, 198.

27   Gabriel, *Une capitale turque: Brousse*, pp. 140–41.

28   For the text of this inscription, see Gabriel, *Monuments turcs d'Anatolie*, 2: 129.

29   *Ibid.*, pp. 29–30.

30   *Ibid.*, p. 33.

31   The foundation charter of Yahşi Bey is dated 1441 (A.H. 845); therefore, it may be assumed that the mosque was erected during the same year or earlier. Yetkin and Eyice accept 1441 as the construction date: Suut Kemal Yetkin, *İslâm Mimârisi*, p. 390; Eyice "Zâviyeler ve Zâviyeli-Camiler," p. 40. Riefstahl gives it as A.H. 735 (1334); Rudolph M. Riefstahl, *Turkish Architecture in Southwestern Anatolia*, p. 33.

32   Ayverdi, *Fâtih Devri Mimarisi*, p. 270.

33   *Ibid.*, p. 221.

34   Gabriel, *Une capitale turque*, p. 46.

35   *Ibid.*, p. 59.

36   Dr. Osman Rıfat, *Edirne Rehnûması*, 1920, p. 35.

37   Cornelius Gurlitt, "Die Bauten Adrianoples," *Orientalisches Archiv*, 1 (Leipzig, 1910–11): 4.

38   *Ibid.*

39   *Ibid.*

40   Oktay Aslanapa, *Edirne'de Osmanlı Devri Âbideleri*, p. 2; Rıfkı Melûl Meriç, "Edirne'nin Tarihî ve Mimarî Eserleri Hakkında," *Türk San'atı Araştırma ve İncelemeleri*, 1: 445; Eyice does not give a date but states that it was probably built by Bayezid I toward the end of the fourteenth century ("Zâviyeler ve Zâviyeli-Camiler," p. 35).

41   Gabriel, *Une capitale turque*, p. 72.

42   Çetintaş contends that it was inaugurated in 1394 (A.H. 797) (Sedat Çetintaş, *Türk Mimarî Anıtları*, 2: 22–23).

43   Some sources note that the construction was halted because of Tamerlane's Anatolian campaign and was later resumed and completed by Bayezid's son Musa Çelebi: Hans Wilde, *Brussa*, p. 20; Diez, *Türk Sanatı*, p. 127; Ali Saim Ülgen, "Bursa Anıtları," *Bursa*, p. 18.

44   For example, the Bedesten (actually a caravanserai) in Alanya (first half of the thirteenth century) and the Mescid of Taş Medrese at Akşehir (1250).

45   Ülgen, "Bursa Anıtları," p. 20.

46   Aslanapa, *Edirne'de Osmanlı Devri Âbideleri*, p. 83.

47   Eyice, "Zâviyeler ve Zâviyeli-Camiler," p. 40.

48   Gabriel, *Une capitale turque*, p. 141.

49   Ayverdi, *Fâtih Devri Mimarisi*, p. 228.

50   *Ibid.*, p. 262.

51   Ali Saim Ülgen, "İnegöl'de İshak Paşa Mimari Manzumesi," *Vakıflar Dergisi*, 4: 191*b*.

52   Gabriel, *Une capitale turque*, p. 108, Fig. 49.

53   Wilde, *Brussa*, pp. 11–12.

54   Albert Gabriel, "Bursa'da Murad I Cami ve Osmanlı Mimarisinin Menşei Meselesi," *Vakıflar Dergisi*, 2: 37.

55   Eyice, Zâviyeler ve Zâviyeli-Camiler," pp. 37–38.

56   Çetintaş, *Türk Mimarî Anıtları*, 1: 18–19.

| 57 | Ayverdi, "Orhan Gazi Devrinde Mi'mârî," pp. 127–31. |
| 58 | Çetintaş, *Türk Mimarî Anıtları*, 1: 20. |

Chapter **3**
The Multi-Unit Mosque

1	Albert Gabriel, *Une capitale turque: Brousse*, p. 146.
2	Ekrem Hakkı Ayverdi, *Fâtih Devri Mimarisi*, p. 179.
3	*Ibid.*, p. 180.
4	Gabriel believes the mosque to be an eleventh-century structure (*Monuments turcs d'Anatolie*, 2: 145–46); Diez shares this point of view: "It is possible that [the mosque] remains from the eleventh-century Danismend era" (Ernst Diez, *Türk Sanatı*, trans. Oktay Aslanapa, p. 64); Erdmann contends that it was built toward the end of the twelfth century (Kurt Erdmann, "Die Sonderstellung der anatolischen Moschee des XII Jhts.," *First International Congress of Turkish Arts* [Ankara, October 19–24, 1959]: *Communications Presented to the Congress* [Ankara, 1961], pp. 94–101).
5	Kâzım Baykal, *Bursa'da Ulu Cami*, p. 21.
6	Gabriel, *Une capitale turque*, p. 31.
7	Gabriel, with obvious error, notes that the inscription plate is on the northeast minaret and consequently cites this minaret as first built.
8	Gabriel, *Une capitale turque*, p. 34.
9	Oktay Aslanapa, *Edirn'de Osmanlı Devri Âbideleri*, pp. 10–11.
10	Cornelius Gurlitt, "Die Bauten Adrianoples," *Orientalisches Archiv*, 1 (Leipzig, 1910–11): 3.
11	H. Kemâli Söylemezoğlu, *İslâm Dini, İlk Camiler ve Osmanlı* Camileri, p. 74.
12	*Ibid.*, p. 72.
13	Gabriel, *Une capitale turc*, p. 134.
14	*Ibid.*, pp. 45–46.
15	Baykal, *Bursa ve Anıtları*, p. 55.
16	Robert Anhegger, "Beitrage zur frühosmanischen Baugeschichte," *Istanbuler Mitteilungen*, 6 (1955): 4–5.
17	Sedat Hakkı Eldem, "Bursa'da Şahadet Camii Konusunda bir Araştırma," *Türk San'atı Tarihi Araştırma ve İncelemeleri*, 1: 313–26.
18	Gabriel, *Une capitale turque*, p. 45. For a comprehensive account of the Mosque of Orhan, which was probably a converted Byzantine church, see Semavi Eyice, "Bursa'da Osman ve Orhan Gazi Türbeleri," *Vakıflar Dergisi*, 5 (1962): 131–47.
19	Baykal, *Bursa ve Anıtları*, pp. 55 and 174.
20	Eldem, "Bursa'da Şahadet Camii Konusunda bir Araştırma," p. 135.
21	Gabriel, *Monuments turcs d'Anatolie*, 2: 45.
22	The one-line inscription above the door is not original but was later painted on.
23	Gabriel, *Monuments turcs d'Anatolie*, 2: 45.
24	*Ibid.*, p. 38.
25	Riefstahl draws attention to the similarity between the triangular vaulted areas in the Ulucami of Manisa and the Üç Şerefeli Cami and finds both solutions unsatisfactory (Rudolf M. Riefstahl, *Turkish Architecture in Southwestern Anatolia*, pp. 8–9).
26	Doğan Kuban, *Osmanlı Dını Mimarisinde İç Mekân Teşekkülü*, p. 19.
27	Semavi Eyice, "Atik Ali Paşa Camiinin Türk Mimârî Tarihindeki Yeri," *Tarih Dergisi*, 14: 110.
28	Tahsin Öz, *Istanbul Camileri*, p. 19.
29	Ayverdi, *Fâtih Devri Mimarisi*, p. 106.
30	The Mosque of Şeyh Vefa (d. 1491) was built during the second half of the fifteenth century. It was destroyed by fire in 1909 and nothing remains of it today except the measured drawings made by Cornelius Gurlitt in 1907.
31	Ayverdi, *Fâtih Devri Mimarisi*, p. 106, Pl. 23.
32	*The Six Voyages of John Baptista Tavernier*, trans. J. Phillips (London, 1678), pp. 72–73.

33   Robert L. Van Nice, who has studied Hagia Sophia in great detail, states that the shells of the halfdomes in Hagia Sophia are no thicker than that of the main dome and that the halfdomes were used not as "functional elements, but purely to enhance the nave's spatial effect" ("The Structure of St. Sophia," *Architectural Forum*, May, 1963, pp. 131–38, 210). No study has as yet been made to ascertain whether the halfdomes in Ottoman architecture were used as structural elements or space definers or both. Until such a survey is conducted, it would be difficult—if not impossible—to comment on this point with accuracy or certainty.

34   A restitution plan of the old Mosque of Fâtih inspired by written descriptions and pictorial presentation of the mosque in sixteenth- and seventeenth-century documents and engravings was first published by Mehmed Ağaoğlu ("The Fâtih Mosque at Constantinople," *Art Bulletin*, Vol. 12.

35   Rıfkı Melûl Meriç, "Bayezid Camii Mimarı," *Yıllık Araştırmalar Dergisi*, 2: 5–67.

36   A Seljuk building restored and Ottomanized by Alâüddevle in 1497–1515.

Chapter 4
Analysis and Conclusion

1   I know of this church through Josef Stryzygowski's book *Origin of Christian Church Art*. The plan is taken from *L'architecture arménienne* of A. Khatchatrian. The reason I prefer this church to others located within the borders of Turkey, such as the Church of the Apostles in Kars (tenth century) which I have seen, studied, and measured, is because its simplicity of massing permits an easier comparison with the Ottoman mosque.

2   Semavi Eyice, "Zâviyeler ve Zâviyeli-Camiler," *Istanbul Üniversitesi İktisat Fakültesi Mecmuası*, Vol. 23.

3   The only exception that I know of is the Tekke (Monastery) at Seyid Gazi near Eskişehir (early thirteenth century), where the main eyvan protrudes from the mass of the rectangular structure. This building, however, was converted from a Byzantine nunnery and therefore cannot be considered representative of indigenous Seljuk architecture.

4   For the site plan, see Albert Gabriel, *Une capitale turque: Brousse*, p. 61.

5   For the site plan, see *ibid.*, p. 66.

6   For the site plan, see *ibid.*, p. 80.

7   William MacDonald, "Design and Technology in Hagia Sophia," *Perspecta*, 4: 23.

Glossary

Arasta	Rows of shops on both sides of a street, sometimes covered by vaults
Bedesten	Large hall for sale of valuable goods
Bimârhane	Hospital
Cami	Mosque equipped with a minber
Çeşme	Fountain
Darüşşifa	Hospital
Dar-ül hadis	Theological school for the study of the religious tradition of the Prophet
Eyvan (iwan)	Vaulted or domed space recessed from a central hall or open court
Hamam	Bath, public or private
Han	Inn
Harem	Inner court, prayer hall
Hünkâr mahfili	Sultan's pew in a mosque, generally elevated and placed to the east of the *mihrab* in sixteenth-century Ottoman mosques
İmâret	Kitchen for the distribution of food to the poor
Kaplıca	Thermal spring
Kıble	Direction to which a Moslem turns when praying (i.e., Mecca)
Külliye	Complex of buildings
Maksure	Protective partition surrounding the *mihrab* and *minber*
Medrese	School for higher learning
Mescid	Small mosque generally, a neighborhood mosque or one attached to another type of building such as a *medrese*
Mihrab	Niche in the *kıble* wall of a mosque, indicating the direction of Mecca
Minare	Minaret
Minber	Pulpit
Mukarnas	Stalactite vault or surface
Mükebbire	Small balcony overlooking the porch in monumental mosques
Revak	Arcade surrounding a court
Saray	Palace
Son cemaat yeri	Porch
Şadırvan	Fountain with pool for ablutions
Şerefe	Balcony of a minaret
Şifahane	Hospital
Tabhane	Hospice
Tekke	Monastery
Türbe	Mausoleum, building over a tomb
Ulucami	Great mosque. *Ulucamis* are built at the center of towns much like a cathedral and serve as the main mosque for Friday prayers
Zâviye	Convent for the Islamic clergy

◆

Chronological List of Early Ottoman Mosques*

Date†			Name	Place	Type	Comments
13th–14th centuries			Mosque of Ertuğrul Gazi	Söğüt, Bilecik	Single-unit	Completely rebuilt
1333	*734*		Mosque of Hacı Özbek	İznik, Bursa	Single-unit	Only foundation exists
1334	*735*		Mosque of Sultan Orhan	İznik, Bursa	Eyvan (axial)	
1335	*736*		Mosque of Alâeddin Bey	Bursa	Single-unit	
1339 (begun)	*740*		Mosque of Orhan Gazi	Bursa	Eyvan (cross-axial)	
First half of 14th century		{	Mosque of Orhan Gazi	Gebze, Istanbul	Single-unit	
			Mosque of Orhan Gazi	Bilecik	Single-unit	
			Mosque of Orhan	Bilecik	Eyvan (axial)	Partially destroyed
			Mosque of Süleyman Paşa	Geyve, Sakarya	Single-unit	
			Mosque of Süleyman Paşa	Göynük, Bolu	Single-unit	Completely rebuilt
			Mosque of Akçakoca	İzmit	Single-unit	
			Mosque of Orhan	İzmit	Single-unit	Completely rebuilt
			Mosque of Orhan	Yarhisar, Bilecik	Single-unit	
			Mosque of Orhan	Yenişehir, Bursa	Single-unit	Completely rebuilt
		{	Geyikli Baba Mosque	Baba Sultan, İnegöl	Single-unit	
1365 (?)			Şehadet Mosque	Bursa	Multi-unit	Partially rebuilt
1365 (begun)	*767*		Mosque of Hüdavendigâr	Bursa	Eyvan (cross-axial)	
1366	*767*		Mosque of Hüdavendigâr	Tuzla	Single-unit	
1374	*776*		Mosque of Hoca Yadigâr	İnönü, Bilecik	Single-unit	
1378 (begun)	*780*		Yeşil Cami	İznik, Bursa	Single-unit	
1382	*784*		Mosque of Asılhan Bey	Kemaller, Çanakkale	Single-unit	
1382	*784*		Mosque of Yıldırım Bayezid	Mudurnu, Bolu	Single-unit	
1390	*793*		Mosque of Yıldırım Bayezid	Alaşehir, Manisa	Multi-unit (5-dome)	
1390 (begun)	*793*		Mosque of Yıldırım	Bursa	Eyvan (cross-axial)	
1393	*796*		Mosque of Ali Paşa	Bursa	Eyvan (axial)	
1396 (begun)	*799*		Ulucami	Bursa	Multi-unit	
1398	*801*		Mosque of Yıldırım	Bergama, İzmir	Multi-unit	
1399	*802*		Saraçhane Mosque	Amasya	Multi-unit	Second unit is a later addition

* The author does not claim that this is a complete inventory. It is simply a first attempt to compile a list of the better-known existing (completely or partially) Ottoman mosques of the fourteenth and fifteenth centuries.

† Dates in italics are A.H.

Date		Name	Place	Type	Comments
		Mosque of Yıldırım	Balıkesir	Multi-unit	Completely rebuilt
		Mosque of Hüdavendigâr	Behramkale, Çanakkale	Single-unit	
		Ulucami	Bolu	Multi-unit	Completely rebuilt
		Mosque of Ebu İshak	Bursa	Eyvan (axial)	Partially destroyed
		Mosque of Timurtaş	Bursa	Eyvan (axial)	Partially destroyed
		Mosque of Hüdavendigâr	Edirne	Eyvan (cross-axial)	
		Mosque of Sarı Hoca	Kırkağaç, Manisa	Single-unit	
Second half of 14th century		Yukarı Cami	Kurşunlu, Bursa	Single-unit	
		Mosque of Umur Bey	Umurbey, Çanakkale	Single-unit	Only foundation exists
		Hızırlık Mosque	Bursa	Single-unit	
		Mosque of Koca Nâib	Bursa	Single-unit	
		Mosque of Somuncu Baba	Bursa	Single-unit	
		Mosque of Demirtaş Paşa	Kütahya	Multi-unit	
		Mosque of Firuz Bey	Milâs	Eyvan (axial)	
		Mosque of Has Hoca	Akhisar, Manisa	Single-unit	Reconstructed
		Mosque of Gülruh Sultan	Akhisar, Manisa	Single-unit	
		Mosque of Ali Paşa	Bursa	Eyvan (axial)	Partially destroyed
		Mosque of Aynalı	Bursa	Single-unit	
1402 (begun)	805	Eski Cami	Edirne	Multi-unit	
1406	809	Mosque of Güzelce Hasan Bey	Hayrabolu, Tekirdağ	Multi-unit	
1412 (begun)	815	Yeşil Cami	Bursa	Eyvan (cross-axial)	
1413	816	Mosque of Çilehan	Amasya	H. A.	
1418	821	Mosque of Ali Bey	Manisa	Single-unit	
1419	822	Mosque of Bayezid Paşa	Amasya	Eyvan (axial)	
1421	825	Mosque of Ali Bey	Manisa	H. A.	
1421	825	Mosque of Çelebi Sultan Mehmed	Dimetoka, Greece	Multi-unit	
1421	825	Mosque of Gazi Mihal	Edirne	Eyvan (axial)	
1424 (begun)	828	Mosque of Murad II	Bursa	Eyvan (cross-axial)	
1426	830	Mosque of Kuşçu Doğan	Edirne	Single-unit	
1427	831	Mosque of Karacabey	Ankara	Eyvan (axial)	
1428	832	Beylerbeyi Mosque	Edirne	Eyvan (axial)	
1428	832	Mosque of Şahmelek Paşa	Edirne	Single-unit	
1428	832	Mosque of Yörgüç Paşa	Amasya	Eyvan (axial)	
1434	838	Dar-ül Hadis	Edirne	Single-unit	
1434	838	Mosque of Sarıca Paşa	Edirne	Single-unit	
1435	839	Muradiye Mosque	Edirne	Eyvan (axial)	
1436	840	Mosque of Hacı Şahabeddin Paşa	Edirne	Single-unit	
1437 (begun)	841	Üç Şerefeli Cami	Edirne	Multi-unit	
1440 (?)		Mosque of İsmail Ağa	Edirne	Single-unit	
1440	844	Mosque of Yanıçoğlu	Bursa	Single-unit	
1440 (?)		İmaret Camii	Plovdiv, Bulgaria	Eyvan (axial)	
1441	845	Mosque of Yahşi Bey	Tire, İzmir	Eyvan (axial)	
1441	845	Mosque of Mezid Bey	Edirne	Eyvan (cross-axial)	
1442	846	Mosque of Mahmud Çelebi	İznik, Bursa	Single-unit	
1445	849	Mosque of Şeyh Sinan	Alaşehir, Manisa	Multi-unit (6-dome)	

Date			Name	Place	Type	Comments
			Güdük Minareli Mosque	Alaşehir, Manisa	Single-unit	
			Mosque of Kadı Şeyh	Alaşehir, Manisa	Single-unit	
			Pazar Camii	Amasya	Single-unit	
			Ulucami	Söğüt, Bilecik	Multi-unit	Completely rebuilt
			Mosque of Emir Sultan	Bursa	Single-unit (?)	Rebuilt in 1804
			Mosque of Altı Parmak	Bursa	Single-unit	
First			Mosque of İbni Bezzaz	Bursa	Single-unit	
half of 15th			Mosque of İsa Bey	Bursa	Single-unit	
century			Mosque of Tuz Pazarı	Bursa	Single-unit	
			Mosque of Umur Bey	Bursa	Single-unit	
			Mosque of Yiğit Köhne	Bursa	Single-unit	
			Mosque of Zeyniler	Bursa	Single-unit	
			İç Kale Mescidi	Manisa	Single-unit	Only foundation walls exist
	(?)		Mosque of Rüstem Çelebi	Tokat	Multi-unit	
1455	860		Mosque of Selçuk Hatun	Edirne	Single-unit	
1456	861		Mosque of Karacabey	Karacabey, Bursa	Eyvan (axial)	
1458	863		Mosque of Eyüp Sultan	Istanbul	Single-unit (?)	Rebuilt in 1789
1459	864		Mosque of Kanberler (Sitti Hatun)	Bursa	Single-Unit	
1462	867		Mosque of Mahmud Paşa	Istanbul	Multi-unit	
1462	867		Mosque of Fâtih	Istanbul	Multi-unit	
1466	871		Mosque of Hacılar	Bursa	Single-unit	
1468	873		Mosque of Ayşe Kadın	Edirne	Single-unit	
1469	874		Mosque of Murad Paşa	Istanbul	Eyvan (axial)	
1471	876		Mosque of Ahmed Daî	Bursa	Single-unit	
1471	876		Mosque of Rum Mehmed Paşa	Istanbul	Eyvan (axial)	
1472	877		Mosque of Gedik Ahmed Paşa	Afyon	Multi-unit	
1474	879		Mosque of Hoca Yahya	Manisa	Single-unit	
1474	879		Mosque of Sinan Bey	Manisa	Single-unit	
1475	880		Hacı İshak	Zile, Tokat	Multi-unit (2-dome)	
1478	883		Mosque of Kasım Paşa	Edirne	Single-unit	
1480	885		Mosque of Attar Hoca	Manisa	Single-unit	Mosque rebuilt; minaret original
1482	887		Mosque of Sitti Hatun	Edirne	Single-unit	
1482	887		Mosque of İshak Paşa	İnegöl, Bursa	Eyvan (cross-axial)	
1484 (begun)		889	Mosque of Bayezid II	Edirne	Single-unit	
1484	889		Mosque of İvaz Paşa	Manisa	Multi-unit (5-dome)	
1485	890		Mosque of Sofular	Amasya	Single-unit	
1485	890		Mosque of Davud Paşa	Istanbul	Single-unit	
1485	890		Hatuniye Mosque	Tokat	Single-unit	
1486	891		Mosque of Sultan Bayezid (II)	Amasya	Multi-unit	
1486	891		Mosque of Mehmed Paşa	Amasya	Single-unit	
1486	891		Mosque of Kileri Süleyman Ağa	Amasya	Single-unit	
1490	896		Mosque of Firuz Ağa	Istanbul	Single-unit	
1490	896		Hatuniye Mosque	Manisa	Multi-unit (5-dome)	

Date		Name	Place	Type	Comments
1493	*899*	Göktaşlı (Gökbaşlı) Mosque	Manisa	Single-unit	
1496	*902*	Mosque of Atik Ali Paşa	Istanbul	Multi-unit	
1498	*904*	İmâret Camii	İnecik, Tekirdağ	Single-unit	
		Paşa Camii	Balıkesir	Multi-unit	Rebuilt in 16th century
		Mosque of Abdal Mehmed	Bursa	Multi-unit	
		Mosque of Başçı İbrahim	Bursa	Single-unit	
		Mosque of Hamza Bey	Bursa	Eyvan (axial)	
		Mosque of Ağalar	Istanbul	Single-unit	
		Mosque of İshak Paşa	Istanbul	Single-unit	
		Merdivenli Mescid	Istanbul	Single-unit	
		Mosque of Samanveren	Istanbul	Single-unit	
		Mosque of Şeyh Vefa	Istanbul	Single-unit	Destroyed at the turn of 20th century
		Mosque of Timurtaş	Istanbul	Single-unit	
		Mosque of Yarhisar	Istanbul	Single-unit	
		Mosque of Yatağan	Istanbul	Single-unit	
		Mosque of Yavaşça Şahin	Istanbul	Single-unit	
		Mosque of Yavuz Ersinan	Istanbul	Single-unit	
		Zincirlikuyu Mosque	Istanbul	Multi-unit	
		Mosque of Bülbül Hatun	Amasya	Multi-unit	
		Mosque of Cumaovası	Cumaovası, İzmir	Single-unit	Only minaret
		Mosque of Hacı Veli Efendi	Cumaovası, İzmir	Single-unit	
Second half of 15th century		Mosque of Cüneyt Bey	Cumaovası, İzmir	Single-unit	
		Mosque of Gazaz	Menemen, İzmir	Single-unit	
		Mosque of Ulamış Village	Seferihisar, İzmir	Single-unit	
		Ulucami	Seferihisar, İzmir	Multi-unit	Restored 19th century
		Mosque of Güdük Minare	Seferihisar, İzmir	Single-unit	Only minaret left
		Mosque of Düzce Village	Seferihisar, İzmir	Multi-unit	Reconstructed 19th century
		Mosque of Hüsameddin	Tire, İzmir	Single-unit	
		Mosque of Kazanoğlu	Tire, İzmir	Eyvan (axial)	
		Mosque of Kazır (Cazır)	Tire, İzmir	Single-unit	
		Mosque of Karahasan	Tire, İzmir	Single-unit	
		Mosque of Yahşi Bey	Urla, İzmir	Single-unit	
		Mosque of Kılıç Ali	Urla, İzmir	Single-unit	
		Mosque of Güdük Minare	Urla, İzmir	Single-unit	
		Mosque of Fâtih İbrahim Bey	Urla, İzmir	Multi-unit (5-dome)	
		Ulucami	Akhisar, Manisa	Multi-unit (5-dome)	
		Mosque of Emir Hıdır Bey	Soma, Manisa	Single-unit	Reconstructed
		Mosque of Ayni (İne) Ali	Manisa	Single-unit	
		Mosque of Serabat	Manisa	Single-unit	Only minaret and one wall exist
		Mosque of Nişancı Paşa	Manisa	(?)	
		Mosque of Çatal	Manisa	Multi-unit (5-dome)	
		Haç Pazarı	Fidi, Erbaa, Tokat	Single-unit	

Bibliography

Ağaoğlu, Mehmed "The Fâtih Mosque at Constantinople," *The Art Bulletin* (New York), Vol. 12 (1930).

Arseven, Celâl Esad *Türk Sanatı Tarihi*. Istanbul: Millî Eğitim Basımevi, 1954–59.

Aslanapa, Oktay *Edirne'de Osmanlı Devri Âbideleri*. Istanbul: Üçler Basımevi, 1949.

"Fatih Devri Âbideleri," *Istanbul G.S.A., Türk San'atı Tarihi Araştırma ve İncelemeleri,* Vol. 1 (1963).

"İznik'te Sultan Orhan İmaret Camii Kazısı," *Sanat Tarihi Araştırmaları* (Istanbul), Vol. 1 (1964).

Ayverdi, Ekrem Hakkı *Fâtih Devri Mimarisi*. Istanbul: Istanbul Matbaası, 1953.

"Orhan Gazi Devrinde Mi'mârî," *Yıllık Araştırmalar Dergisi*, Vol. 1 (1956).

"Dimetoka'da Çelebi Sultan Mehmed Camii," *Vakıflar Dergisi*, Vol. 3 (1956).

"Yugoslavya'da Türk Âbideleri ve Vakıfları," *Vakıflar Dergisi*, Vol. 3 (1956).

"Osmanlı Mimarisinin İlk Asrı," *Milletlerarası Birinci Türk Sanatları Kongresi (19–24 Ekim 1959), Tebliğler*. Ankara: Türk Tarih Kurumu Basımevi, 1962.

"Mudurnu'da Yıldırım Bayezid Manzûmesi ve Taş Vakfiyesi," *Vakıflar Dergisi*, Vol. 5 (1962).

Baykal, Kâzım *Bursa'da Ulu Cami*. Istanbul: İbrahim Horoz Basımevi, 1950.

Bursa ve Anıtları. Bursa, 1950.

Charles, M. A. "Hagia Sophia and the Great Imperial Mosques," *The Art Bulletin* (New York), Vol. 12 (1930).

Çetintaş, Sedat *Türk Mimarî Anıtları. Bursa'da İlk Eserler*. Istanbul: Millî Eğitim Basımevi, 1946.

Türk Mimarî Anıtları. Bursa'da Murad I ve Bayezid I Binaları. Istanbul: Millî Eğitim Basımevi, 1952.

Yeşil Cami ve Benzerleri Cami Değildir. Istanbul, 1958.

Creswell, K. A. C. *The Muslim Architecture of Egypt*. Oxford, 1952.

Diez, Ernst *Türk Sanatı*. Translated from the German by Oktay Aslanapa. Istanbul: Üniversite Matbaası Komandit Şti., 1946.

Eldem, Sedat Hakkı "Bursa'da Şahadet Camii Konusunda bir Araştırma," *Istanbul, G.S.A., Türk San'atı Tarihi Araştırması ve İncelemeleri*, Vol. 1 (1963).

Erdmann, Kurt "XIII. Yüzyıl Anadolu Camilerinin Özel Durumu," *Milletlerarası Birinci Türk Sanatları Kongresi (19–24 Ekim 1959), Tebliğler*. Ankara: Türk Tarih Kurumu Basımevi, 1962.

Ethem, Halil *Camilerimiz*. Istanbul: Kanaat Kütüphanesi, 1933.

Nos mosquées de Stamboul. Translated from the Turkish by Ernest Mamboury. Istanbul: Kanaat Kütüphanesi, 1934.

Eyice, Semavi "İlk Osmanlı Devrinin Dinî—İçtimaî bir Müessesesi: Zâviyeler ve Zâviyeli-Camiler," *Istanbul Üniversitesi İktisat Fakültesi Mecmuası*, Vol. 23, Nos. 1–4.

"Atik Ali Paşa Camiinin Türk Mimârî Tarihindeki Yeri," *Tarih Dergisi*, Vol. 14, No. 19 (1964): 99–114.

"Osmanlı-Türk Mimarisinin İlk Devrinin Bir Cami Tipi Hakkında," *Milletlerarası Birinci Türk Sanatları Kongresi (19–24 Ekim 1959), Tebliğler*. Ankara: Türk Tarih Kurumu Basımevi, 1962.

Son Devir Bizans Mimarisi. Istanbul: Baha Matbaası, 1963.

Gabriel, Albert	*Les mosquées de Constantinople*. Syria, 1926.
	Une capitale turque: Brousse. 2 vols. Paris: E. de Boccard, 1958.
	Monuments turcs d'Anatolie. 2 vols. Paris: E. de Boccard, 1931, 1934.
	"Bursa'da Murad I Cami ve Osmanlı Mimarisinin Menşei Meselesi," *Vakıflar Dergisi*, Vol. 2 (1942).
Godard, André	*The Art of Iran*. London, 1965.
Gurlitt, Cornelius	"Die Bauten Adrianoples," *Orientalisches Archiv* (Leipzig) Vol. 1 (1910–11).
Kızıltan, Ali	*Anadolu Beyliklerinde Cami ve Mescitler*. Istanbul: Güven Basımevi, 1958.
Kuban, Doğan	*Osmanlı Dini Mimarisinde İç Mekân Teşekkülü*. Istanbul: Güven Basım ve Yayınevi, 1958.
	Anadolu–Türk Mimarisinin Kaynak ve Sorunları. Istanbul: Özaydın Matbaası, 1965.
Kunter, Halim Baki, and Ülgen, Ali Saim	"Fatih Camii," *Vakıflar Dergisi*, Vol. 1 (1938).
Kuran, Aptullah	*İlk Devir Osmanlı Mimarisinde Cami*. Ankara: Ajans Türk Matbaası, 1964.
	"The Mosque of Yıldırım in Edirne," *Belleten* (Ankara), Vol. 28, No. 3 (1964).
MacDonald, William	"Design and Technology in Hagia Sophia," *Perspecta: The Yale Architectural Journal*, Vol. 4 (1957).
Meriç, Rıfkı Melûl	"Bayezid Camii Mimarı," *Yıllık Araştırmalar Dergisi* (Ankara), Vol. 2 (1957).
	"Edirne'nin Tarihî ve Mimarî Eserleri Hakkında," *Istanbul, G.S.A., Türk San'atı Tarihi Araştırması ve İncelemeleri*, Vol. 1 (1963).
Nice, Robert L. Van	"The Structure of St. Sophia," *Architectural Forum*, May, 1963.
Otto-Dorn, Katharina	*Das islamische Iznik*. Berlin, 1941.
Öz, Tahsin	*Istanbul Camileri*. Ankara: Türk Tarih Kurumu Basımevi, 1962.
Rice, David Talbot	*The Byzantines*. London: Thames and Hudson, 1962.
Rice, Tamara Talbot	*The Seljuks*. London: Thames and Hudson, 1961.
Riefstahl, Rudolf M.	*Turkish Architecture in Southwestern Anatolia*. Cambridge, Mass., 1931.
Sayılı, Adnan	"Higher Education in Medieval Islam," *Ankara Üniversitesi Yıllığı*, 2 (1948).
Söylemezoğlu, H. Kemâli	*İslâm Dini, İlk Camiler ve Osmanlı Camileri*. Istanbul: Pulhan Matbaası, 1955.
Strzygowski, Josef	*Origin of Christian Church Art*. Translated from the German by O. M. Dalton and H. J. Braunholtz. Oxford: Clarendon Press, 1923.
(Uzunçarşılı) İsmail Hakkı	*Kitâbeler*. Istanbul, 1929.
Ülgen, Ali Saim	"Kırşehir'de Türk Eserleri," *Vakıflar Dergisi*, Vol. 2 (1942).
	"Bursa Anıtları," *Bursa*. Istanbul: Doğan Kardeş Yayınları A. Ş. Basımevi, 1948.
	"İznik'te Türk Eserleri," *Vakıflar Dergisi*, Vol. 1 (1938).
	"Türk Mimarisinin Felsefî ve Estetik Özellikleri," *Milletlerarası Birinci Türk Sanatları Kongresi (19–24 Ekim 1959), Tebliğler*. Ankara: Türk Tarih Kurumu Basımevi, 1962.
	"İnegöl'ün Kurşunlu Abideleri," *Istanbul, G.S.A., Türk San'atı Tarihi Araştırma ve İncelemeleri*, Vol. 1 (1963).
	"İnegöl'de İshak Paşa Mimarî Manzumesi," *Vakıflar Dergisi*, Vol. 4 (1958).
Ünsal, Behçet	*Turkish Islamic Architecture*. London: Alec Tiranti, 1959.
Vogt-Göknil, Ulya	*Les mosquées turques*. Translated from the German by Jean Paul Haymoz. Zurich: Orgio Verlag, 1953.
Wilde, Hans	*Brussa*. Berlin: Ernst Wasmuth, 1909.
Yetkin, Suut Kemal	*İslâm Mimârisi*. Ankara: Ankara Üniversitesi Basımevi, 1959.
	L'architecture turque en Turquie. Paris: Maisonneuve et Larose, 1962.

Index